Fodor's InFocus
PANAMA

12
TOP EXPERIENCES

Panama offers terrific experiences that should be on every traveler's list. Here are Fodor's top picks for a memorable trip.

1 Panama Beaches

With some 1,500 miles total of Pacific and Caribbean coastlines and with no spot in the country more than 50 miles from a coast, Panama is fringed by beautiful beaches. *(Ch. 3–7)*

2 Handicraft Markets

Exploring Panama City's handicraft markets is a must even for non-shoppers. Browse the colorful stalls and learn about local cultures from shop owners who are often indigenous people. *(Ch. 1)*

3 The Panama Canal

One of the world's remarkable engineering achievements, the Panama Canal is all the more amazing when you consider its construction took place a century ago. *(Ch. 3)*

4 Barro Colorado

Hop a boat on Gatún Lake to explore the island of Barro Colorado, one of the world's first wildlife reserves and home to more than 400 bird species and 120 kinds of mammals. *(Ch. 3)*

5 Rain Forests

Panama's accessible rain forests surround the capital, back the beaches of Bocas del Toro, and stretch to remote regions in the east, providing easy day-hikes or deeper jungle adventures. *(Ch. 1, 2, 3, 5)*

6 Bicoastal Diving

In Panama you can dive the Pacific and Caribbean on the same day. Pacific dives have bigger schools of fish; Caribbean sites offer sponge, coral, and wreck diving. *(Ch. 3, 4, 5, 7)*

7 The Emberá

Many of Panama's indigenous Emberá people live in villages in protected parks. Guided tours provide a fascinating glimpse into their traditional lifestyle and culture. *(Ch. 1, 2, 6)*

8 Surf Tours

Hot-shot surfers flock to Panama for the challenging reef breaks, but many operators offer lessons for beginners. Take a surf tour to access Panama's best waves. *(Ch. 4, 5, 7)*

9 Seafood

A trip to a country whose name means "abundance of fish" isn't complete without a fresh seafood meal. One Panamanian specialty not to be missed is ceviche (marinated, raw fish). *(Ch. 1, 2)*

10 Bocas del Toro Town

Slow down and unwind in Bocas Town, where there are almost no cars but plenty of bicycles. Stroll or pedal its wide streets lined with brightly colored, wooden Caribbean houses. *(Ch. 5)*

11 Casco Viejo

Stroll beneath latticework balconies on brick streets and discover this historic Panama City neighborhood, a World Heritage Site with a pastel patchwork of ancient churches, convents, shops, and homes. *(Ch. 2)*

12 Land of the Guna

The indigenous Guna people hold the deed to what is arguably Panama's most stunning scenery: white-sand beaches, coconut palms, and 300-plus islands off the northeast Caribbean coast. *(Ch. 6)*

CONTENTS

MAPS

ABOUT THIS GUIDE

Fodor's Ratings

Everything in this guide is worth doing—we don't cover what isn't—but exceptional sights, hotels, and restaurants are recognized with additional accolades. Fodor'sChoice★ indicates our top recommendations; highlights places we deem highly recommended. Care to nominate a new place? Visit Fodors.com/contact-us.

Trip Costs

We list prices wherever possible to help you budget well. Hotel and restaurant price categories from **$** to **$$$$** are noted alongside each recommendation. For hotels, we include the lowest cost of a standard double room in high season. For restaurants, we cite the average price of a main course at dinner or, if dinner isn't served, at lunch. For attractions, we always list adult admission fees; discounts are usually available for children, students, and senior citizens.

Hotels

Our local writers vet every hotel to recommend the best overnights in each price category, from budget to expensive. Unless otherwise specified, you can expect private bath, phone, and TV in your room. For expanded hotel reviews, facilities, and deals visit Fodors.com.

Restaurants

Unless we state otherwise, restaurants are open for lunch and dinner daily. We mention dress code only when there's a specific requirement and reservations only when they're essential or not accepted. To make restaurant reservations, visit Fodors.com.

Credit Cards

The hotels and restaurants in this guide typically accept credit cards. If not, we'll say so.

Top Picks
★ **Fodor's**Choice

Listings
⊠ Address
⊠ Branch address
🕮 Mailing address
🕾 Telephone
🖷 Fax
⊕ Website
✍ E-mail

🎫 Admission fee
☉ Open/closed times
Ⓜ Subway
↔ Directions or Map coordinates

**Hotels &
Restaurants**
🏠 Hotel
🛏 Number of rooms
🍴 Meal plans

✕ Restaurant
🍸 Reservations
👔 Dress code
▭ No credit cards
$ Price

Other
⇨ See also
☞ Take note
🏌 Golf facilities

1

EXPERIENCE
PANAMA

WHAT'S WHERE

1 Panama City. The capital is an obligatory stop, and a surprisingly pleasant hub for exploring the country. It is a vibrant and diverse metropolis with excellent dining, lodging, and nightlife, and an abundance of day-trip options.

2 The Canal and Central Panama. Central Panama holds an array of landscapes and attractions in a relatively small area. The Panama Canal is the region's biggest attraction, literally, and it can be admired from half a dozen vantage points or navigated on day trips.

3 Chiriquí Province. The western province of Chiriquí comprises everything from cloud forest to coral reefs, and white-water rivers to white-sand beaches. World-class surfing, river rafting, sportfishing, bird-watching, skin diving, and hiking make Chiriquí a destination meant for lovers of the great outdoors.

4 Bocas del Toro Archipelago. The Bocas del Toro Archipelago holds an impressive mix of beaches, jungle, idyllic cays, and coral reefs. The archipelago's dozens of islands are surrounded by turquoise waters and lined with pristine strands that provide access to great skin diving or surfing, according to the season.

5 Guna Yala. Guna Yala is Panama at its wildest. This region also has the country's best sportfishing and fishing lodges and beautiful island beaches.

Caribbean Sea

Golfo de
Mosquitos

Portobelo
El Porvenir
Colón
Rio Sidra
Naraganá
Sabanitas
GUNA YALA
Chilibre
El Llano
Ailigandí
2 **1**
Ustupu
COLÓN
Pacora
PANAMA
Arraiján
⭐ **PANAMA CITY**
Mulatupu
COCLÉ
La Chorrera
Puerto
Obaldia
a Fé La Pintada
Cerro
Gaital
Nueva
Gorgona
Bahía de
Panamá
Peñonomé
San Carlos
Meteti
RAGUAS
Anton
Farallon
San Miguel
La Palma
ntiago **Aguadulce**
Isla del Rey
Yaviza
Divisa
DARIÉN
El Real
HERRERA **Chitré**
Golfo de
Garachiné
Sambú
Minas **Las Tablas**
Panamá
LOS SANTOS
Pocrí
Puerto Piña
Tonosí
Pedasí
Punta Piña
Jaqué

COLOMBIA

CEAN

0   50 mi

0   50 km

PANAMA TODAY

Panama's natural attractions, culture, and history are the main draws for travelers, and the country's penchant for modernization makes it an international destination. Panama has had one of the fastest growing economies in the Western Hemisphere for most of the past decade, and that prosperity is apparent in Panama City's proliferation of skyscrapers, malls, new restaurants, and fancy cars.

Canal and Infrastructure Expansion

Successive governments have invested tax revenues and borrowed funds into an array of infrastructure improvements, the most expensive of which is the $5.25 billion expansion of the Panama Canal to accommodate more, larger ships. When the Panama Canal's centennial was celebrated on August 15, 2014, work was well underway on the construction of a third set of locks, which should begin functioning in early 2016. Those locks will accommodate much larger ships than the "Panamax" vessels that have been a shipping standard for much of the past century, and shipyards and ports around the world are already preparing for the next generation of cargo ships.

Other new infrastructure includes dozen's of shiny skyscrapers—including apartments, office towers, and hotels—and Panama City's first subway line, The Metro, which connects the interior district of San Miguel with the city center and Allbrook. The Biomuseo, a modern museum designed by the architect Frank Gehry and dedicated to the country's extraordinary biodiversity, is one of the city's major new attractions.

Stable Democracy

These improvements have been accompanied by a steady consolidation of Panama's democracy, which was long manipulated by the country's military. The election of President Juan Carlos Varela in May of 2014 marked the fifth free and peaceful elections since the U.S. invasion of December 1989 ousted military dictator Manuel Noriega and restored the country's democracy. Though ongoing investigations of graft in the last administration indicate that corruption remains a problem, Panama's government is relatively efficient and it is one of the safest countries in Latin America. Despite the country's stability, tourism growth has slowed in recent years, yet the number of hotels and attractions have increased. This is good news for travelers, because the ample supply of rooms and services and moderate demand should make a Panama vacation a relative bargain, at least for awhile.

WHEN TO GO

Hotels often fill up between Christmas and Easter, especially on weekends. Reserve rooms weeks or months in advance if you plan to be here during Christmas week or Semana Santa (Holy Week). Holidays mean crowded times at the beach, but they hardly affect Guna Yala. Check the Panama Tourism Authority's website (⊕ *www. visitpanama.com*) for holiday and festival dates.

Most visitors come during the December through May dry season, but there's no bad time to visit. Just choose your activity.

Bird-watching is best from October to March, when northern migrants boost the native population.

Fishing excels from January to March, though Pacific sailfish run from April to July, and there are plenty of fish biting from July to December.

Surfing is best from June to December in the Pacific, whereas the Caribbean gets more waves between November and March, and some swells in July and August.

White-water rafting and **kayaking** are best June to December, when you have half a dozen rivers to choose from.

Scuba diving varies according to the region. The Caribbean's best diving conditions are between August and November, though March and April can also be good. The Gulf of Panama has better visibility from June to December, but the trade winds make the sea progressively colder and murkier there from December to May. Those winds have less of an impact on the Gulf of Chiriquí and Isla de Coiba, where the diving is best from December to July.

Dry Season/Wet Season

Panama is an unmistakably tropical country, where temperatures fluctuate between 70°F and 90°F year-round, and humidity hovers around 80%. The country experiences only two seasons: dry, from late December to May, and rainy from early May to December. January through April are the sunniest months for most of the country. Panama experiences a mini dry season in July and August, where you may have long stretches of sunny days. Count on downpours most afternoons in May, June, September, October, and November. Bocas del Toro province gets plenty of rain in December and January, but less than the rest of the country in September and October.

PANAMA PLANNER

Getting Here and Around

Air Travel: Copa, a United partner, is Panama's flagship carrier. It operates flights from Atlanta, Boston, Chicago, Dallas, Denver, Fort Lauderdale, Houston, Las Vegas, Los Angeles, Miami, Newark, New Orleans, New York–JFK, Orlando, San Francisco, Toronto, and Washington Dulles. Copa also flies to many Central and South American cities. You can fly to Panama from Houston and Newark on United; from Atlanta on Delta; from Miami, Dallas, New York, and Newark on American; and from Fort Lauderdale on Spirit.

Air Panama is Panama's domestic carrier and serves destinations all over the country, including Guna Yala, Bocas del Toro, David, and the Darién. Domestic flights usually cost $100 to $250 round-trip; you can buy tickets directly from the airline or through a travel agent. Air Panama offers charter flights as well, although these tend to be quite pricey.

Car Travel: Driving is a great way to explore Central Panama and Chiriquí Province, but Panama City can be confusing, and you'll want to fly to and from the other provinces. The Panamerican Highway runs between Panama City and David, Chiriquí, passing most of the country's beach resorts, and with a car, you can also visit small villages and explore remote areas more easily. Most secondary roads are well signposted and in reasonable condition.

Compact car rentals like a Ford Fiesta or Toyota Yaris start at around $35 a day; midsize cars are from $40–$50. Four-wheel-drive pickups start at $70 a day. International agencies sometimes have cheaper per-day rates, but locals undercut them on longer rentals. Stick shift is the norm in Panama, so check with the rental agency if you only drive an automatic.

Where to Stay

"Hotel" isn't the only tag you'll find in Panama: *hospedaje, pensión, casa de huespedes,* and *posada* also denote somewhere to stay. Hotels and *posadas* tend to be higher-end, whereas *hospedajes, pensiones,* and *casas de huespedes* are sometimes smaller and family run. A *residencial* might be a by-the-hour sort of place.

Resorts: Big international chain hotels (Westin, Radisson, Marriott, and more) are found throughout Panama City. They have rooms and facilities equal to those at home, but can lack a sense of place. If five-star luxury isn't your top priority, the best deals are undoubtedly with mid-range local hotels.

Rentals: Short-term furnished rentals are increasingly common in

Panama. Airbnb has rentals listed in several regions of Panama. Villas International offers premium villa and apartment rentals, mostly near beaches. Sublet.com and VRBO offer an array of short-term rentals, primarily in Panama City or on beaches.

Bed-and-Breakfasts: In Panama the term *B&B* is frequently extended to luxury hotels that happen to include breakfast in their price. There is a decent selection of small B&Bs in Panama City and several provinces listed on Bed & Breakfast.com and BnB Finder.

Eco-Lodges: Found primarily in Guna Yala, the country's eco-lodges are rustic but comfortable. Most are well off the beaten path, so plan on staying a few nights. The term *eco-lodge* sometimes describes a property in a rural or jungle location rather than somewhere that is truly sustainable. The International Ecotourism Society has online resources to help you pick somewhere green.

Tips and Safety
Packing: Insect repellent, sunscreen, and sunglasses are essential to help protect you from the relentless sun and persistent mosquitoes. Panama's rainy season lasts from mid-April to December, and rain is common at other times, too, so a foldable umbrella or waterproof jacket is advisable.

Trouble Spots: Poorer neighborhoods in the capital (shaded on our Panama City maps), the city of Colón (other than the Colón 2000 cruise port, the free zone, the train station, and the hotels we list), and the border area with Colombia in the Darién are best avoided. Using standard travel precautions, the majority of visitors have a hassle-free trip here.

Visitor Resources
The Panamanian Tourism Authority, ATP, is Panama's official tourism organization. Its website (⊕ *www.visitpanama.com*) is an excellent pre-trip planning resource with overviews of Panama's regions and points of interest.

ATP has 17 offices around Panama, open weekdays 8–3:30. The English-speaking staff at ATP offices are friendly and helpful. Their resources—mostly brochures—tend to plug local tour companies rather than aid independent exploration.

Other resources include *The Visitor,* a small, free paper found at most hotels and travel agencies, and *Panama Planner,* an excellent tourism magazine, available at large hotels.

IF YOU LIKE

Diving

Panama is a world-class dive destination. Its Caribbean reefs are adorned with dozens of sponge and coral species and an array of fish and invertebrates. The Pacific has the country's most spectacular dives, with schools of big fish, sharks, and other creatures.

Bocas del Toro. With plenty of coral reefs and several dive shops, this popular Caribbean archipelago is perfect for scuba divers and snorkeling enthusiasts alike.

Escribano Bank, Central Caribbean Coast. This barrier reef east of Isla Grande holds some of the country's healthiest coral. It is so remote that few divers visit it, but it lies near the eco-resort Coral Lodge.

Isla Coiba, Chiriquí Province. Protected within a vast national park, Coiba Island is surrounded by excellent diving, with rocky reefs that attract legions of fish. Explore it on one-week dive cruises or shorter trips from Playa Santa Catalina.

Islas Secas, Chiriquí Province. This remote archipelago in the Gulf of Chiriquí has extensive reefs teeming with marine life that can be explored from the exclusive resort on the islands, or on day trips from Boca Chica.

History

The site of the first Spanish colony on the American mainland, Panama has remnants of five centuries of European influence, including ancient fortresses and colonial churches, as well as indigenous cultures that have hardly changed since Columbus sailed down the country's coast.

The Canal. The Panama Canal's creation only a century ago was a historic event that is celebrated by displays in the visitor center at Miraflores Locks and murals in the Canal Administration Building.

Casco Viejo. Panama City's historic quarter holds an enchanting mix of colonial churches, abandoned monasteries, 19th-century buildings, and timeless plazas that are perfect for a drink or meal.

Indigenous Panama. The country's indigenous communities are living history, preserving centuries-old customs. Visiting them provides glimpses of the Panama that Spanish explorers discovered five centuries ago.

Panama Viejo. The ruins of Panama's first city—founded almost five centuries ago, and sacked by the pirate Henry Morgan in 1671—evoke the nation's start as a trade center.

Beaches

Panama holds a panoply of *playas* (beaches) ranging from pristine to full-blown resorts. The latter are on the Central Pacific coast, though Isla Contadora also has some splendid strands. The country's most spectacular beaches, however, are on the Caribbean isles of Bocas del Toro Archipelago and Guna Yala.

Playa Kobbe, Panama City. The closest beach to Panama City, Playa Kobbe (aka Playa Bonita) is backed by massive resorts and overlooks the Panama Canal's Pacific entrance, with dozens of ships moored in the distance.

Playa Farallón, Central Pacific Coast. Panama's longest beach, Playa Farallón (aka Playa Blanca) has a selection of resorts, golf courses, restaurants, bars, and casinos to complement the sand, sun, and sea.

Playa Cacique, Central Pacific Islands. The most picturesque beach on Isla Contadora, one of the Pearl Islands, Playa Cacique's beige sand and aquamarine sea are a short boat or plane trip from Panama City, yet a world apart.

Isla Bolaños, Chiriquí Province. The ivory sand and tropical foliage of this uninhabited island a short boat trip from Boca Chica are the stuff of tropical fantasies.

Red Frog Beach, Bocas del Toro. This pristine beach on Isla Bastimientos is named for the tiny amphibians that abound in the adjacent jungle, but it is also popular with sea turtles and globetrotters.

Cayos Zapatillas, Bocas del Toro. With coconut palms towering over white sand and crystalline waters washing across acres of coral, these twin atolls in Parque Nacional Marino Isla Bastimentos are the crown jewels of the Bocas del Toro Archipelago.

San Blas Islands, Guna Yala. Though none of them have names, there are countless idyllic beaches on the remote San Blas Islands, many of which can be visited on excursions from the region's eco-lodges.

GREAT ITINERARIES

CITY, CANAL, AND BEYOND

This quintessential three-day Panama itinerary is perfect for a long weekend beginning and ending in Panama City. You get the capital, the canal, and a taste of adventure in the interior. It requires a bit of planning, but it's entirely possible to get a sampling of the best of Panama's urban and wilderness offerings in a brief time, thanks to short distances and the number of attractions easily reached from Panama City.

Tips

Transit tour scheduling: Partial canal transit tours operate one or two days a week; full canal transits operate one or two days a month.

Use taxis in the city. They are much cheaper and easier than renting a car, particularly for short trips to the outskirts of town.

In Colón, arrange a pick-up in advance through a tour company or take a shuttle to Colón 2000 cruise port (these shuttles always meet the Panama Railway trains), and hire a taxi there, not at the train station.

Days 1 and 2: Panama City and Canal

On your first day, get an early start to avoid the midday heat. Head to Casco Viejo, the capital's restored colonial quarter, for a morning of old-world exploration. The pastel colors and latticework gates evoke old New Orleans, sans Bourbon Street of course. In the afternoon, head to Miraflores, just outside the city, for a front-row seat to the spectacle of huge ships passing through the locks. Narration in English and Spanish describes the fascinating process, and an adjoining museum documents the history of the canal. A visit to the Biomuseo or an afternoon of shopping in an air-conditioned mall such as Allbrook, Multiplaza, or SOHO Panama comfortably rounds out a Panama City day. The port facility at Calzada de Amador is a great place for sunset cocktails or dinner.

If you want to be on the canal waterway rather than alongside it, skip Miraflores on Day 1 and schedule a canal transit for Day 2. Partial transits, billed as half-day tours, frequently take up three-quarters of a day. Less-frequently offered full canal transits travel end to end and take up a full day with a return to Panama City in the evening.

Day 3: Railway and Nature

Get up early on your third day to take the Panama Canal Railway to Colón. Here, you can spend the day exploring the country's Caribbean coast, fortresses, rain forest, or the beaches of Portobelo or San Lorenzo. You'll leave Panama City at 7:15 am and return at 5:15 pm, which allows plenty of time to see the coast. Another option keeps you closer to the capital: Spend one or two days at the Gamboa Rainforest Resort, which is less than an hour north of Panama City by taxi. This option includes several choices of outdoor activities, including the popular rain-forest aerial tram and trips onto Lago Gatún. No matter what you choose, you're sure to be amazed by such pristine wilderness so close to a major urban area.

THE BEST OF PANAMA

With some serious picking and choosing you can put together an almost perfect dream itinerary. Panama's decent highway system makes travel quite easy, and its good domestic air network puts even the farthest-flung places an hour or less from the capital.

Days 1 to 3: Panama City and Canal

The "City, Canal, and Beyond" itinerary makes a good base from which to start. The capital, canal, and Central Panama are a good introduction to the country for most visitors. Added time gives you more flexibility to include other Central Panama destinations. Active travelers may prefer to head to El Valle de Antón for bird-watching, hiking, biking, or

horseback riding. Several excellent lodging choices will make sure you sleep in comfort and eat in style. You could also combine a night at Sierra Llorona or Burbayar Lodge (both in the highlands northeast of Panama City) with a visit to an indigenous Emberá village.

Days 4 to 7: Bocas del Toro

An early-morning flight from Panama City puts you in Bocas del Toro in less than an hour, and you'll be pleasantly surprised at how quickly you slow down to island time. Check into your hotel in Bocas town, where most visitors stay. ■TIP→ **If you're staying at one of the outer islands, arrange to have a hotel representative meet you at the airport and transfer you by boat. The farther-flung lodgings lie 45–60 minutes away.** Nearby botanical and butterfly gardens on the main island can occupy your first day. Your second day should be spent on Isla Bastimentos, about 15 minutes away by boat. Traditionally, visitors come here to visit the indigenous Ngöbe communities, the islands' original inhabitants. These days, more Bastimentos visitors head for the popular zip-line canopy tour at Red Frog Beach. Don't worry, there's time enough to do both. Bocas means underwater activities, too. If you've always wanted to try scuba diving, the several dive shops here offer a one-day intro course. You

TIPS

■ If flying domestically, opt for morning flights during the rainy season. Skies are usually clearer, and you'll appreciate the smoother conditions on Air Panama's small-ish planes.

■ Do not schedule international-to-domestic flight connections (or vice-versa) the same day. Delays are not uncommon.

■ The small airstrips in the Darién and Guna Yala receive one early-morning flight from Panama City. David and Bocas del Toro offer morning and afternoon flight options.

■ The trip from David to Almi-rante, the ferry port for Bocas del Toro, is three hours overland, making it easy to combine Boquete and Bocas without backtracking to Panama City.

■ Elevation makes all the difference at these latitudes. Lowland Panama swelters year-round, but you'll appreciate long sleeves at highland elevations such as Bo-quete and El Valle de Antón.

won't get certified, but you'll see if you want to pursue the activity. Of course, a full diving course will take up several days here. And for much less muss and fuss, anyone who can swim can snorkel.

Days 7 to 9: Boquete and Chiriquí

Fly to the western city of David, a business hub where travelers rarely linger. Rent a car or take a taxi for the 45-minute drive over a new four-lane highway to highland Boquete. The elevation change makes temperatures noticeably cooler. Get your bearings that first day exploring the town. Early European settlers created a community that could have been transported from the Swiss Alps. Any number of expert guides can take you bird-watching—this is one of Panama's premier destinations and is the haunt of the beautiful resplendent quetzal. An early-morning horseback tour can kick off your third day. The highlands are Panama's coffee country, and a few processors offer tours that acquaint you with the life and times of the dark beverage. If you're a rafter, you've likely come to Chiriquí for white-water sports. The Estí, Dolega, and one sector of the Chiriquí Viejo rivers are apt for beginners and take up full- or half-day excursions.

PANAMANIAN CUISINE

Signature dishes and flavors

One of Panama's typical dishes, *carimañola*, consists of the tuber yuca, ground and boiled and made into a dumpling that's filled with minced beef or chicken and pieces of boiled egg. It's a Panamanian breakfast staple. *Sancocho* is the other dish that truly says "Panama." This chicken and yuca soup—sometimes prepared as thick as a stew—is flavored with *culantro* (think "cilantro," but slightly more aromatic.) It's reputed to be good for whatever ails you and also makes for a surprisingly cooling dish on a sweltering day. To make the descriptively named *ropa vieja* ("old clothes"), a Panamanian cook stews beef with tomato and onion until it can be shredded with a fork and then serves it with rice. Ropa vieja is one of the few Panamanian dishes that can be spicy.

Cooks here make a variation on Mexican tamales—the singular is *tamal*—with a filling of chicken, peas, onions, and cornmeal boiled inside tied plantain leaves. You eat the filling but not the leaves, and certainly not the string. Every Latin American country claims its own variation on empanadas. Panamanians make semicircular ones with a filling of ground beef, chicken, or cheese deep fried and served as a snack or appetizer. Caribbean cooks often add plantain to the filling.

Almojábana, corn-flour bread, and *patacones,* salted green plantains fried golden brown and pounded into crispy chips, accompany many meals. *Hojaldras* (fried bread) is a popular alternative to toast with breakfast. It can also be eaten sweet, sprinkled with sugar, like doughnuts.

Seafood

With 1,500 miles of coastline, seafood is everywhere. Corvina, a white sea bass, frequently shows up as the main ingredient in ceviche. Whatever kind of cubed pieces of fish or seafood is used, Panamanian ceviche is marinated in lime juice, with onion and celery and sometimes hot pepper and served chilled as an appetizer.

Beverages

Seco, a distilled sugarcane firewater, is commonly tempered with chilled milk. For a smooth easy beverage, try *chicheme,* a blend of milk, cornmeal, cinnamon, and vanilla. And beverages don't come more basic than the ubiquitous *pipa*. Poke a hole in an unripe coconut, stick in a straw, and you have a refreshing drink of coconut juice. Roadside stands everywhere sell them.

OUTDOOR VACATIONS

The options for enjoying Panama's great outdoors range from hiking through the cloud forest to paddling down a white-water river. The country's world-class fishing, surfing, diving, and bird-watching draw plenty of people focused on just one activity, but Panama is also a great destination for travelers who want to dabble in several outdoor experiences.

Multisport Outfitters

Ancon Expeditions Panama and EcoCircuitos Panama handle everything from beach stays to hiking excursions, and they are recommended in numerous categories.

Ancon Expeditions of Panama. ☎ 888/760–3426 *in North America, 507/269–9415 in Panama* ⊕ *www.anconexpeditions.com.*

EcoCircuitos Panama. ☎ 800/830–7142 *in North America, 507/315–1305 in Panama* ⊕ *ecocircuitos. com.*

Beaches

Season: Year-round. **Locations:** Bocas del Toro, Guna Yala. **Cost:** from $1,500 for seven days from Panama City.

Escape the crowds on Panama's Caribbean coast where pristine beaches are reachable only by boat. The beaches of the Bocas del Toro Archipelago are backed by lush rain forest and lie near multicolored coral reefs. The San Blas Islands are some of the most stunning and serene isles in the world and are home to the indigenous Guna. There are just a few small guesthouses here, but the waters are crystal clear and the marine life is abundant. Adventure Life, Ancon Expeditions of Panama, and Wildland Adventures offer trips that combine the canal and mountain forests with time on the beaches of either Bocas del Toro or the San Blas Islands, whereas EcoCircuitos Panama has a tour that visits both Bocas del Toro and Guna Yala.

Adventure Life. ☎ 406/541–2677 ⊕ *www.adventure-life.com.*

Wildland Adventures. ☎ 800/345–4453 ⊕ *www.wildland.com.*

Bird-Watching

Season: Year-round. **Locations:** Central Panama, Chiriquí, Darién. **Cost:** From $115.

Panama has more than 960 bird species and is home to rare species such as the spectacular rainbow-billed toucan and resplendent quetzal. It's also a place to witness hawk and vulture migrations or island rookeries where thousands of seabirds gather. The best months for birding are October to April, when northern migrants boost the local population, so you might spot an emerald toucanet and a Baltimore oriole in the same tree.

The best regions are Central Panama, the mountains of western Chiriquí Province, and the jungles of the Darién. The most popular central area is Parque Nacional Soberanía, where the Panama Audubon Society has held many world-record Christmas bird counts. The mountain valleys of Chiriquí's Boquete and Cerro Punta host birds you won't find in other parts of the country, including the quetzal.

Ancon Expeditions has excellent guides and a comprehensive, 12-day "Birds of Panama" tour. The smaller Advantage Tours Panama and EcoCircuitos Panama offer comparable trips. Canopy Tower Family has two terrific birding lodges and good guides. Field Guides and Exotic Birding sell Ancon Expeditions' tours but send an expert guide along, whereas Victor Emanuel Nature Tours does the same thing using the Canopy Tower Family lodges. The Panama Audubon Society offers inexpensive weekend excursions.

Canopy Family. ☎ *800/617–7451 in North America, 507/264–5720 in Panama ⊕ www.canopytower.com.*

Exotic Birding. ☎ *877/247–3371 in North America ⊕ www.exoticbirding.com.*

Field Guides. ☎ *800/728–4953 in North America ⊕ www.fieldguides.com.*

Panama Audubon Society. ☎ *507/232–5977 in Panama ⊕ www.audubonpanama.org.*

Victor Emanuel Nature Tours (*VENT*). ☎ *800/328–8368 in North America ⊕ www.ventbird.com.*

Diving

Season: Year-round (conditions vary by region). **Locations:** Central Caribbean, Gulf of Panama, Isla Coiba, Gulf of Chiriquí, Bocas del Toro, Guna Yala. **Cost:** From $70 for two-tank boat dive to $350 per day for an Isla Coiba dive cruise.

Panama is the only country where you can dive in the Pacific and the Atlantic on the same day. The Atlantic has more coral and sponge diversity and warmer water. The waters of Isla Coiba are home to more than 700 fish species, big schools, and lots of sharks. Scuba Coiba and Panama Divers run trips that include nights in rustic rooms on the island. Coiba Dive Expeditions offers nights on the 115-foot M/V Yemaya. Diving around Golfo de Chiriquí is available at the Islas Secas. More accessible sites in the Golfo de Panama can be explored from Isla Contadora with Coral Dreams, or out of Panama City with Scuba Panama, which also offers diving in the Panama Canal.

The most accessible Atlantic diving areas are near Portobelo, where Panama Divers and Scuba Panama provide access to miles of barrier reef, sunken ships, and a plane wreck. To the east there's the Escribano Bank, with exceptionally healthy coral, and Guna Yala's San Blas Islands, where only snorkeling is permitted. Bocas del Toro, in Western Panama, has dozens of dive spots and an array of accommodations. Bocas Watersports and Starfleet Scuba offer dives at the impressive Cayos Zapatillas and Tiger Rock, among other sites.

Bocas Water Sports. ⊠ *Bocas del Toro* ☎ *507/757–9541 in Panama* ⊕ *www.bocaswatersports.com.*

Coiba Dive Expeditions. ☎ *507/ 314–9350 in Panama* ⊕ *www. coibadiveexpeditions.com.*

Coral Dreams. ☎ *507/6536–1776 in Panama* ⊕ *www.coral-dreams.com.*

Panama Divers. ☎ *507/448–2293 in Panama* ⊕ *www.panamadivers. com.*

Scuba Coiba. ☎ *507/6980–7122 in Panama* ⊕ *www.scubacoiba.com.*

Scuba Panama. ☎ *507/261–3841 in Panama* ⊕ *www.scubapanama. com.*

Starfleet Scuba. ⊠ *Bocas del Toro* ☎ *507/757–9630* ⊕ *www.starfleet-scuba.com.*

Fishing

Season: Year-round (best January and February). **Locations:** Gulf of Panama, Chiriquí, Gatún Lake. **Cost:** From $350 per day for Gatún Lake to $1,600 per day for fishing cruises or lodge packages.

"Panama" means "abundance of fish," and although Caribbean fishing is average, the Pacific waters have some of the best fishing in the Western Hemisphere. The Golfo de Chiriquí, in western Panama, is a close second, with lots of marlin, sailfish, and other big fighters near the Hannibal Banks, Isla Montuosa, and Isla de Coiba. Those waters can be fished out of lodges with Gone Fishing Panama, Panama Big Game Fishing Club, Pesca Panama, or Coiba Adventure Sport Fishing. Between those two regions lie the Pearl Islands, where good angling is accessible from Isla Contadora or Panama City with Panama Fishing & Catching. A less expensive alternative to deep-sea fishing is light-tackle angling on Gatún Lake, in the Panama Canal, or the Bayano River to the east. Panama Canal Fishing has family packages and can guarantee you'll catch fish.

Coiba Adventure Sport Fishing. ☎ *800/800–0907 in North America* ⊕ *www.coibadventure.com.*

Gone Fishing Panama. ☎954/378-9429 *in North America, 507/6930–4215 in Panama* ⊕*www.gonefishingpanama.com.*

Panama Big Game Fishing Club. ☎786/600–1672 *in North America* ⊕*www.panama-sportfishing.com.*

Panama Canal Fishing. ☎*507/315–1905 in Panama* ⊕*www.panamacanalfishing.com.*

Panama Fishing & Catching. ☎*507/6622–0212 in Panama* ⊕*www.panamafishingandcatching.com.*

Pesca Panama. ☎*800/946–3474 in North America* ⊕*www.pescapanama.com.*

Hiking

Season: Year-round. **Locations:** Central Panama, Chiriquí. **Cost:** $30 to $175 per day for expeditions.

Options for getting into the country's forests range from an early-morning hike through Panama City's Parque Natural Metropolitano to a weeklong trek along the remains of the Spanish mule trail Camino Real. Ancon Expeditions of Panama, EcoCircuitos Panama, and Sendero Panama are the hiking specialists, offering day hikes and multiday trips that include camping in rain forest. The most challenging of these is the seven-day Camino Real trek, which takes you through pristine forest. Various lodges with private reserves and trail systems serve as excellent bases for day hikes, such as Finca Lérida, Los Quetzales Lodge, Punta Patiño Lodge, and the Canopy Family lodges. The mountains hold some of the most popular trails, namely El Valle de Antón and Chiriquí's Volcán Barú and La Amistad national parks, near Boquete and Cerro Punta.

Sendero Panama. ☎*507/390–5526* ⊕*www.senderopanama.com.*

Surfing

Season: Year-round. **Locations:** Central Pacific, Chiriquí, Bocas del Toro. **Cost:** $75–$150 per day.

Panama's best surf is at Santa Catalina, on the Azuero Peninsula, and the islands of the Gulf of Chiriquí and Bocas del Toro Archipelago.

Surf tours are an excellent option because some of Panama's breaks are quite remote and are often accessible only by boat. Panama Surf Tours has a rustic lodge in Santa Catalina and offers guided trips to the country's best spots. The Morro Negrito Surf Camp, on an island in the Golfo de Chiriquí, provides access to five isolated breaks that are seldom surfed.

Panama Surf Tours. ☎*507/6671–7777 in Panama* ⊕*www.panamasurftours.com.*

Puerto Limón

Parque Nacional Cahuita

Caribbean Sea

Bribri · Las Tablas
Guabito
Changuinola · *Isla Colón*
Reserva Forestal Palo Seco · Bocas del Toro
BOCAS DEL TORO · Almirante · *Parque Nacional Marino Isla Bastimentos*
Parque Internacional La Amistad · 11 · Chiriquí Grande · *Golfo de los Mosquitos* · COLÓN

COSTA RICA · Cerro Punta · Bajo Boquete · NGÖBE BUGLE · COCLÉ
Volcán · Caldera · *Parque Nacional Omar Torrijos* · La Pintada · El Valle de Antón
Paso Canosas · CHIRIQUÍ · La Concepción · 4 · Santa Fe · Penonomé
Puerto Armuelles · David · San Félix · VERAGUAS · 91 · Antón
Quebrada del Medio · 1 · Aguadulce
Punta Burica · *Parque Nacional Marino Golfo de Chiriquí* · Interamericana · Divisa · *Parque Nacional Sariqua*
Soná · Santiago · Ocú · 3 · Chitré
Las Minas · HERRERA · Los Santos
Isla de Coiba · *Parque Nacional Coiba* · *Golfo de Montijo* · Macaracas · Las Tablas
Parque Nacional Cerro Hoya · *Parque Nacional La Tronosa* · Tonosí
LOS SANTOS · *Reserva Forestal La Tronosa*

KEY	
🔭	*Bird watching*
🐟	*Diving/Snorkeling*
🎣	*Fishing*
⛳	*Golf*
🥾	*Hiking*
🐴	*Horseback riding*
🛶	*Kayaking*
🛟	*Rafting*
🏄	*Surfing*

National Parks and Activities

Portobelo

Parque Nacional Portobelo

Colón

Sabanitas

Chilibre

Gamboa

Arraiján

La Chorrera

Cerro Gaitál

Nueva Gorgona

Playa Coronado

San Carlos

Farallón

Pocrí

Pedasí

El Porvenir

Carti Suitupo

Burbayar

Parque Nacional Chagres

El Llano

Pacora

Chepo

Naraganá

Rio Sidra

GUNA YALA

Ailigandí

Ustupu

Mulatupu

Puerto Obaldia

Panama City

PANAMÁ

Interamericana

Bahia de Panama

San Miguel

Isla del Rey

Isla San José

Golfo de Panamá

Meteti

La Palma

DARIÉN

Yaviza

El Real

Garachiné

Sambú

Puerto Piña

Punta Piña

Jaqué

Parque Nacional Darién

COLOMBIA

PACIFIC OCEAN

0   40 miles

0   40 kilometers

LIVING IN PANAMA

Panama gets high marks as the Western Hemisphere's up-and-coming retirement destination.

Moderate cost of living, ease of owning real estate for foreigners, quality health-care facilities in the hub cities of Panama City and David, decent in-country transportation and communication, and proximity to the United States draw thousands of Americans, who make up the majority of foreigners who retire to Panama.

The expat population congregates mostly in four enclaves around Panama. The former Canal Zone came ready-made with U.S.-style housing and amenities and a California or Florida look and feel when Panama took over the canal in 1999. In the northwest, Bocas del Toro is Panama's version of slow-paced Caribbean-island life. Central Panama's El Valle de Antón and Chiriquí province's Boquete offer higher-elevation respites from the lowland heat. The latter, in particular, is growing at an astonishing pace. Each is rich in opportunities for foreigners to meet up for events or volunteer work.

Retirement and relocation give you three status options to look into:

Pensioner. Most popular for foreigners is the *pensionado* route. You need a guaranteed monthly income from a pension, public or private, of at least $1,000. You are allowed a one-time duty-free import of your household goods up to $10,000 as well as the tax-free purchase of a car every two years. In addition, various Panamanian businesses and institutions offer a wide variety of discounts.

Investor. As an *inversionista,* you incorporate a business under Panamanian law and provide full-time employment to at least five citizens. (Household employees do not count.)

Person of Means. To qualify for *solvencia económica propia,* you must deposit at least $300,000 in a fixed-term account in a Panamanian bank for at least three years.

Note that none of these options permits you to work, and all require a clean police record. A good attorney here can help navigate the bureaucracy.

Don't fall prey to "Sunshine Syndrome." Pause and take a deep breath if you find yourself uttering the words, "Honey, we met that nice real estate agent in the hotel bar. Let's buy a house." Some succumb and move to Panama, only to find that living here bears scant resemblance to vacationing here. Experts suggest a trial run. Rent a house or apartment for a few months and see if day-to-day life in Panama agrees with you.

PANAMA CITY

Updated
by Mark
Chesnut

FOUNDED NEARLY FIVE CENTURIES AGO, Panama city is steeped in history, yet much of it is remarkably modern. The baroque facades of the city's old quarter appear frozen in time, while the area around Punta Paitilla (Paitilla Point) is positively vaulting into the 21st century, with gleaming skyscrapers towering over the waterfront.

Panama City is home to races, religions, and cultures from around the world. Whereas the high-rises of Punta Paitilla and the Area Bancária (banking district) create a skyline more impressive than that of Miami (really!), the brick streets and balconies of the Casco Viejo evoke the French Quarter of New Orleans. The tree-lined boulevards of Balboa are a mixture of early-20th-century American architecture and exuberant tropical vegetation. The islands reached by the nearby Calzada de Amador (Amador Causeway) are full of bars and restaurants and a marina.

The city's proximity to tropical nature is astounding, with significant patches of forest protected within city limits on Cerro Ancón (Ancón Hill) and in Parque Metropolitano, and the national parks of Camino de Cruces and Soberanía just to the northwest of town. You could spend a morning hiking through the rain forest of the Parque Metropolitano to see parrots and toucans, then watch pelicans dive into the sea while sipping a sunset drink at one of Amador Causeway's restaurants. There are plenty of spots in and around the city to view massive ships moving in and out of the Panama Canal.

An array of restaurants, an abundance of shops and handicraft markets, and a vibrant nightlife scene round out Panama City's charm. Panama City can also serve as a base for a bunch of day trips, including Panama Canal transit tours, a boat ride to Isla Taboga or Isla Contadora, a trip on the Panama Canal Railway, a day exploring the colonial fortresses, beaches, and coral reefs of Portobelo, or hikes through various rain-forest reserves.

Included in Panama City's colorful contrasts are many of the unfortunate aspects of urban life in the developing world. It has its fair share of slums, including several around must-see Casco Viejo. Traffic is often downright terrible, and the ocean along its coast is very polluted. Crime is a problem in some neighborhoods. Be careful where you walk around alone, especially at night. The city as a whole is quite safe, especially the downtown area, where you'll find bustling hotels, restaurants, and bars.

TOP REASONS TO GO

The Panama Canal. Eighty kilometers (50 miles) long, the interoceanic canal is literally Panama's biggest attraction. There are half a dozen spots in or near the capital from which to admire it. The Calzada de Amador, the Balboa Yacht Club, and the visitor center at Miraflores Locks all offer impressive vistas of the "big ditch."

Casco Viejo. The balconies, brick streets, and quiet plazas of the historic Casco Viejo have a European air, and the neighborhood's ancient churches and monasteries stand as testimony to the country's rich colonial history. Though much of it is dilapidated, the neighborhood has some of the city's nicest restaurants and bars.

Calzada de Amador. Stretching 3 km (2 miles) into the Pacific to connect three islands to the mainland, the Amador Causeway has panoramic views of the city's skyline, the canal's Pacific entrance, and the Bay of Panama, as well as a good selection of restaurants and bars—all of them cooled by ocean breezes.

Day Trips. Panama City is close to some of the most accessible rain forests in the world; jungle trails are a short drive from most hotels. In addition to boat trips on the Panama Canal or wildlife-watching on Gatún Lake, you can visit an Emberá Indian village; go white-water rafting, fishing, kayaking, or hiking through the jungle; ferry out to Isla Contadora or Isla Taboga; or visit the Caribbean fortresses of Portobelo, where the history is complemented by beaches and coral reefs.

ORIENTATION AND PLANNING

GETTING ORIENTED

Panama City sprawls for 20 km (12 miles) along the Bahía de Panamá (Bay of Panama), on the Pacific Coast, and deep into the sultry hinterland. Most of its attractions and accommodations are within a few miles of one another in the city's southwest corner, near the Panama Canal's Pacific entrance. Panama snakes west to east, so the canal cuts across running north from the Pacific to the Atlantic. The eastern edge of the canal's entrance includes the Calzada de Amador (the breakwater connecting several islands to the mainland) and the neighborhoods of Balboa, Albrook, and Cerro Ancón, a forested hill topped by a big Panamanian flag that is a landmark visible from much of the city. The city is largely divided into neighborhoods old and new, upscale and lower class, with some overlap. Neighborhoods just to the east of Cerro Ancón, beyond busy Avenida de los Mártires, include the slums of Chorrillo and Santa Ana, both of which are best avoided (although they can be visited on tours) and San Felipe, which includes the historic and stylish Casco Viejo. Newer neighborhoods like El Cangrejo, Obarrio, Paitilla, and San Francisco are home to the majority of large hotels, offices, and restaurants.

Avenida Balboa, one of the city's main east–west routes, runs along the Bay of Panama between the Casco Viejo and modern Paitilla Point. It runs through an attractive waterfront promenade called the Cinta Costera. The neighborhood along its western half is sketchy, but the park-like Cinta Costera itself is a pleasant place to stroll. Avenida Balboa ends at Punta Paitilla, with its Multicentro shopping mall, skyscrapers, and private hospitals. There it branches into the Corredor Sur, an expressway to the international airport, and the inland Vía Israel, which eventually turns into Avenida Cincuentenario and leads to the ruins of Panamá Viejo.

The main eastbound street to the north of Avenida Balboa is Avenida Justo Arosemena, which runs east from Plaza Cinco de Mayo and flows into Calle 50 (Cincuenta, also called Calle Nicanor de Obarrio). The main westbound route is Vía España, a busy boulevard lined with banks and shopping centers that curves south to become Avenida Central, which in turn becomes a pedestrian mall at Plaza Cinco de Mayo, after which it curves eastward to become the main avenue in the Casco Viejo.

Casco Viejo. Panama City's oldest inhabited neighborhood has an eclectic mix of colonial architecture and historic attractions like the towering cathedral, Teatro Nacional (National Theater), as well as peaceful squares, museums, galleries, trendy restaurants and clubs, and boutique hotels.

Cerro Ancon, Balboa, and the Calzada de Amador. Activities in these neighborhoods, located along the Pacific entry to the Panama Canal, include wandering the lush rain forest of Ancon, visiting cultural sites in the historic Panama Canal zone around Balboa, and enjoying ocean-side biking and dining in the Calzada de Amador.

Parque Natural Metropolitano, Miraflores, and Summit. Just outside of the city center, both Parque Natural Metropolitano and Parque Municipal Summit offer easy-access wilderness getaways, while the nearby Miraflores visitor center is *the* spot to view the locks of the Panama Canal.

Downtown Panama City. For simplicity, we lump several of the newer, upscale neighborhoods into "downtown" as a sort of mega-neighborhood, but locals often refer specifically to each area by name (El Cangrejo, Obarrio, Area Bancaria, Paitilla). The wide variety of dining, shopping, and hotels makes this section of the capital a preferred area for international visitors.

Panamá Viejo. The ruins of Panamá Viejo offer a fascinating glimpse into the life of Panama City's first settlers.

Playa Bonita. Also known as Playa Kobbe, this beach destination is backed by two large resorts that offer the only all-inclusive beach stays in the city.

PLANNING

WHEN TO GO

Unlike the rest of the country, Panama City hardly has a low season, because the bulk of its visitors are business travelers. Most tourists head here during the dry season, from December to May; this is when the city's hotels are packed. Carnaval, around mid-February, is a fun time to be in the capital, because that long weekend is celebrated with parades and lots of partying. The city is fairly quiet during Easter week, on the other hand, since many businesses close from Thursday to Easter Sunday and every resident who can leaves town.

May, June, and September through November are the rainiest months in Panama City, though most of that rain falls in the afternoon or evening. The rains let up a bit in July and August, which is a good time to visit, because you can share the place with fewer tourists than during the dry season.

Because Panama City has the country's only international airport and is the transportation hub for domestic flights and buses, you may return here several times during your trip. This means you can explore the capital bit by bit over the course of your stay in the country.

PLANNING YOUR TIME

Panama City is a large metropolis with a variety of noteworthy neighborhoods and daunting traffic. You can explore some areas on foot, but many neighborhoods are quite far apart, making a taxi necessary to travel between them. It's best to group your preferred activities and attractions by neighborhood and tackle one area of the city at a time. Start early and plan for lunch during the hottest midday hours, then head out again. The Casco Viejo is a destination unto itself and should be treated as such, whereas it's easy to combine visits to the parks and the Miraflores locks visitor center in a day trip. Panamá Viejo is a bit removed from other attractions, so plan it as a separate morning or afternoon excursion. Shopping, dining, and nightlife are easy to squeeze in no matter the weather, thanks to large malls like MultiPlaza, Albrook, MultiCentro, and Soho. If you're here during the rainy season, you can expect downpours nearly every afternoon; they usually only last for about 20 minutes, so you can duck into a restaurant and have a cup of coffee or a drink until the deluge subsides. Most, though not all, museums are closed on Monday. Farmacia Arrocha has a dozen large pharmacies scattered around the city that are open 24 hours. Maps, brochures, and basic information are available at the Autoridad de Turismo Panama stands in the the Tocumen and Allbrook airports.

GETTING HERE AND AROUND

AIR TRAVEL

All international flights (except for a handful of flights from San José, Costa Rica and Medellín, Colombia) land at Panama City's Aeropuerto Internacional de Tocumen (PTY), 26 km (16 miles) northeast of Panama City. Panama has one domestic airline, Air Panama, which flies to about two-dozen destinations (as well as to San José and Medellín) out of Aeropuerto Marcos A. Gelabert, next to Albrook Mall.

CAR TRAVEL

Driving a car in Panama City is not an undertaking for the meek, but renting a car is an excellent way to explore the surrounding countryside. Growth in the number of rental-car companies has driven prices down in recent years; rentals can dip as low as $4 per day, whereas four-wheel-drive vehicles can cost as little as $11 a day (plus taxes and service fees). All the big car-rental companies offer GPS rentals, and have offices downtown and at the airports.

2

TAXI TRAVEL

Taxis in Panama City are all independently owned, tend to be smaller cars, and don't have meters. The city is divided into zones, the flat fare for one person being $1.50, to which they add 50¢ each time you cross into another zone, plus 50¢ for each additional person. Fares also increase about 20% after 10 pm and on Sunday. But don't expect any of these guidelines to be followed consistently if you're a foreigner; fares are commonly inflated even if you speak Spanish, so be sure to agree on a fare before boarding the taxi. A short trip should cost about $4 for two people, whereas a trip to the domestic airport in Albrook or the Calzada de Amador can run about $60. Tips are not expected. You will be charged double, or several times the standard rate, by the taxi drivers who wait outside hotels, but they drive vans or SUVs, and are likely to speak some English. Flagging a cab in the street is widely considered to be safe. If you're alone, you may be expected to share a taxi, a common practice in Panama, as is sitting in the passenger seat next to the driver.

Panamataxi Turismo provides personal transportation and various cultural tours for individuals and small groups.

Contacts Panamataxi Turismo. ✉ *Panama City* ☎ *507/263–8311, 507/6663–0192* ⊕ *www.panamataxi.com.*

TRAIN TRAVEL

Central America's first modern urban rail system, the Panama Metro opened its first line in 2014, and operates daily (5 am until 10 pm Monday through Saturday and 7 am until 10 pm on Sunday), costs 35¢ per ride (plus $2 to buy the reusable Metro card) and offers an efficient, traffic-free option for travelers, with air-conditioned cars and stations. For foreign visitors, Line 1—the only one currently operating—is mostly best for traveling between the tourist-heavy neighborhood called El Cangrejo, Albrook Mall, and the city's main bus station. It's also possible to walk from the station at Plaza 5 de Mayo to the Casco Antiguo, but it's a bit of a hike.

Contacts Title Metro de Panama. ✉ *Panama City* ☎ *507/504–7200* ⊕ *www.elmetrodepanama.com.*

PRICES

WHAT IT COSTS IN U.S. DOLLARS			
$	**$$**	**$$$**	**$$$$**
Restaurants Under $10	$10–$15	$16–$20	over $20
Hotels Under $100	$100–$160	$161–$220	over $220

Restaurant prices are per person for a main course at dinner. Hotel prices are for two people in a standard double room, excluding service and 10% tax.

SAFETY

Most of the city is safe for walking, even at night, especially El Cangrejo, the Area Bancária, the Casco Viejo, and Paitilla, where the bulk of the city's hotels and restaurants are located. The Avenida Central pedestrian mall is safe by day, but after dark don't wander west of Calle 10, or Plaza Herrera. Even during the day you should leave most valuables and money in your hotel safe. At night you should travel to and from the Casco Viejo only by taxi or rental car, but by day walking there from Plaza Cinco de Mayo on Avenida Central is fine. The increasing gentrification of the Casco Viejo, as well as the presence of police in the neighborhood, have made this area safe both by day and night, making it one of the most popular places to dine and go bar hopping. If you're on foot and feel any apprehension about where you've ended up, flag down the first taxi, even if it has another passenger in it, and go someplace you know is safe. Between 11 am and 3 pm, the heat is usually oppressive, so serious strolling should be limited to the morning and evening hours.

■ TIP➔ **Areas that should be avoided are El Chorrillo and Santa Ana, just west of the Casco Viejo (although guided tours are safe); the southwestern half of Calidonia, including Avenida Balboa west of the Balboa Monument; and Curundú, just to the west of Caledonia.**

TOURS

⇨ *For information on Tours of the Panama Canal, see the Panama Canal section in Chapter 3.*

Panama City has many tour companies offering tours of the city, canal, and nearby parks. But not all of them have guides of the same caliber, and few have true naturalist guides. An inexpensive city tour option is to board one of the hop-on/hop-off, red double-decker buses of **City-sightseeing Panama** (⊕ *citytourspanama.com*), which stop at the Amador Causeway, Miraflores Locks, Casco Viejo, and several malls once an hour, allowing you to get off, explore, then board the next bus.

TOUR COMPANIES

Advantage Panama. With a strong focus on bird-watching and nature tours, Advantage uses guides trained in tourism and biology, and offers multiday and single-day excursions into rain forests and national parks. ✉ *1040 Calle 11 Este, Parque Lefevre* ☎ *507/6676–2466* ⊕ *www.advantagepanama.com.*

Ancon Expeditions. Panama's highest-profile tour operator provides an array of options, including whale watching, Panama Canal boat excursions, and adventure travel in Bocas del Toro. The company is a preferred operator for Virtuoso, the upscale travel network. ✉ *Calle Elvira Mendez, Edificio El Dorado No. 3* ☎ *507/269–9415* ⊕ *www.anconexpeditions.com.*

EcoCircuitos Panama. One of Panama's best tour operators focused on ecotourism and nature travel, EcoCircuitos offers complete, multiday escorted packages into the country's interior, as well as day trips from Panama City that visit some of the region's best natural attractions. They also do city tours and Panama Canal excursions. ✉ *Albrook Plaza, No. 31, Urbanización Albrook* ☎ *507/315–1305, 800/830–7142 toll-free in U.S.* ⊕ *www.ecocircuitos.com.*

Rain Forest Adventures by Panama Excursions. This tour operator, a division of a larger company that also operates in Costa Rica, Jamaica, and St. Lucia, offers a variety of well-organized group and individual tour options, including Panama Canal full and partial transits, Panama Canal Railway excursions, eco-cruises on Gatún Lake, and visits to Emberá villages. ✉ *Av. Roberto Chiari #722, Balboa, Panama City* ☎ *507/314–0820* ⊕ *www.rainforestadventure.com.*

VISITOR INFORMATION

Autoridad de Turismo Panama (*ATP*). The Autoridad de Turismo Panama has a decent website and information offices in the Tocumen and Allbrook airports where they answer basic questions and hand out brochures. ✉ *Aeropuerto de Tocumen* ☎ *507/238–4356* ⊕ *www.visitpanama.com.*

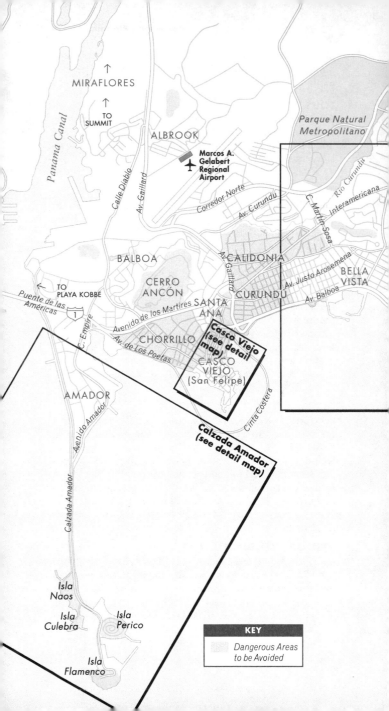

BETANIA

TO
BAHA'I TEMPLE

Ricardo J. Alfaro (Tumba Muerto)

**Downtown Panama City
(see detail map)**

Via Simón Bolívar

EL
CANGREJO

Via Brasil

Gran Morrison Via España

Rio Matasnillo

Via España

Av. Ernesto T. Lefevre

Rio Gallinera

OBARRIO

Parque
Recreativo
OMAR

Av. Santa Elena

Av. Nicanor de Obarrio

Av. Balisario Porras

Via Cincuentenario

PANAMÁ
VIEJO

MARBELLA

SAN
FRANCISCO

Via Cincuentenario

Av. Balboa

SAN
SABASTIÁN

Via Israel

Corredor Sur

PUNTA
PAITILLA

PUNTA
PACÍFICA

TO
TOCUMEN INT'L. AIRPORT

Bahía de Panama

0 _____ 1/2 mile
0 _____ 1/2 kilometer

*PACIFIC
OCEAN*

Panama City

EXPLORING

Panama City is a hassle-free place to explore on your own: many people speak English, the U.S. dollar is legal tender, and there are ATMs, restaurants, pharmacies, shops, and taxis just about everywhere. You can explore some areas on foot, though distances between neighborhoods make taxis (or perhaps the shiny new Metro rail system, depending on your destination) necessary for most trips. If you ever feel uneasy about a location or situation and there aren't any police around, just flag down a taxi, which are safe and everywhere. Be sure to agree on the fare before boarding the taxi, as drivers are notorious for overcharging foreigners. Tourism police patrol the Casco Viejo and Panamá Viejo on bicycles. If you have a medical problem, go to Hospital Punta Pacífica, the best private clinic in the city. It also has a dental clinic.

CASCO VIEJO

Panama City's historic quarter is known as the Casco Viejo (pronounced CAS-coh Bee-EH-hoh; also called the Casco Antiguo, which translates as "old shell"). It's spread over a small point in the city's southeast corner, where timeless streets and plazas are complemented by views of a modern skyline and the Bahía de Panamá. The Casco Viejo's narrow brick streets, wrought-iron balconies, and intricate cornices evoke visions of Panama's glorious history as a major trade center. A stroll here offers opportunities to admire a beautiful mix of Spanish colonial, neoclassical, and art nouveau architecture. And though many of its buildings are in a lamentable state of neglect, and some of the neighborhood is poor, it is nevertheless a lively and colorful place, where soccer balls bounce off the walls of 300-year-old churches and radios blare Latin music, even as trendy restaurants, bars, shops, and hotels welcome an increasingly stylish clientele. Movie fans may spot a few places used as settings for the James Bond movie *Quantum of Solace*—Panama stood in for both Bolivia and Haiti in the movie, with the shell-like remnants of the Club Unión used for a party scene, and the National Institute of Culture serving as a fictional hotel in Bolivia (Daniel Craig actually stayed in the Casco Antiguo during shooting).

TIMING AND PRECAUTIONS

The Casco Viejo is best explored on foot, though due to the intensity of the tropical heat, try to do your walking in the morning or late in the afternoon. Four o'clock in the afternoon is a great time to stroll around, when you can enjoy the evening light at Plaza Francia, have a drink on Plaza Bolívar, then dine at a nearby restaurant. Give yourself at least two hours to tour this neighborhood, more if you plan to shop.

Even with ongoing renovations and gentrification, Casco Viejo still has many poor pockets, but it isn't as dangerous as it may look. Nevertheless, precautions should be taken: leave jewelry and passports in your hotel safe and don't bring heaps of money. The crime problem is not so much in Casco Viejo but in the adjacent neighborhoods. The area is patrolled by Tourism Police, who work out of a station behind the Teatro Nacional.

TOP ATTRACTIONS

Iglesia de San José (*Saint Joseph's Church*). This church is an exact replica of the temple of the same name in Panamá Viejo. It is the sanctuary of the country's famous golden altar, the most valuable object to survive pirate Henry Morgan's razing of the old city. According to legend, a wily priest painted the altar with mud to discourage its theft. Not only did Morgan refrain from pilfering it, but the priest even managed to extract a donation from the pirate. The ornate baroque altar is made of carved mahogany covered with gold leaf. It is the only real attraction of the small church, though it does have several other wooden altars and a couple of lovely stained-glass windows. ⊠ *Av. A at Calle 8* ⧉ *Free* ☉ *Mon.–Sat. 9–noon and 2–5, Sun. 8–11:30 am.*

Palacio de las Garzas (*Palacio Presidential*). The neoclassical lines of the stunning, white presidential palace stand out against the Casco Viejo's skyline. Originally built in the 17th century by an official of the Spanish crown, the palace was a customs house for a while, and passed through various mutations before being renovated to its current shape in 1922, under the administration of Belisario Porras. President Porras also started the tradition of keeping pet herons, or egrets, in the fountain of the building's front courtyard, which led to its popular name: "Palace of the Herons." Because the building houses the president's offices and is surrounded by ministries, security is tight in the area, though nothing compared to the White House. During the

CHORRILLO

Bahía de Panama

Casco Viejo

Parque Santa Ana

Av. Eloy Alfaro

La Compañía

City Wall

Club Unión

Iglesia de La Merced, **4**

Iglesia de San José, **6**

La Catedral, **2**

Las Bóvedas, **9**

Museo del Canal Interoceánico, **3**

Palacio de las Garzas, **14**

Paseo Esteban Huertas, **10**

Plaza Bolívar, **12**

Plaza Catedral, **1**

Plaza de Francia, **8**

Plaza Herrera, **5**

Salón Bolívar, **13**

Santo Domingo, **7**

Teatro Nacional, **11**

0   1/8 mile

0   1/8 kilometer

KEY

Dangerous Areas to be Avoided

day the guards may let you peek into the palace's Moorish foyer at its avian inhabitants, but to get inside you'll need to reserve a free tour by email (*gbernal@presidencia. gob.pa*) at least two weeks ahead of time. Tours are given Tuesday through Thursday. ⊠ *Av. Alfaro, 2 blocks north of Plaza Catedral* ☎ *507/527–9656* ⊕ *www.presidencia.gob.pa.*

Paseo Esteban Huertas. This promenade built atop the old city's outer wall is named for one of Panama's independence leaders. It stretches around the eastern edge of the point at Casco Viejo's southern tip. From the Paseo you can admire views of the Bay of Panama, the Amador Causeway, the Bridge of the Americas, the tenements of El Chorrillo, and ships awaiting passage through the canal. As it passes behind the Instituto Nacional de Cultura, the Paseo is shaded by a bougainvillea canopy where Kuna women sell handicrafts and couples cuddle on the benches. Bougainvillea arches frame the modern skyline across the bay, creating a nice photo op: the new city viewed from the old city. ⊠ *Plaza Francia, between the stairway at the back of the plaza and Calle 1* ⊠ *Free.*

★ **Fodors Choice Plaza Bolívar.** A small plaza surrounded by 19th-century architecture, this is one of Casco Viejo's most pleasant spots, especially at night, when people gather at its various cafés for drinks and dinner, and street musicians perform for tips. It's centered around a monument to the Venezuelan general Simón Bolívar, the "Liberator of Latin America," with decorative friezes marking events of his life and an Andean condor perched above him. In 1926 Bolívar organized a meeting of independence with leaders from all over Latin America in the Franciscan monastery in front of the plaza, which, in the end, he was unable to attend. The original San Francisco Church was destroyed by fire in the 18th century and restored twice in the 20th century. At this writing, the church was closed for yet another round of renovations, and was to reopen to the public in 2016 (open hours had not yet been announced). The former monastery is now occupied by a Catholic school. Across the plaza from it, on the corner of Avenida B and Calle 4, is the smaller church, **Iglesia de San Felipe de Neri,** which was recently restored and is open daily. The **Hotel Colombia,** across the street from it, was one of the country's best when it opened its doors in 1937, but it fell into neglect during the late 20th century until it was renovated in the 1990s and converted to luxury apartments. ⊠ *Av. B between Calles 3 and 4.*

Plaza Catedral. The old city's main square is also known as Plaza Mayor, or Plaza de la Independencia, since the country's independence from both Spain and Colombia were celebrated here. Busts of Panama's founding fathers are scattered around the plaza, at the center of which is a large gazebo. The plaza is surrounded by historic buildings such as the Palacio Municipal, the Museo del Canal Interoceánico, and the Hotel Central, which once held the city's best accommodations and is slowly being renovated. Plaza Catedral is shaded by some large *tabebuia* trees, which are ablaze with pink blossoms in January and February. The plaza is the site of ocassional craft fairs, weekend concerts, and other events. ⊠ *Av. Central between Calles 5 and 7.*

★ **Fodors Choice Plaza de Francia.** Designed by Leonardo de Villanueva, this attractive plaza on the southeastern corner of the Casco Viejo peninsula is dedicated to the French effort to build the canal, and the thousands who perished in the process. An obelisk towers over the monument at the end of the plaza, where a dozen marble plaques recount the arduous task. Busts of Ferdinand de Lesseps and his lieu-

FAMILY

tenants gaze across the plaza at the French Embassy—the large baby-blue building to the north of it. Next to them is a bust of Dr. Carlos Finlay, a Cuban physician who later discovered that yellow fever, which killed thousands during the French effort, originated from a mosquito bite—information that prompted the American campaign to eradicate mosquitoes from the area before they began digging. The plaza itself is a pleasant spot shaded by poinciana trees, which carry bright-orange blossoms from May to July. At the front of the plaza is a statue of Pablo Arosemena, one of Panama's founding fathers and one of its first presidents. The plaza covers part of a small peninsula that served as a bastion for the walled city's defense during its early years. The former dungeons of Las Bóvedas line the plaza's eastern edge, and next door stands a large white building that was once the city's main courthouse but now houses the Instituto Nacional de Cultura (National Culture Institute). ⊠ *End of Calle 1 Este.*

WORTH NOTING

Iglesia de La Merced (*Mercy Church*). One of the oldest structures in the Casco Viejo, La Merced's timeworn, baroque facade was actually removed from a church of the same name in Panamá Viejo and reconstructed here, stone by stone, in 1680. Flanked by white bell towers and tiny chapels, it's a charming sight, especially in late-afternoon light. The interior was destroyed by fires and rebuilt in the early 20th century, when some bad decisions were made, such as covering massive cement pillars with bathroom tiles. ⊠ *Calle 9 and Av. Central* ☉ *Weekdays 6:30 am–noon and 2–7, Sat. 4–7 pm, Sun. 6:30–11 am.*

La Catedral (*Catedral de Nuestra Señora de la Asunción*). Built between 1688 and 1796, Panama City's stately cathedral is one of Casco Viejo's most impressive structures. The interior is vast, but rather bleak, but for the marble altar, made in 1884, beautiful stained glass, and a few religious paintings. The stone facade, flanked by painted bell towers, is quite lovely, with its many niches filled with small statues. The bell towers are decorated with mother-of-pearl from the Pearl Islands, and the bells in the left tower were salvaged from the city's first cathedral, in Panamá Viejo. ⊠ *Av. Central and Calle 7* ☉ *Weekdays 8:30–3:30, Sat. 9–2, Sun. 9–11.*

Las Bóvedas. The arched chambers in the wall on the eastern side of Plaza Francia, which originally formed part of

2

the city's battlements, served various purposes during the colonial era, from storage chambers to dungeons. Dating from the late 1600s, when the city was relocated to what is now Casco Viejo, the Bóvedas were abandoned for centuries. In the 1980s the Panama Tourist Board initiated the renovation of the cells, two of which are used by the Instituto Nacional de Cultura for ocassional art exhibits. Three cells hold a French restaurant called Las Bóvedas, which hosts live music on some evenings and also has tables on the plaza where you can enjoy drinks in the afternoon or evening. ⊠ *Plaza Francia, Calle 1* ☎ *507/228–8058* ☞ *Free.*

Museo del Canal Interoceánico (*Interoceanic Canal Museum*). Once the only museum dedicated to the Panama Canal, the Museo del Canal Interoceánico has been put to shame by the visitors' center at Miraflores Locks. The museum is packed with artifacts, paintings, photographs, and videos about the Panama Canal, with most information posted in English and Spanish, although you may want to spend $5 for a recorded tour in English. Though the building was constructed in 1875 to be the Gran Hotel, it soon became the offices of the Compagnie Universelle du Canal Interoceanique, the French company that made the first attempt to dig a canal in Panama. After that effort went bust, the building became government property, and before being converted to a museum in the 1990s it was the central post office. ⊠ *Plaza Catedral* ☎ *507/211–1995* ⊕ *museodelcanal. com* ☞ *$2, audio guide $5* ☉ *Tues.–Sun. 9–5.*

Plaza Herrera. This large plaza a block off Avenida Central is surrounded by some lovely old buildings, several of which have been renovated or are in the process of renovation. The largest building on the square is home to the stylish American Trade Hotel, which has a lobby bar, restaurant, and jazz club, as well as outdoor dining and imbibing on the square some evenings. At the center of the plaza is a statue of local hero General Tomás Herrera, looking rather regal on horseback. Herrera fought in South America's wars for independence from Spain and later led Panama's first attempt to gain independence from Colombia, in 1840. Half a block west of it stands the last remaining chunk of the ancient wall that once enclosed Casco Viejo, called the Baluarte de la Mano de Tigre (Tiger's Hand Bulwark), beyond which the neighborhood grows somewhat sketchy. A company called Fortaleza Tours, which operates out of the American Trade Hotel, offers walking tours through the poorer blocks where gangs once ruled the streets; the fact that former gang members lead the tours lends even more authenticity to the experience. ⊠ *Av. A and Calle 9.*

Salón Bolívar. The hall in which Simón Bolívar's 1926 meeting of independence took place, next to the Iglesia de San Francisco, holds a small museum. ⊠ *Calle 3, Plaza Bolívar* ☎ *507/511–4100* ⊕ *www.inac.gob.pa* 🖾 *$1* ⊘ *Weekdays 8–4.*

Santo Domingo. A catastrophic fire ruined this 17th-century church and Dominican monastery centuries ago. What's left at the entrance is the Arco Chato, or flat arch, a relatively precarious structure that served as proof that the country was not subject to earthquakes, tipping the scales in favor of Panama over Nicaragua for the construction of the transoceanic canal. The arch finally collapsed in 2003, without the help of an earthquake, but the city fathers considered it such an important landmark that they had it rebuilt. ⊠ *Av. A at Calle 3* ☎ *507/209–6300 museum.*

NEED A BREAK? Gran Clement. Exploring Casco Viejo's narrow streets can be a hot and exhausting affair, which makes the gourmet ice-cream shop of Gran Clement an almost obligatory stop. Located in the ground floor of a restored mansion one block west of the Policía de Turismo station, the shop serves a wide assortment of ice creams including ginger, coconut, passion fruit, and mango. Gran Clement is also open at night, and until 9:30 pm on weekends. ⊠ *Av. Central and Calle 3* ☎ *507/228–0737* ⊕ *www.granclement.com* ⊘ *Mon.–Thurs. 11:30–8, Fri. and Sat. 11:30–9:30, Sun. noon–8.*

Teatro Nacional (*National Theater*). The interior of this theater is truly posh, with ceiling murals, gold balconies, and glittering chandeliers—a little bit of Europe in the heart of old Panama City. After serving as a convent and, later, an army barracks, the building was remodeled by Italian architect Genaro Ruggieri in 1908. Paintings inside by Panamanian artist Roberto Lewis depict Panama's history via Greek mythology. Check the local papers, or call to find out if the national symphony orchestra, or another group, is playing while you're in town, as attending a concert is the best way to experience the building. ⊠ *Av. B and Calle 3* ☎ *507/501–4107* ⊕ *www.inac.gob.pa* 🖾 *$1* ⊘ *Weekdays 8:30–3:30.*

CERRO ANCÓN AND BALBOA,

For the better part of the 20th century, the area to the west of Casco Viejo held the border between the American Canal Zone and Panama City proper, and it continues to be an area of stark contrasts. Busy Avenida de Los Mártires (which separates the neighborhoods of El Chorrillo and Santa Ana from Cerro Ancón [Ancón Hill]) was once lined with a chain-link fence; it was named for Panamanian students killed during demonstrations against American control of the zone in 1964. To the west of that busy avenue, which leads to the Bridge of the Americas and the other side of the canal, rises the stately buildings of the former Canal Zone, whereas the area to the east of it is dominated by slums. Aside from Casco Viejo, and the pedestrian mall on Avenida Central south of Plaza Cinco de Mayo, the areas to the east of that avenue should be avoided. The eastern side of Cerro Ancón holds the Museo de Arte Contemporáneo (Museum of Modern Art) and the tourist village of Mi Pueblito. The western slope of Cerro Ancón holds the stately Edificio de la Administración del Canal (Panama Canal Administration Building), which overlooks the lawns, trees, and buildings of Balboa from a ridge.

TIMING AND PRECAUTIONS

As with most of Panama City, you are better off exploring Balboa and Cerro Ancón in the morning or late afternoon. Balboa is perfectly safe, but you'll want to avoid the neighborhoods on the other side of Avenida de los Martires from Cerro Ancón.

TOP ATTRACTIONS

Balboa. The heart of the former Canal Zone is quite a switch from the rest of Panama City, with its wide tree-shaded lawns and stately old buildings. It sometimes feels like a bit of a ghost town, especially after you spend time on the busy streets of Panama City proper, but it's a peaceful area with lots of greenery. You may spot toucans, or *agoutis* (large jungle rodents) on the slopes of Ancon Hill, or near the Panama Canal Administration Building. The Friday's restaurant next to the Country Inn & Suites Panama Canal has a front-row view of the canal and Bridge of the Americas. ✉ *Av. Arnulfo Arias and Av. Amador.*

Edificio de la Administración del Canal (*Panama Canal Administration Building*). Well worth a stop is this impressive structure set atop a ridge with a dramatic view of Balboa and the canal—a site chosen by the canal's chief engineer,

George W. Goethals. The building, designed by New York architect Austin W. Lord, was inaugurated in 1914, one month before the SS *Ancon* became the first ship to navigate the canal. Since it holds the offices of the people in charge of running the canal, most of the building is off-limits to tourists, but you can enter its lovely rotunda and admire the historic murals of the canal's construction. The murals were painted by William B. Van Ingen, who also created murals for the U.S. Library of Congress and the Philadelphia Mint. They're quite dramatic, and capture the monumental nature of the canal's construction in a style that is part Norman Rockwell, part Frederic Edwin Church. The rotunda also houses busts of the three canal visionaries: Spain's King Carlos V, who first pondered the possibility in the 16th century; the Frenchman Ferdinand de Lesseps, who led the first attempt to dig it; and President Theodore Roosevelt, who launched the successful construction effort. The doors at the back of the rotunda are locked, but if you walk around the building you'll be treated to a view of the neat lawns and tree-lined boulevards of Balboa. ⊠ *Calle Gorgas* ☎ *507/272–7602* ⊕ *www. micanaldepanama.com* ⊗ *Daily 7–4.*

WORTH NOTING

Cerro Ancón Summit. The rain forest that covers most of Cerro Ancón is a remarkably vibrant natural oasis in the midst of the city. The best area to see wildlife is on the road to the Cerro Ancón Summit, which is topped by radio towers and a giant Panamanian flag. The road ascends the hill's western slope from the luxuriant residential neighborhood of Quarry Heights, above Balboa. There is also a trail into the forest behind the offices of ANCON, Panama's biggest environmental group. If the gate at the end of Quarry Heights is locked, it should take 20-30 minutes to hike to the summit. It is best done early in the morning or late in the afternoon, when you are likely to see animals such as the abundant agoutis (large rodents), keel-billed toucan, and Geoffrey's tamarind—Panama's smallest simian. If you have a taxi drop you off at the trailhead (ask the driver to take you to the "Oficinas de ANCON" in Quarry Heights), you can hike down the other side of the hill to Mi Pueblito, where you should be able to flag a cab. ⊠ *Quarry Heights,, 400 meters south of ANCON.*

Calzada Amador

Bahía de Panama

PACIFIC OCEAN

| 0 | 1/2 mile |
| 0 | 1/2 kilometer |

Centro de Exhibiciones Marinas Punta Culebra, **3**

Isla Flamenco, **5**

Isla Naos, **2**

Isla Perico, **4**

Museo de la Biodiversidad, **1**

Punta Culebra

THE CALZADA DE AMADOR

Just south of Balboa is the former U.S. military base of Amador, a relatively empty area that is connected to three islands by a breakwater called the Calzada de Amador (Amador Causeway). The Causeway was constructed as a breakwater from the trainloads of rock and earth removed while digging the canal. Years later, a road was paved atop it, which is now lined with a sidewalk and palm trees. It stretches almost 3 km (2 miles) into the Pacific Ocean to connect the mainland to three islands: Isla Naos, Isla Perico, and Isla Flamenco, which hold strip malls, dozens of bars and restaurants, and a couple marinas. Those islands are a popular destination for people who want to escape the heat and traffic jams, and enjoy the views of the surrounding sea, massive ships passing through the adjacent canal, and the city's modern skyline.

The Calzada de Amador is a great spot for lunch, a sunset cocktail, or nighttime revelry. On Sunday afternoon, the promenade fills with joggers and bikers.

TOP ATTRACTIONS

Museo de la Biodiversidad (*Museum of Biodiversity*). The triangle of land where the Causeway begins is the site of the eye-catching Museo de la Biodiversidad. Also called the "BioMuseo," the museum was designed by the American architect Frank O. Gehry, famous for the Guggenheim Museum in Bilbao, Spain, and the pavilion at Chicago's Millennium Park. Gehry's colorful, jutting architecture is a big part of the attraction; inside you'll find exhibits on the remarkable biodiversity of Panama's forests and oceans, as well as the isthmus's role as a biological bridge between North and South America. Large-screen videos and life-size animal sculptures make dramatic visual statements, and plans call for a small inside aquarium to display marine life. The admission price is a bit steep considering the modest size of the museum, but it's still a noteworthy attraction, and the grounds offer lovely views of the canal entrance and the city skyline. ✉ *Beginning of Causeway* ☎ *507/830–6700* ⊕ *www.biomuseopanama.org* ⊒ *$22 foreign adults, $11 foreign students and visitors under age 18 ($12 for adult residents)* ⊘ *Mon. and Wed.–Fri. 10–4, weekends 10–5.*

WORTH NOTING

FAMILY **Centro de Exhibiciones Marinas Punta Culebra** (*Marine Exhibition Center*). Though it doesn't compare to the aquariums of other major cities, the Centro de Exhibiciones Marinas is worth a stop. It was created by the scientists and educators at the STRI and is located on a lovely, undeveloped point with examples of several ecosystems: beach, mangrove forest, rocky coast, and tropical forest. A series of signs leads visitors on a self-guided tour. There are several small tanks with fish and sea turtles, as well as pools with sea stars, sea cucumbers, and other marine creatures that kids can handle. The spyglasses are great for watching ships on the adjacent canal. Be sure to visit the lookout on the end of the rocky point. ✉ *Punta Culebra, Isla Naos* ☎ *507/212–8793* ⊕ *www.stri.si.edu/english/visit_us/index.php* ⊒ *$5, children $1* ⊘ *Tues.–Fri. 1–5, weekends 10–6 during school year; otherwise Tues.–Sun. 10-6.*

Isla Perico. The second island on the causeway, Isla Perico, holds a long strip mall, called Brisas de Amador, that has an array of restaurants and bars, most of which have terraces that face the canal's Pacific entrance, so you can watch the ships passing.

Isla Naos. The first island that you'll reach on the Amador Causeway, Isla Naos is dominated by the marine research laboratories of the Smithsonian Tropical Research Institute (STRI). On the far side of the island are various restaurants, a large marina, which is where you catch the ferry to Isla Taboga, and the STRI Marine Exhibition Center on Punta Culebra. The dirt road that leads to the marina and Punta Culebra is on the right just in front of the restaurant Mi Ranchito, which has a high thatch roof. Just south of Mi Ranchito is a small strip mall with several bars, a bicycle rental company, and restaurants, one of which has a swimming pool that costs a few dollars to use.

Isla Flamenco. The Amador Causeway ends at Isla Flamenco, which has two shopping centers and an assortment of restaurants. The Flamenco Marina is a popular mooring spot for yachts and fishing boats; it's the disembarkation point for cruise-ship passengers, most of whom board tour buses. Several restaurants and bars overlook the marina, which also has a great view of the city's skyline, making it a popular destination night and day.

PARQUE NATURAL METROPOLITANO, MIRAFLORES, AND SUMMIT

The area to the north of Balboa, which was also part of the American Canal Zone, has undergone considerable development since being handed over. The former U.S. Army airfield of Albrook is now Panama City's domestic airport, Aeropuerto Marcos A. Gelabert (often called simply Albrook airport); next to that are the massive Albrook Mall and the city's bustling bus terminal, the Terminal de Transporte Terrestre, called "Terminal de Buses" by locals. To the northeast of Albrook is a large swath of rain forest protected within Parque Natural Metropolitano, which is home to more than 200 bird species. To the northwest, the former army base of Clayton is now called Ciudad del Saber, or City of Knowledge; many of its buildings are occupied by international organizations and the area is also home to the Holiday Inn Panama Canal. Across the road is the first set of locks on the Pacific side of the canal, the Esclusas de Miraflores (Miraflores Locks), an area that is much more visitor-friendly than it was when the canal was U.S. property. The Panamanian administration built a state-of-the-art visitor center, with a museum and observation decks, making it one of Panama City's top attractions. From there the road follows the canal northwest through the rain forest of Soberanía National Park to the small canal port and community of Gamboa, on the shore of Gatun Lake.

Follow the road north from the locks through the forest of Camino de Cruces National Park to the former American enclave of Summit, which holds Panama City's only golf course, a botanical garden and zoo, and one of the city's best hotels.

TIMING AND PRECAUTIONS

You should visit Parque Natural Metropolitano as early in the day as you can, or late in the afternoon, because those are the times when birds and other animals are most active. Bring insect repellent with you, stay on the trails, and watch your footing, because there are poisonous snakes in these areas. The visitor center at Miraflores Locks is air-conditioned, so it is one of the few places in Panama City that you can comfortably visit in the late morning or early afternoon.

TOP ATTRACTIONS

★ Fodor'sChoice **Esclusas de Miraflores** (*Miraflores Locks*). The FAMILY four-story visitor center next to these double locks provides a front-row view of massive ships passing through the lock chambers. It also houses an excellent museum about the canal's history, engineering, daily operations, and environmental demands. Because most of the canal lies at 85 feet above sea level, each ship that passes through has to be raised to that level with three locks as they enter it, and brought back to sea level with three locks on the other end. Miraflores has two levels of locks, which move vessels between Pacific sea level and Miraflores Lake, a man-made stretch of water between Miraflores Locks and the Pedro Miguel Locks. Due to the proximity to Panama City, these locks have long been the preferred place to visit the canal, but the visitor center has made it even more popular.

There are observation decks on the ground and fourth floors of the massive cement building, from which you can watch vessels move through the locks, as a bilingual narrator explains the process and provides information about each ship, including the toll they paid to use the canal. The museum contains an excellent combination of historic relics, photographs, videos, models, and even a simulator of a ship passing through the locks. There is also a gift shop and a snack bar (the second-floor restaurant was closed for renovations as of press time). While the canal is busier at night, the largest ships pass during the day. You can call at 9 am the day before your visit to ask what time the largest ships are due through the locks. ⊠ *Road to Gamboa, across from Ciudad del Saber* ☎ *507/276–8325* ⊕ *www. visitcanaldepanama.com* ⊠ *$15, children $10* ⊙ *Daily 9–5 (last tickets sold at 4:15).*

FAMILY **Parque Natural Metropolitano** (*Metropolitan Natural Park*). A mere 20-minute drive from downtown, this 655-acre expanse of protected wilderness is a remarkably convenient place to experience the flora and fauna of Panama's tropical rain forest. It's home to 227 bird species ranging from migrant Baltimore orioles to keel-billed toucans. Five well-marked trails, covering a total of about 4.8 km (3 miles), range from a climb to the park's highest point to a fairly flat loop. On any given morning of hiking you may spot such spectacular birds as a gray-headed chachalaca, a collared aracari, or a mealy parrot. The park is also home to 45 mammal species, so keep an eye out for dark brown agoutis (large jungle rodents). Keep your ears perked for tamarins, tiny monkeys that sound like birds.

There's a visitor center near the southern end of the park, next to El Roble and Los Caobas trails, where the nonprofit organization that administers the park collects the admission fee and sells cold drinks, snacks, and nature books. This is the best place to begin your exploration of the park, since you can purchase a map that shows the trails. Call two days ahead to reserve an English-speaking guide ($25).

Across the street from the visitor center is a shorter loop called Sendero Los Momótides. The Mono Titi and La Cieneguita trails head into the forest from the road about 1 km (½ mile) north of the visitor center and connect to each other to form a loop through the park's most precipitous terrain. The Smithsonian Tropical Research Institute (STRI) has a construction crane in the middle of the forest near the Mono Titi trail that is used to study life in the forest canopy, which is where the greatest diversity of flora and fauna is found. El Roble connects with La Cieneguita, so you can hike the northern loop and then continue through the forest to the visitor center; the total distance of that hike is 3½ km (2¼ miles).

Be sure to bring water, insect repellent, and binoculars, and be careful where you put your feet and hands, since the park does have poisonous snakes, biting insects, and spiny plants. ⊠ *Av. Juan Pablo II* ☎ *507/232–5552* ⊕ *www.parque-metropolitano.org* ⊠ *$4 for foreign visitors* ⊙ *Daily 7–5.*

WORTH NOTING

Cementerio Francés (*French Cemetery*). The pastoral Cementerio Francés sits on the left side of the road just before Summit and serves as a testament to the human toll once taken by grand construction projects. Hundreds of crosses line a hill in this pretty cemetery and mark the resting place of a fraction of the 20,000 workers who died during France's brief attempt to construct a canal across the isthmus.

Museo Antropológico Reina Torres de Araúz (*Reina Torres de Araúz Anthropological Museum*). After decades of being on display in a former railway station, the government's collection of pre-Columbian artifacts is now housed in a larger facility with more than 50,000 square feet of exhibit space, not far from the Parque Natural Metropolitano visitor center. The museum is named for Panama's pioneering anthropologist, Reina Torres de Araúz, who first opened this and a half-dozen other museums in the country. The facility has a rather impressive collection of more than 15,000 pieces of jewelry, ceramics, stone, and other prehispanic artifacts. ⊠ *Av. Juan Pablo II, Llanos de Curundú* ☎ *507/501–4731* ⊕ *www.inac.gob.pa* ☑ *$2.50* ☉ *Tues.–Sun. 9–4.*

FAMILY **Parque Municipal Summit** (*Jardín Botánico Summit, or Summit Botanical Garden*). About 13 miles northwest of Balboa, this large garden and zoo is surrounded by rain forest. Started in 1923 as a U.S. government project to reproduce tropical plants with economic potential, it evolved into a botanical garden and a zoo in the 1960s. The gardens and surrounding forest hold thousands of species, but the focus is on about 150 species of ornamental, fruit, and hardwood trees from around the world that were once raised here. These range from coffee and cinnamon to the more unusual candle tree and cannonball tree. The zoo is home to 40 native animal species, most of them in cages that are depressingly small, though a few have decent quarters. Stars include jaguars, ocelots, all six of the country's monkey species, several macaw species, and the harpy eagle, Panama's national bird. A neat thing about Summit is that most of the animals exhibited in the zoo are also found in the surrounding forest, so you may spot parrots, toucans, and agoutis on the grounds. ⊠ *22 km (13 miles) northwest of downtown on road to Gamboa* ☎ *507/232–4850* ☑ *$5* ☉ *Daily 9–4.*

DOWNTOWN

The area northeast of the old city, stretching from the neighborhoods of El Cangrejo to Punta Paitilla, is where you'll find most of the city's office towers, banks, hotels, restaurants, and shops. As Panama City's economy grew and diversified during the 20th century, those who had money abandoned Casco Viejo and built homes in new neighborhoods to the northeast; apartment buildings and office towers soon followed. Many of Panama City's best hotels and restaurants are clustered in El Cangrejo and the Area Bancária (Financial District), which flank busy Via España. Calle 50, another of the city's main arteries, defines the southern edge of the Area Bancária. A few blocks southeast of Calle 50 is Avenida Balboa, another of the city's major thoroughfares, which curves along the coast between the Casco Viejo and Punta Paitilla and is lined by the parks and waterfront promenade of La Cinta Costera. Between Calle 50 and Avenida Balboa you'll find the neighborhoods of Bella Vista and Marbella, which hold an interesting mix of apartment towers, aging mansions, shops, and government offices. Just to the east of Marbella is Punta Paitilla, a small point packed with skyscrapers and a few hotels.

TIMING AND PRECAUTIONS

The neighborhoods mentioned in this section are safe to explore, although you should be careful crossing its main streets. La Cinta Costera is best strolled in the morning or early evening; it skirts some rough neighborhoods to the west of the Balboa Monument, but even this section of the Cinta is generally considered safe for visiting during these hours.

WORTH NOTING

Area Bancária (*Financial District*). Narrow streets shaded by leafy tropical trees make the city's financial district a pleasant area to explore, though the trees are being cut to make room for more skyscrapers. Together with El Cangrejo, which lies across Vía España from it, the Area Bancária holds a critical mass of hotels and restaurants. You'll find two of the city's highest concentrations of bars and restaurants in El Cangrejo and the area around Calle 48 (Calle Uruguay), between Calle 50 (Nicanor de Obarrio) and Avenida Balboa. ⊠ *Between Vía España and Calle 50.*

La Cinta Costera. The busy waterfront boulevard Avenida Balboa and the linear park running alongside it are lined with palm trees and graced with great views of the Bay of Panama and Casco Viejo. The sidewalk that runs along the bay and the park wedged between the avenue lanes is a popular strolling and jogging route. To the west of the Miramar towers and the Yacht Club is a small park with a monument to Vasco Nuñez de Balboa, who, after trudging through the rain forests of the Darién in 1501, became the first European to set eyes on the Pacific Ocean. That gleaming white **Monumento a Balboa** is topped by a steel sculpture of the conquistador gazing out at the Pacific. The statue was a gift to the Panamanian people from Spain's King Alfonso XIII in 1924. Walking is best to the east of the Monumento, since it passes some rough neighborhoods to the west—although the newer area near the fish market and entrance to Casco Viejo has become popular for walking, relaxing, and outdoor exercising (there's an open-air workout area). Unfortunately, a stroll along the waterfront may be punctuated by wiffs of Panama City's raw sewage, which pours into the bay from a series of pipes just off the Cinta Costera, and is especially noxious at low tide. The government is building the city's long-overdue sewage system, but it will take years to complete. ⊠ *Av. Balboa.*

PANAMÁ VIEJO

Crumbling ruins are all that's left of Panamá Viejo (sometimes called Panamá la Vieja), the country's first major Spanish settlement, which was destroyed by pirate Henry Morgan in 1671. Panamá Viejo was founded in 1519 by the conquistador Pedroarias Dávila. Built on the site of an indigenous village that had existed for centuries, the city soon became a busy colonial outpost. Expeditions to explore the Pacific coast of South America left from here. When Francisco Pizarro conquered the Incan empire, the copious gold and silver he stole arrived in Panamá Viejo, where it was loaded onto mules and taken across the isthmus to Spain-bound ships. For the next 150 years Panamá Viejo was a vital link between Spain and the gold and silver mines of South America. Year after year, ships came and went; mule trains carried precious metals to Panama's Caribbean coast and returned with Spanish goods bound for the southern colonies. The city's merchants, royal envoys, and priests accumulated enough gold to make a pirate drool. At the time of Morgan's attack, Panamá Viejo had a handful of convents and churches, one hospital, markets, and luxurious mansions. The fires started during the pirate attack reduced much of the city to ashes within days. The paucity of the remaining ruins is not due entirely to the pirates' looting and burning: the Spanish colonists spent years dismantling buildings after they decided to rebuild their city in the neighborhood now known as Casco Viejo or Casco Antiguo, on the peninsula to the southwest, which was deemed easier to defend against attack. The Spanish carried everything that could be moved to the new city, including the stone blocks that are today the walls of the city's current cathedral and the facade of the Iglesia de la Merced. Panamá Viejo is part of all city tours, which can be a good way to visit the site, if you get a knowledgeable guide. There are also sometimes guides at the Plaza Mayor who provide free information in Spanish. The collections of walls that you'll pass between the Visitor Center and Plaza Mayor are all that remain of several convents, the bishop's palace, and San Juan de Dios Hospital. Plaza Mayor is approximately 1 km (½ mile) from the visitor center, so you may want to drive or take a cab. Try to visit this site before 11:00 am or after 3:00 pm.

TIMING AND PRECAUTIONS

As with any outdoor attraction in often-sweltering Panama City, it's best to visit Panamá Viejo first thing in the morning or later in the afternoon. ■TIP➔ **The museum closes at 4:30 pm, so make sure this is one of your first stops.** The ruins are patrolled by tourism police on mountain bikes, but the neighborhood is less tourist-friendly, so don't wander too far from the main road—Vía Cincuentenaria—and the Plaza Mayor.

WORTH NOTING

Centro de Visitantes (*Visitor Center*). Start your visit to Panamá Viejo at the Centro de Visitantes—a large building on the right as you enter Panamá Viejo on Vía Cincuentenaria. From ATLAPA, that street heads inland for 2 km (1 mile) through a residential neighborhood before arriving at the ruins, which are on the coast. Once you see the ocean again, look for the two-story visitor center on your right. It holds a large museum that chronicles the site's evolution from an indigenous village to one of the wealthiest cities in the Western Hemisphere. Works on display include indigenous pottery made centuries before the arrival of the Spanish, relics of the colonial era, and a model of what the city looked like shortly before Morgan's attack. Keep that model in mind as you explore the site, since you need a good dose of imagination to evoke the city that was once home to between 7,000 and 10,000 people from the rubble that remains of it. ✉ *Vía Cincuentenaria, 2 km (1 mile) east of ATLAPA* ☎ *507/226–1757* ⊕ *www. panamaviejo.org* ✍ *$8 for foreigners to visit museum and ruins* ☉ *Tues.–Sun. 8:30–4:30.*

Plaza Mayor (*Main Plaza*). Vía Cincuentenaria curves to the left in front of what was once the city's **Plaza Mayor** (Main Plaza), a simple cobbled square backed by a stone tower that is the only part of Panamá Viejo that has undergone any significant renovation. Show your admission ticket for the Visitor Center at the entrance here, or buy a separate ticket to enter the plaza alone. Climb the metal staircase inside the **Torre de la Catedral** (Cathedral Tower)—the former bell tower of Panama's original cathedral—for a view of the surrounding ruins. The structure just south of the tower was once the city hall; walls to the north and east are all that remain of homes, a church, and a convent. The extensive ruins are shaded by tropical trees, which attract plenty of birds, so the nature and scenery are as much of an attraction as the ancient walls. ✉ *Av. Cincuentenario, about 3 km (2 miles) east of ATLAPA* ☎ *507/226–8915* ⊕ *www. panamaviejo.org* ✍ *$8 for foreigners to visit museum and ruins* ☉ *Tues.–Sun. 8:30–4:30.*

PLAYA KOBBE (PLAYA BONITA)

7 km (4 miles) southwest of Panama City.

With a long beach on a cove of calm water backed by tropical forest, Playa Kobbe is a lovely spot. It's the closest beach to Panama City, less than 20 minutes from downtown. Since Kobbe Beach lies on the other side of the Canal, the water there is considerably cleaner than near Panama City, but it may at times still be tinged with oil from the area's abundant ships, so it is not always ideal for swimming or snorkeling. Once a popular picnic spot for locals, Playa Kobbe is now dominated by two resort-style hotels, the Dreams Buenaventura Panama (a revamp of the former InterContinental Playa Bonita, which is scheduled to debut in 2016), and the Westin Playa Bonita (*See Where to Stay*). Both of these properties restrict access to the beach, even though all beaches are public property under Panamanian law. The name Playa Bonita (beautiful beach) is a fairly recent PR invention, but it is rapidly replacing Playa Kobbe, named for the U.S. military base that once stood nearby, as the beach's moniker.

GETTING HERE
To drive to Kobbe from Panama City, take Avenida de los Martires to the Bridge of the Americas and take the first exit after crossing the canal, turning left and following the signs to the Intercontinental Play Bonita Resort. A taxi should cost $25.

2

WHERE TO EAT

It's not quite New York or Paris, but Panama City's restaurant scene is impressive. Panamanians like to eat out, and enough of them have incomes that allow for regular dining on the town, which has resulted in a growing cadre of restaurants. Many of the best restaurants are clustered in Casco Viejo, El Cangrejo, Area Bancária, and nearby Calle Uruguay, which are also the neighborhoods where you'll find most of the best hotels. Java junkies will rejoice that a good cup of coffee can be found just about anywhere; even the inexpensive restaurants have espresso machines.

Cuisine selection spans the globe, from Indian and Italian to Lebanese and Panamanian (obviously). The seafood tends to be quite fresh, which shouldn't come as a surprise, since the word "*Panama*" means "abundance of fish," and it's relatively inexpensive, with the exception of lobster and crab. Panama produces decent beef, but the best beef is imported from the United States and can be more expensive. A typical entrée at an expensive restaurant runs about $17, whereas a main dish at a less expensive eatery averages around $9. It's customary to tip at least 10%, but some restaurants automatically add a 10% *servicio* charge, so be sure to have a good look at the check.

Some restaurants close Sunday, and many close between lunch and dinner (approximately 2:30 to 6:30). Reservations aren't usually required, but are a good idea on weekends. Jackets and ties aren't necessary, but don't wear shorts and sandals unless the restaurant is outdoors.

CASCO VIEJO

Here you'll find some of Panama City's best restaurants, as well as the city's best ambience. Even if you stay downtown, you should head here for at least one meal, and a drink on Plaza Bolívar. ■TIP→ **Many restaurants here close between lunch and dinner, so call ahead if you want to eat between 2 and 7.**

0 ___ 1/8 mile
0 ___ 1/8 kilometer

Bahía de Panamá

KEY

Dangerous Areas to be Avoided

1 Restaurants

Casco Viejo Dining

The Dining Room at American Trade Hotel, **2**

Ego y Narcisco, **6**

Las Clementinas Café & Bar, **1**

L'Ostería, **4**

Manolo Caracol, **8**

Mostaza, **9**

René Café, **5**

Super Gourmet, **7**

Tantalo, **3**

★ **Fodor's**Choice ✕ **The Dining Room at American Trade Hotel.** *Interna-*
$$$$ *tional.* Set in the high-ceilinged lobby of the American Trade
Hotel, The Dining Room is an elegant venue that pays great
attention to detail. The stylish decor blends antique and
contemporary touches, and the cuisine is largely the work
of chef Clara Icaza, a well-regarded culinary expert who
was named one of the top 20 young chefs by the Spanish-
language *Gato Pardo* magazine. Top dinner choices feature
an array of meat and seafood creations, including corn-
dusted filet of cobia served with spicy piccata sauce, and
beef tenderloin served with a sweet potato tamale and guava
sauce. The wine list is equally impressive, with varietals
from regions including Argentina, Australia, Chile, Italy,
and Spain. ⓢ *Average main: $22* ✉ *American Trade Hotel,
Plaza Herrera, Panama City* ☎ *507/211–2200* ⊕ *www.
acehotel.com/panama.*

$$$ ✕ **Ego y Narciso.** *Italian South American.* This small restau-
rant has tables on Plaza Bolívar, overlooking the Iglesia de
San Francisco, making it one of Panama City's more charm-
ing dinner spots. If you can't handle the heat, though, you
can always move into the air-conditioned dining room in
the historic building across the street. The menu is a mix

of Latin American and Italian cuisines, an example being chicken ravioli with a spicy Peruvian cream sauce called *ají de gallina*. They offer several other fresh pastas, as well as seafood and meat dishes. Popular starters include seafood carpaccio, Peruvian ceviche, and *mini brochetas*: try the breaded pork option with sesame seeds and tamarind sauce. Those tapas and the gorgeous setting make this a good spot for cocktails and appetizers even if you dine elsewhere. [$] *Average main: $19* ✉ *Calle 3 Este y Av. Sucre, on Plaza Bolívar* ☎ *507/262–2045.*

$$$ ✕ **Las Clementinas Café & Bar.** *Eclectic.* An eclectic blend of Panamanian, European, and Asian cuisines and the choice of dining in an old-world café or a distinctly tropical patio make a meal at Las Clementinas a memorable experience. The bright dining room evokes a Parisian bistro, with its large, arched windows, tile floors, and long, marble-topped bar, and the lush garden patio is a lovely spot for an intimate dinner. The menu ranges from sea bass with jasmine rice and roasted eggplant to three-chili-braised goat tacos with homemade corn tortillas. They offer several cuts of beef and a selection of sandwiches, soups, and salads, and a popular Sunday brunch. It can get quite lively on weekend nights, when reservations are recommended, but as soon as things calm down, the manager usually sits down at the piano and plays a song. [$] *Average main: $20* ✉ *Av. B and Calle 11* ☎ *507/228–7613* 🌐 *www.lasclementinas.com* ⏲ *Closed Mon.*

$$$ ✕ **L'Ostería.** *Italian.* Quality Italian cuisine served amid ancient walls make L'Ostería a popular dinner option. The restaurant is located under the Casa del Horno boutique hotel, in a restored colonial building, and the back patio, with its stone walls and small garden, is a lovely spot to spend a couple hours. The menu includes a small selection of pizzas, pastas, meat, and seafood dishes. Try the pennette with a zucchini and almond pesto sauce, *corvina alla piastra* (sautéed sea bass served with grilled vegetables), or one of the excellent pizzas. [$] *Average main: $20* ✉ *Av. B between Calle 7 and Calle 8* ☎ *507/212–0809* 💳 *No credit cards* ⏲ *No lunch.*

★ **Fodor'sChoice** ✕ **Manolo Caracol.** *Mediterranean.* Owned by
$$$$ Spanish chef Manolo Madueño, this restaurant-cum-art gallery in a restored colonial building is dedicated to the joy of dining, with a different prix-fixe menu consisting of 8 to 10 items offered each night. All you need to do is choose your beverage—perhaps a beer or a Spanish wine—and wait for the succession of succulent surprises that the waiters

will deliver shortly after you scrape each plate clean. Meals tend to be strong on seafood, but there are always a couple of meat dishes. Manolo's is for people who like to eat big, so if you're a light eater, or are on a budget, you should head elsewhere. With its eclectic shrine to the Virgin Mary, and ancient, whitewashed walls hung with modern art, it's a charming spot to spend a few hours, which is how long dinner will take, especially when Manolo is there working the crowd. It gets noisy on weekend nights, when it can be hard to carry on a conversation, and it can get awfully hot at the tables near the cooking area, which is in the central back part of the dining area. ⓈAverage main: $41 ⊠ Av. Central and Calle 3 Este ☎507/228–4640 ⊕www. manolocaracol.net ⚭ Reservations essential.

$$$$ ✕**Mostaza.** Latin American. Nestled in a restored colonial building across the street from the ruins of Santo Domingo, Mostaza offers a cozy and delicious dining experience in the heart of the historic quarter. Start with a drink on the plaza, then move into one of the two narrow dining rooms, one of which has a centuries-old exposed stone wall. The Argentine and Panamanian owners are usually in the kitchen, preparing an eclectic mix of local seafood and meat dishes that range from lenguado (sole) in a mushroom sauce to pork tenderloin in a maracuya (passion fruit) sauce. They offer some inventive fresh pastas, such as seafood ravioli in a vodka salmon sauce, and langostinos (prawns) sautéed with Gran Marnier, but meat lovers will want to try the classic Argentine bife de chorizo (a thick cut of tenderloin) with chimichurri: an olive oil, garlic, and parsley sauce. ⓈAverage main: $35 ⊠ Av. A and Calle 3 ☎507/228–3341 ⊙ Closed Mon. No lunch weekends.

$$$$ ✕**René Café.** Latin American. After managing Manolo Caracol for years (see review), René opened his own place, while following Manolo's popular formula of offering a set menu that changes daily and consists of about a dozen items served in five or six courses. The difference is a more intimate setting, more Caribbean influence, and lower prices. René is almost always there, making sure his guests are happy. The small restaurant is in a historic building on the northwest corner of Plaza Catedral, with a high ceiling and white walls that are invariably decorated with the work of local artists. There are also several tables on the sidewalk with cathedral views. The dining experience is a sort of culinary journey, in which fresh dishes appear every time you complete a course, and you happily chew your way forward, toward a light dessert. Simpler, inexpensive

lunches are an alternative to René's seemingly endless dinners. [$] *Average main: $25* ✉ *Plaza Catedral, Calle Pedro J. Sossa* ☎ *507/262–3487* ⏲ *Closed Sun.* ✍ *Reservations essential.*

$ FAMILY ✕ **Super Gourmet.** *Deli.* This American-owned deli, in a historic building behind the Palacio Municipal, is a popular breakfast and lunch spot thanks to its selection of sandwiches, salads, and homemade soups. The ample breakfast menu includes several English muffin sandwiches and a house version of eggs Benedict, as well as excellent coffee. In addition to a dozen sandwiches, they offer a good selection of salads and such treats as homemade hummus and a Brie and fruit plate. They also make good cookies and other desserts. The central location and free Wi-Fi make this a popular hangout for local expats. [$] *Average main: $8* ✉ *Av. A and Calle 7* ☎ *507/212–3487* 🌐 *www.supergourmetcascoviejo.com* 💳 *No credit cards* ⏲ *No dinner.*

$$ ✕ **Tántalo.** *International.* This trendy tapas restaurant packs in the locals on weekend nights, but it's a fun place for a meal any time. Seating is at long, high tables, which different groups share under a tangle of wires and hanging lamps. The tapas are an international mix of flavors: from Greek salad to coconut cashew chicken to a selection of Panamanian empanadas (fried pastries stuffed with sausage and potato or beans and cheese). The portions vary in size, but the best thing is to start with two per person, and share. The atmosphere is hip, with house and other contemporary music on the stereo and original art on the walls. You may want to head up to the rooftop bar—a popular night spot with an impressive view—once you've had your fill of tapas. The restaurant's weekday lunch specials are reasonably priced and make for a nice break while touring the historic neighborhood. [$] *Average main: $15* ✉ *Av. B and Calle 8* ☎ *507/262–4030* 🌐 *www.tantalohotel.com* 💳 *No credit cards* ✍ *Reservations essential.*

CALZADA DE AMADOR

The best thing about eating on the Amador Causeway is that you usually get an ocean view with your meal. A great place for lunch, the Causeway is also a popular dinner destination, and its restaurants tend to serve food late.

$$$ ✕ **Alberto's.** *Italian.* The best tables here are across the drive from the main restaurant, overlooking the Flamenco Marina and the city skyline beyond, but they are also the first ones to fill up. The other options are to sit on the

large covered terrace, cooled by ceiling fans, or in the air-conditioned dining room. The food here is good, but the service can be leisurely. The menu has something for everyone, including a good selection of pizzas and pastas, but seafood is usually the best choice. You can start with *duo de mar* (corvina and lobster in béchamel sauce) or *mero* (grouper) carpaccio, and move on to pizza, salmon ravioli in a creamy tomato sauce, *corvina al cartucho* (sea bass and julienne vegetables broiled in foil), or *langostinos provençal* (prawns sautéed with fine herbs and tomatoes). You may want to walk around the island a few times before visiting their Italian ice cream shop. [$] *Average main: $16* ✉ *Edificio Fuerte Amador, Isla Flamenco* ☎ *507/314–1134*.

$$ 🍴 **Mi Ranchito.** *Latin American.* FAMILY Topped by a giant thatch roof that has become an Amador Causeway landmark, Mi Ranchito has a great view of the city across the bay and is one of the best places in town to sample Panamanian cuisine. The food isn't gourmet, but it's authentic and inexpensive. House specialties include various ceviches, *corvina entera frita* (a whole fried sea bass), *crema de mariscos* (seafood chowder), *camarones a la criolla* (shrimp in a tomato and onion sauce), *corvina al ajillo* (sea bass in a garlic sauce), and a rib-eye steak *encebollado* (smothered in onions). They serve tasy *batidos* (frozen fruit drinks) made from papaya, *piña* (pineapple), and other tropical fruits; this is an excellent spot for a drink at sunset, when the skyline glows. At night, you can enjoy the live Latin music, often traditional Panamanian. [$] *Average main: $15* ✉ *Isla Naos* ☎ *507/228–4909* 🌐 *www.restaurantemiranchito.com*.

$$$$ 🍴 **Restaurante Barko.** *Seafood.* This open-air restaurant is known for serving large portions of fresh seafood, prepared a variety of ways, with an ocean breeze. The specialties are all from the surrounding sea, such as ceviche, *corvina con hongos* (sea bass with a mushroom sauce) and crispy *langostinos* (prawns) served with coconut rice and *guandú* (pigeon peas). The name is a misspelling of the word *barco* (boat), and you'll probably see a few as you dine, because most tables face the canal, whereas the rest overlook the bay and city, beyond the parking lot. The wine list has 10 vintages from various countries. It's the first restaurant in the Brisas del Amador shopping center, on the left as you arrive at Isla Perico. [$] *Average main: $22* ✉ *Isla Perico* ☎ *507/314–0000*.

DOWNTOWN PANAMA CITY

Not only does the downtown area have a high concentration of restaurants, it also has the greatest variety of cuisines and prices. Many of these are within walking distance of hotels, and the area is very safe. It also has plenty of bars.

$$ 🍴 **Beirut.** *Lebanese.* The interior of this Lebanese restaurant goes a bit overboard, with faux-stone columns and arches, but the food is consistently good, and the waitstaff is attentive. The extensive menu goes beyond the Middle East to include dishes such as grilled salmon and pizzas, but the best bets are the Lebanese dishes, which include an array of starters such as falafel, baba ghanoush, and nearly a dozen salads that can make for an inexpensive, light meal. It's a good choice for vegetarians. Be sure to order some fresh flat bread to go with your meal. Belly dancers perform on Thursday, Friday and Saturday nights at 9 pm. There is a collection of hookahs for smoking on the patio, which is a nice place to eat at night, as long as it isn't full of hookah smokers. The owner also has a restaurant on the Amador Causeway. [$] *Average main: $15* ✉ *Calles 52 and Ricardo Arias, across from Panama Marriott Hotel* ☎ *507/214–3815.*

$$ 🍴 **Caffé Pomodoro.** *Italian.* Decent Italian food at reasonable prices served amidst tropical foliage make this restaurant in the Hotel Las Vegas a local favorite. Though there is a small air-conditioned dining room, the nicest tables are on the hotel's large interior patio, with its tropical trees, potted plants, and palms decorated with swirling Christmas lights. At lunch, it feels like a jungle oasis in the heart of the city, with birds singing in the branches above. The food is standard Italian, with eight varieties of homemade pastas served with any of a dozen different sauces, a variety of broiled meat and seafood dishes, personal pizzas, and focaccia sandwiches. For dessert, choose from chocolate cheesecake, tiramisu, and other treats. There is usually a guitarist playing at dinnertime Monday through Saturday, and the Wine Bar next door has acoustic Latin music until late. [$] *Average main: $11* ✉ *Vía Veneto and Calle Eusebio A. Morales* ☎ *507/269–5836* 🌐 *www.caffepomodoro.com.*

$ 🍴 **El Trapiche.** *Latin American.* El Trapiche is a popular spot for traditional Panamanian food, thanks to its convenient location and reasonable prices. The menu includes all the local favorites, from *ropa vieja* (stewed beef) to *cazuelo de mariscos* (seafood stew) and *sancocho* (chicken soup). They serve inexpensive set lunches, and typical Panama-

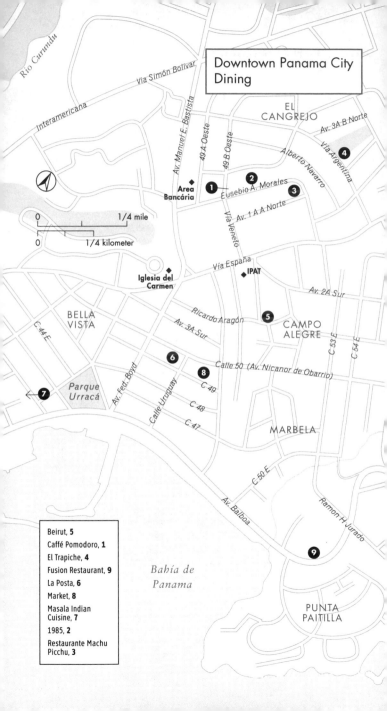

Downtown Panama City Dining

Río Curundú

Interamericana

Via Simón Bolívar

EL CANGREJO

Av. 3A B Norte

Av. Manuel E. Bastista

49 A Oeste

49 B Oeste

Alberto Navarro

Via Argentina

4

Area Bancária

1 Eusebio A. Morales

2

3

Via Veneto

Av. 1 A A Norte

0 ——— 1/4 mile

0 ——— 1/4 kilometer

Iglesia del Carmen

Via España

IPAT

Av. 2A Sur

BELLA VISTA

Ricardo Aragón

Av. 3A Sur

5

CAMPO ALEGRE

C. 53 E

C. 54 E

C. 44 E

Calle 50 (Av. Nicanor de Obarrio)

6

8

C. 49

Av. Fed. Boyd

Parque Urracá

Calle Uruguay

C. 48

C. 47

MARBELA

7 ←

C. 50 E

Ramon H. Jurado

Av. Balboa

9

Beirut, **5**

Caffé Pomodoro, **1**

El Trapiche, **4**

Fusion Restaurant, **9**

La Posta, **6**

Market, **8**

Masala Indian Cuisine, **7**

1985, **2**

Restaurante Machu Picchu, **3**

Bahía de Panama

PUNTA PAITILLA

nian breakfasts, which include *bistec encebollado* (skirt steak smothered in onions), *tortillas* (thick deep-fried corn patties), and *carimañolas* (cassava croquets stuffed with ground beef). The decor is appropriately folksy, with drums, Carnaval masks, and other handicrafts hanging on the walls, and a barrel-tile awning over the front terrace, at the end of which is the old *trapiche* (traditional sugarcane press) for which the place is named. The owners also have a branch location at Albrook Mall. [$] *Average main: $8* ✉ *Vía Argentina, 2 blocks off Vía España* ☎ *507/269–4353.*

$$$ 🍴 **Fusion Restaurant.** *Eclectic.* This restaurant combines wild decor with an inventive menu that melds the cuisines of three continents. The central dining area looks like something out of a Hollywood adventure movie, dominated by a 20-foot bust reminiscent of the statues on Easter Island. By day, sunlight glistens down through portholes in the bottom of the pool on the roof. If the statue is a bit too much for you, look for a table in the other dining area, where the artistic decor includes giant vases and a wall of TVs broadcasting fire images. The menu matches the atmosphere with an inventive mix of Continental, Asian, and Latin American cuisines that is true to the restaurant's name. You can start your dinner with Peruvian ceviche or turkey ginger spring rolls, then dive into some shrimp and vegetables in a coconut curry, lamb ribs with a sweet and spicy sauce, or creamy lobster risotto with palm fruit. [$] *Average main: $19* ✉ *Hotel Decapolis, Av. Balboa, next to Multicentro* ☎ *507/215–5000* 🌐 *www.radisson.com.*

★ Fodor's Choice 🍴 **La Posta.** *Latin American.* Elegant ambience

$$$ and an innovative mix of Latin American and European flavors have kept La Posta one of Panama City's most popular restaurants. Located in a refurbished house just off Calle Uruguay, it has a classic Caribbean feel, with ceiling fans, cane chairs, colorful tile floors, and potted palms. There is usually Latin music playing, and the shiny hardwood bar stretching down one end of the dining room is the perfect place to sip a mojito. The menu changes regularly, but it always includes fresh seafood, USDA beef, and organic pork and chicken prepared in inventive ways, plus a few risottos and pastas. You can check current offerings on the restaurant's website. Reserve a table in the back, overlooking the small, tropical garden, and try your best to save room for dessert. [$] *Average main: $20* ✉ *Calle 47 and Calle Uruguay, next to Waldorf Astoria* ☎ *507/269–1076* 🌐 *www.lapostapanama.com* ⏲ *Closed 2:30–7; closed Sun.*

★ $$$ **Fodor's Choice** 🍴 **Market.** *Steakhouse.* This trendy steak house a block off busy Calle Uruguay is the best option for a meat lover, whether you're in the mood for filet mignon or a cheeseburger. You can get USDA Omaha beef here, but it costs considerably more than the Panamanian beef. The chicken and pork are organic and free-range from the restaurant's own farm. You can also get such American classics as a Cobb salad or a side of macaroni and cheese, which are no doubt novelties for the predominantly Panamanian clientele. The steaks are excellent, but so is the Moroccan-style chicken with couscous, and the salmon *grille beurre maitre d'hôtel*. There's an extensive wine list, and the service is excellent. You may want to reserve a table on weekends, when this place gets packed and noisy. They also serve brunch from 11:30 to 2:30 on weekends. [$] *Average main: $17* ✉ *Calle 48 between Calle Uruguay and Aquino de La Guardia* ☎ *507/226–9401* 🌐 *www.marketpanama.com* 🕒 *Closed Mon.–Wed. 2:30–6:30; closed Thurs. and Fri. 3:30–6:30.*

$$$$ 🍴 **Masala Indian Cuisine.** *North Indian.* Panama City's best Indian restaurant is also one of your surest bets for going vegetarian in a town short on options for herbivores. The shrine behind the bar shows a traditionally dressed Indian woman making the gesture meaning "welcome," and owners Koreena Bajwa and César Marín certainly make guests feel that way. Their authentic north Indian cuisine is served in cozy, colorfully decorated dining rooms, which include an area for shoeless dining on the floor on plush cushions. Just about any of the dozens of vegetarian, chicken, and lamb options on the menu are guaranteed to make your taste buds smile. A great nonmeat option is the *thali*, a plate that includes four hefty samplers including beans or lentils and a yogurt-based dish. This popular restaurant is small, so reservations are essential. [$] *Average main: $27* ✉ *Justo Arosemena, between Calles 44 and 45* ☎ *507/225–0105* 🕒 *Closed Sun.* ✍ *Reservations essential.*

$$$ 🍴 **1985.** *French Swiss.* Named for the year it opened, this restaurant serves traditional French and Swiss cuisine in an eclectic mix of dining rooms. It holds the strange distinction of occupying the only building in Panama City that resembles a Swiss chalet. The owner, chef Willy Dingelman, trained in Lausanne then moved to Panama three decades ago, and has since developed a small restaurant and wine-importing empire. They consequently have an excellent wine cellar. When President Ricardo Martinelli was on the campaign trail, Dingelman promised he'd share

a $15,000 bottle if he won the election; there's a photo of the post-election moment on the wall at the entrance. Dingelman's original Swiss restaurant, called the Rincón Suizo, is now a rustic dining room in the back of 1985—two menus under one roof. The decor is a bit of this and a bit of that, with a cluttered collection of chairs and couches in the long entrance, but people come here for the food, such as chicken *cordon bleu*, tenderloin in green peppercorn sauce, raclette, bratwurst, or *Zürcher Geschnetzeltes* (veal chunks in a mushroom cream sauce). [$] *Average main: $20* ✉ *Calle Eusebio A. Morales, in front of Sevilla Suites hotel* ☎ *507/263–8541*.

$$ 🍴 **Restaurante Machu Picchu.** *Peruvian.* This popular Peruvian restaurant named after that country's famous Inca ruins occupies an unassuming house a short walk from the hotels of El Cangrejo. Its relatively small dining room, decorated with paintings of Peruvian landscapes and colorful woven tablecloths, is often packed with Panamanians at night. The food they come for is traditional Peruvian, with a few inventions such as *corvina Hiroshima* (sea bass in a shrimp, bell pepper, and ginger sauce) and *langostinos gratinados* (prawns au gratin). You can't go wrong with such Peruvian classics as ceviche, *ají de gallina* (shredded chicken in a chili-cream sauce), *seco de res* (Peruvian stewed beef with rice), and *sudado de mero* (grouper in a spicy soup). Be careful how you apply the *ají* hot sauce; it's practically caustic. [$] *Average main: $13* ✉ *Calle Eusebio A Morales No. 18* ☎ *507/264–9308* 🌐 *www.restaurantemachupicchu.com*.

WHERE TO STAY

Panama City has a good hotel selection, with something for every taste and budget. Casco Viejo has stylish boutique hotels in historic settings, but they lack the facilities of the bigger hotels and can be noisy on weekends. There are various large hotels scattered around the city, but most are clustered in El Cangrejo and the Area Bancária, which are busy, but have plenty of restaurants and nightlife. For a quieter alternative (albeit farther removed from most activities and attractions), head to Balboa, Cerro Ancón, or one of the areas just outside the city, such as Summit, or Playa Kobbe.

Because of a recent boom in hotel construction, you won't need to reserve too far ahead except for the small B&Bs and boutique hotels. ■ **TIP→ Because of an oversupply of big** hotels, you can often get a room for a fraction of the rack rate if you book online, especially on weekends. The city's best hotels are quite nice and varied enough in what they offer to suit most tastes, but some can suffer from poor service. Travelers on a budget can find a variety of comfortable accommodations for less than $120, which often includes a swimming pool. All hotels listed here have private bathrooms with hot water, air-conditioning, and Wi-Fi; most have a telephone and cable TV in the room.

Hotel reviews have been shortened, for full information visit Fodors.com.

CASCO VIEJO

Casco Viejo has various small hotels in refurbished buildings dating from the early 20th or late 19th centuries, with great decor and views. They are an excellent option for those who want to experience life in the city's colorful historic quarter. ■TIP➜ **Casco Viejo has a critical mass of bars, and some hotels suffer party noise into the wee hours on weekends.**

★ **Fodor's**Choice ☒ **American Trade Hotel.** *Hotel.* The style-con-
$$$$ scious folks of the U.S.-based boutique hotelier Ace Hotels are partly responsible for the American Trade, one of the city's most beautiful boutique hotels. A former 1930s apartment building—which had sat abandoned and neglected for decades—has been recast as a one-of-a-kind luxury hotel, with a high-ceilinged lobby with a pristine tile floor and comfy furnishings, as well as a pricey-but-worth-it restaurant and lobby bar. **Pros:** stylish; central Casco Viejo location; on-site bar, restaurant, and jazz club. **Cons:** pricey; small pool. Ⓢ *Rooms from: $229* ☒ *Plaza Herrera, Casco Viejo, Panama City* ☏ *507/211–2000* ⊕ *www.acehotel.com/panama* ⌁ *50 rooms* ⦿*No meals.*

★ **Fodor's**Choice ☒ **Las Clementinas.** *B&B/Inn.* The six bright,
$$ spacious suites in this refurbished, early-20th-century apartment building are as charming as they are comfortable, which together with the friendly staff and an excellent restaurant make this a premier Casco Viejo lodging option. **Pros:** tasteful decor; friendly staff; great restaurant; conveniently located. **Cons:** noisy neighbors. Ⓢ *Rooms from: $150* ☒ *Calle 11 at Av. B* ☏ *507/228–7613, 877/889–0351* ⊕ *www.lasclementinas.com* ⌁ *6 suites, 3 rooms* ⦿*Breakfast.*

$$ ☒ **Los Cuatro Tulipanes.** *Rental.* These charming apartments in a refurbished, historic building lack hotel services, but offer some of the quietest accommodations in Casco Viejo, and are a great option for independent travelers. **Pros:** lovely building and decor; quiet; great location; good value. **Cons:** ground-floor rooms are dark; few guest services. [$] *Rooms from: $125* ✉ *Av. Central between Calle 3 and Calle 4* ☎ *507/6679–8431, 609/643–4811* 🌐 *www.loscuatrotulipanes.com* 🛏 *7 apartments* 🍴 *No meals.*

$ 🏨 **Magnolia Inn.** *Hotel.* This American-run hotel is in a refurbished, 18th-century building behind the cathedral. **Pros:** friendly owners; lovely historic building; good value; great views. **Cons:** noisy on weekend nights. [$] *Rooms from: $88* ✉ *Calle 8 between Av. Central and Av. B* ☎ *507/202–0872, 507/6551–9217* 🌐 *www.magnoliapanama.com* 🛏 *16 private rooms, 6 shared* 🍴 *No meals.*

★ **$$** **Fodor'sChoice** 🏨 **Tántalo.** *Hotel.* Eco-conscious luxury meets a hip, creative attitude at this 13-room hotel. **Pros:** friendly service; excellent bar and dining scene; centrally located. **Cons:** lively nightlife nearby may not appeal to some travelers. [$] *Rooms from: $115* ✉ *Av. B and Calle 8* ☎ *262–4030* 🌐 *www.tantalohotel.com* 🛏 *12 rooms* 🍴 *No meals.*

CERRO ANCÓN, BALBOA, AND THE CALZADA DE AMADOR

Hotels in the former Canal Zone offer clean air, tranquility, greenery, and priceless views. Another bonus: They are a short taxi trip from the Calzada de Amador or Casco Viejo.

$ FAMILY 🏨 **Country Inn & Suites Panama Canal.** *Hotel.* A front-row view of the Panama Canal and the peace and fresh air that come with an out-of-town location make this hotel a great option, especially for families. **Pros:** great canal views; peaceful; big pool; good value. **Cons:** public areas need work; "garden views" disappointing; could be better maintained and managed. [$] *Rooms from: $65* ✉ *Calzada de Amador and Calle Pelícano* ☎ *507/211–4500, 888/201–1746 in the U.S.* 🌐 *www.countryinns.com* 🛏 *161 rooms, 94 suites and apartments* 🍴 *Breakfast.*

DOWNTOWN PANAMA CITY

Panama City's critical mass of accommodations is found in this amalgam of neighborhoods that extends from Bella Vista to Punta Paitilla. Many of them are found near the intersection of Vía España and Vía Veneto, the heart of El Cangrejo. Several are scattered through the nearby Area Bancária, the city's financial district, whereas a few more are on or near the coast, either on the Cinta Costera, or

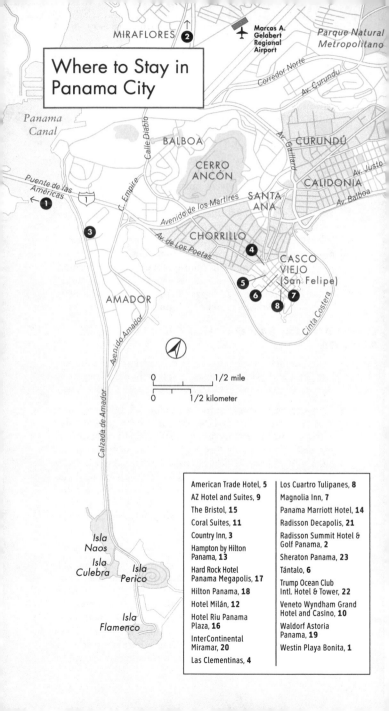

Where to Stay in Panama City

MIRAFLORES **2**

Marcos A. Gelabert Regional Airport

Parque Natural Metropolitano

Corredor Norte

Av. Curundú

Panama Canal

BALBOA

CERRO ANCÓN

CURUNDÚ

Av. Gaillard

Av. Justo

CALIDONIA

Av. Balboa

Puente de las Américas **1**

C. Empire

Calle Diablo

Avenido de los Martires

SANTA ANA

3

Av. de Los Poetas

CHORRILLO

4

CASCO VIEJO (San Felipe)

5

6 **7**

8

AMADOR

Avenido Amador

Cinta Costera

0   1/2 mile

0   1/2 kilometer

Calzada de Amador

Isla Naos

Isla Culebra

Isla Perico

Isla Flamenco

American Trade Hotel, **5**
AZ Hotel and Suites, **9**
The Bristol, **15**
Coral Suites, **11**
Country Inn, **3**
Hampton by Hilton Panama, **13**
Hard Rock Hotel Panama Megapolis, **17**
Hilton Panama, **18**
Hotel Milán, **12**
Hotel Riu Panama Plaza, **16**
InterContinental Miramar, **20**
Las Clementinas, **4**

Los Cuartro Tulipanes, **8**
Magnolia Inn, **7**
Panama Marriott Hotel, **14**
Radisson Decapolis, **21**
Radisson Summit Hotel & Golf Panama, **2**
Sheraton Panama, **23**
Tántalo, **6**
Trump Ocean Club Intl. Hotel & Tower, **22**
Veneto Wyndham Grand Hotel and Casino, **10**
Waldorf Astoria Panama, **19**
Westin Playa Bonita, **1**

Bahía de Panama

PACIFIC
OCEAN

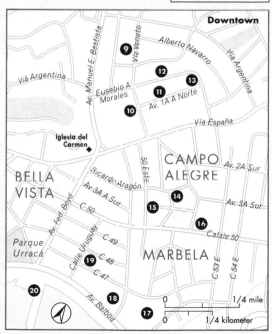

Punta Paitilla. This area is safe for walking and is sprinkled with restaurants, shops, nightlife, and other diversions.

$$ **⚈ AZ Hotel and Suites.** *Hotel.* On a quiet street just a short walk from the bars and restaurants of El Cangrejo, AZ Hotel and Suites is a reincarnation of the former Las Huacas hotel, and is a good option if you're on a budget. **Pros:** bright rooms; convenient location; quiet neighborhood. **Cons:** inconsistent service; rooms can be musty. ⓢ *Rooms from: $125 ⊠ Calle 49, 1½ blocks north of Salsa's Bar and Grill ☎ 507/213–2222 ⊕ www.az-hotelespanama.com ⇘ 73 rooms ⦿ Breakfast.*

$$$$ **⚈ The Bristol.** *Hotel.* Much like a European boutique hotel, the Bristol—a member of the consortium Leading Hotels of the World—is gorgeous and classy, with personalized service and attention to detail to boot. **Pros:** excellent service; great rooms; convenient location; nice restaurant. **Cons:** pricey; small pool. ⓢ *Rooms from: $229 ⊠ Av. Aquilino de la Guardia, between Calle 50 and Vía España ☎ 507/264–0000, 800/223–6800 in the U.S. ⊕ www.thebristol.com ⇘ 125 rooms and suites ⦿ No meals.*

$ **⚈ Coral Suites.** *Hotel.* Popular with travelers on a budget, Coral Suites offers mini apartments with many of the same amenities you'll find in luxury hotels for less money. **Pros:** affordable; lots of amenities; great location. **Cons:** pool is small; no restaurant. ⓢ *Rooms from: $88 ⊠ Calle D, half a block east of Vía Veneto ☎ 507/269–3898 ⊕ www.coral-suitespanama.com ⇘ 62 rooms ⦿ Breakfast.*

$$ **⚈ Hard Rock Hotel Panama Megapolis.** *Hotel.* "Mega" is the right prefix for this 66-floor tower, starting with its expansive lobby and mezzanine of bars—a popular night spot—but the rooms are attractive, and the ocean views, impressive. **Pros:** hip vibe; abundant nightlife; attractive rooms; ocean views. **Cons:** inconsistent service; can be a zoo when full; overwhelming size. ⓢ *Rooms from: $127 ⊠ Av. Balboa, next to Multicentro ☎ 507/380–1111 ⊕ www.hardrockhotels.com ⇘ 1,500 rooms ⦿ No meals.*

$ **⚈ Hampton by Hilton Panama.** *Hotel.* One of the newest hotels
FAMILY   in the popular El Cangrejo neighborhood, the Hampton by Hilton Panama has a great location within walking distance of restaurants and a Metro station. **Pros:** great location; modern and attractive. **Cons:** limited on-site dining options. ⓢ *Rooms from: $89 ⊠ Calle Eusebio A. Morales, Panama City ☎ 507/301–0000 ⊕ www.hilton.com ⇘ 108 rooms ⦿ Breakfast.*

★ **Fodor'sChoice** 🏨 **Hilton Panama.** *Hotel.* The newest luxury hotel
$$$ on Avenida Balboa offers some of the city's best views of the Cinta Costera and Pacific Ocean. **Pros:** great views; attentive service. **Cons:** lack of economical dining options on-site; charge for parking. [$] *Rooms from: $179* ✉ *Av. Balboa at Aquilino de la Guardia, Panama City* ☎ *507/280–8001* 🌐 *www.hilton.com* 🛏 *347 rooms* 🍴 *No meals.*

$ 🏨 **Hotel Milán.** *Hotel.* With clean, reasonably priced rooms near some of the best restaurants in El Cangrejo, the Hotel Milán is one of the city's best options for budget travelers, especially considering its 15% discount if you pay cash. **Pros:** great location; decent rates. **Cons:** no pool; rooms lack personality. [$] *Rooms from: $70* ✉ *Calle Eusebio A. Morales No. 31* ☎ *507/263–6130* 🌐 *www.hotelmilan.com.pa* 🛏 *93 rooms, 14 suites* 🍴 *No meals.*

$$ 🏨 **Hotel Riu Panama Plaza.** *Hotel.* Towering over busy Calle
FAMILY 50, this chic hotel caters to vacationers with its tropical decor, attractive rooms, large pool area, selection of bars and restaurants, and convenient location at the edge of the Area Bancária (its meeting space, location, and dining options also appeal to business travelers). **Pros:** attractive; nice pool area; often offers discounted rates. **Cons:** big; caters to tour groups. [$] *Rooms from: $119* ✉ *Calle 50 at Calle 53 Este* ☎ *507/378–9000, 507/269–1000, 888/748–4990 toll-free in U.S.* 🌐 *www.riuplaza.com* 🛏 *610 rooms, 34 suites* 🍴 *Breakfast.*

$$ 🏨 **InterContinental Miramar.** *Hotel.* Amazing ocean views, elegant rooms, and an attractive pool area make this 25-story tower a good choice for business travelers and vacationers alike. **Pros:** amazing view; lovely pool; good breakfasts; good value. **Cons:** inconsistent service; slightly isolated; cold rooms. [$] *Rooms from: $148* ✉ *Miramar Plaza, Av. Balboa at Av. Federico Boyd* ☎ *507/206–8888* 🌐 *www.miramarpanama.com* 🛏 *186 rooms, 14 suites* 🍴 *Breakfast.*

★ **Fodor'sChoice** 🏨 **Panama Marriott Hotel.** *Hotel.* From the airy
$$ lobby, with its marble floors and potted palms, to the sumptuous guest rooms, this 20-story hotel, which in 2014 opened a 14-story second tower in the heart of the financial district, is one of the city's best. **Pros:** good location; friendly staff; lovely rooms; some great views. **Cons:** small pool; some mediocre views; Wi-Fi is extra. [$] *Rooms from: $129* ✉ *Calle 52 and Calle Ricardo Arias* ☎ *507/210–9100, 888/236–2427 in the U.S.* 🌐 *www.marriott.com* 🛏 *366 rooms, 23 suites* 🍴 *No meals.*

★ **Fodor'sChoice** 🏨 **Radisson Decapolis.** *Hotel.* Though most of the
$$ guests are business travelers, this modern, 29-story high-rise

is a great place for vacationers, thanks to its circular pool, spa, chic lobby bar, and restaurant. **Pros:** hip atmosphere; friendly staff; some great views; good restaurant; close to shops and entertainment. **Cons:** some mediocre views; small pool. $ *Rooms from: $110* ✉ *Av. Balboa, next to Multicentro* ☎ *507/215–5000, 800/333–3333 in the U.S.* ⊕ *www.radisson.com* ⮑ *240 rooms* ⦿ *Breakfast.*

$$ ⛝ **Trump Ocean Club International Hotel & Tower.** *Hotel.* The ocean views from the sleek guest rooms and 13th-floor pool terrace of this impressive skyscraper are the big selling points, but the restaurants, facilities, and friendly staff close the deal. **Pros:** first-class service; great pool area; ocean views. **Cons:** far from most sites and restaurants. $ *Rooms from: $159* ✉ *Calle Punta Colón* ☎ *507/215–8800, 885/225–9640 in U.S.* ⊕ *www.trumphotelcollection.com* ⮑ *328 rooms, 41 suites* ⦿ *No meals.*

$ ⛝ **Veneto Wyndham Grand Hotel and Casino.** *Hotel.* The Veneto's massive marquee with flashing colored lights, and its large and lively casino, are Panama City's answer to Las Vegas, but its spacious rooms and competitive prices make it a decent option for non-gamblers as well. **Pros:** centrally located; hopping casino. **Cons:** lobby may be too busy for some; indifferent service; definitely not a family-friendly atmosphere. $ *Rooms from: $79* ✉ *Vía Veneto and Av. Eusebio A. Morales* ☎ *507/340–8686, 888/611–9840 in the U.S.* ⊕ *www.venetocasino.com* ⮑ *300 rooms, 26 suites* ⦿ *No meals.*

★ Fodor'sChoice ⛝ **Waldorf Astoria Panama.** *Hotel.* The Panama
$$ hotel scene ascended to the next level with the 2013 arrival of this five-star favorite, located downtown near the business hubs and nightlife-lined Calle Uruguay, featuring best-in-class service, modern decor, and a pool with skyline views. **Pros:** five-star service; pool with a view; spacious and sophisticated rooms; diverse dining options; near business and nightlife. **Cons:** expensive Wi-Fi in the rooms (free in public areas); surrounding nightlife area can get noisy. $ *Rooms from: $119* ✉ *Calle 47 and Calle Uruguay* ☎ *507/340–3500* ⊕ *www.waldorfastoriapanama.com* ⮑ *130 rooms* ⦿ *No meals.*

SAN FRANCISCO

The predominantly residential neighborhood of San Francisco offers a decent supply of restaurants and one large hotel, the Sheraton, which is next door to the ATLAPA Convention Center.

$$ **Sheraton Panama.** *Hotel.* One of the city's original luxury
FAMILY hotels, the Sheraton Panama remains one of its best, in no small part thanks to its spacious pool area and lobby. **Pros:** quiet; nice pool; friendly staff; quick trip to the airport. **Cons:** far from many attractions; small bathrooms. $ *Rooms from: $100 ✉ Vía Israel and Calle 77, next to ATLAPA convention center ☎ 507/305–5100, 800/325–3535 in the U.S. 🌐 www.sheratonpanama.com.pa 333 rooms, 23 suites 🍴 No meals.*

PARQUE NATURAL METROPOLITANO, MIRAFLORES, AND SUMMIT

★ Fodor'sChoice **Radisson Summit Hotel & Golf Panama.** *Hotel.*
$ This comfortable hotel has one of the country's best golf
FAMILY courses, and the rooms overlooking the rain forest make it a good choice for anyone who prefers peace and nature to urban lodging, too. **Pros:** 18-hole golf course; friendly staff; quiet; surrounded by nature; good value. **Cons:** 20–30 minutes from most restaurants and nightlife. $ *Rooms from: $80 ✉ Av. Omar Torrijos, 20 km (12 miles) northwest of Panama City Paraiso ☎ 507/232–3700, 800/395–7046 in U.S. and Canada 🌐 www.radisson.com 103 rooms 🍴 Breakfast.*

PLAYA KOBBE

$$ **Westin Playa Bonita.** *Resort.* Families, couples, and busi-
FAMILY ness travelers looking for the amenities of a full-service resort, the feel of a destination beach-retreat, and proximity to Panama City's best attractions will find that the Westin elegantly unites all these features in one towering complex. **Pros:** great beach getaway close to downtown Panama City; beautiful common areas with sea views; wide array of amenities and activities make it a great place for a multigeneration vacation. **Cons:** guests who opt for all-inclusive have to wear a plastic bracelet; poolside snack fare is mediocre. $ *Rooms from: $160 ✉ Road to Veracruz, Km 6 ☎ 507/304–6600 🌐 www.westin.com/playabonita 611 rooms 🍴 All-inclusive; Breakfast; Some meals.*

NIGHTLIFE AND PERFORMING ARTS

There is plenty to do in Panama City once the sun sets, though it is much more of a party town than a cradle of the arts. Because it is so hot by day, the night is an especially inviting time to explore the city. The entertainment and nightlife centers are Casco Viejo, El Cangrejo, and the Calle Uruguay area. Entertainment tends more toward high culture in Casco Viejo, with its Teatro Nacional and jazz venues, while the scene in the other areas is more about casinos, drinking, and dancing the night away.

PERFORMING ARTS

Panama may be a commercial cen ter, but its arts scene is lacking. There are occasional dance or classical music performances in Teatro Nacional and jazz or Latin music can be found at various bars and nightclubs. For information on concerts, plays, and other performances, check out the listings in the free tourist newspaper called *The Visitor* or the ATP website (⊕ *www.visitpanama.com*).

FOLK DANCING

Panamanians love their folk dancing, which forms an important part of regional festivals and other major celebrations. The typical folk dances have their roots in popular Spanish dances of the 18th century, but they also have African and indigenous influences. The easiest way to experience them is at Las Tinajas restaurant in the Area Bancária.

Las Tinajas. Las Tinajas is an attractive Panamanian restaurant with a convenient location in the financial district that offers a folk-dancing show every Tuesday, Thursday, Friday, and Saturday night. The hour-long show starts at 9 pm and costs $5—plus you need to consume $12 worth of food and drink. Reserve ahead of time and arrive early to choose a good table, since the stage is at the center of the room and not all tables have great views. ⊠ *Calle 51, No. 22, near Av. Federico Boyd* ☎ *507/269–3840* ⊕ *www. tinajas.com.pa.*

JAZZ

Panama has long had a jazz scene, especially in the Caribbean port of Colón, but its best musicians have always moved abroad. The city's prodigal son, Danilo Pérez, a celebrated pianist who has played with the best, lives in the States. Other notable Panamanian jazz musicians have included saxophonist Maurice Smith, who played with everyone from Charlie Mingus to Dizzy Gillespie, and pianist Victor Boa. Some very good musicians live in the city, though most have to play salsa and other popular genres to survive. The best time for jazz fans to visit the city is late January, during the **Panama Jazz Festival,** which features concerts by international stars. For information on the next festival, check the website (⊕ *www.panama-jazzfestival.com*). Jazz fans have several opportunities per week to hear good music in Casco Viejo.

★ **Fodor's**Choice **Danilo's Jazz Club.** Named for Panamanian jazz legend Danilo Pérez, this 50-seat venue has quickly become one of Panama City's premier live music venues. Small and intimate, Danilo's serves an array of cocktails and hosts a steady rotation of local and international talent. ⊠ *Plaza Herrera, next to American Trade Hotel, Panama City* ☎ *507/211–2000* ⊕ *www.acehotel.com/panama/jazz-club.*

Jeronimo. This attractive venue in Casco Viejo features art exhibits in the front, comfortable seating, and a bar in back, with live jazz by local groups like the talented young Alex Testa Quartet. Every month features different talent, so call or drop by to check the schedule. ⊠ *Av. B at Calle 10, Panama City* ☎ *507/211–2758.*

Las Bóvedas. The bar at the French restaurant Las Bóvedas, on Plaza Francia, usually has live jazz on Friday night. There's a mellower atmosphere than the Latin vibe at nearby Platea, and they play earlier, starting around 7 pm. Call to confirm that the band is playing. ⊠ *Plaza Francia* ☎ *507/228–8058* ⊕ *lasbovedasrestaurante.com.*

Platea. Located on the ground floor of a restored colonial building, Platea sometimes hosts live Latin jazz; the venue is only open on Friday and Saturday nights. Call to confirm. ⊠ *Calle 1 Oeste, Edificio 13, Local 13, in front of the old Club Union* ☎ *507/228–8210* ⊕ *www.barplatea.com.*

NIGHTLIFE

Panama City's after-dark offerings range from a quiet drink on historic Plaza Bolívar to dancing until dawn at one of the clubs on Calle Uruguay, with plenty of options in between. Although there are bars everywhere, nightlife is concentrated in Casco Viejo, El Cangrejo, and Calle Uruguay, though there are also a few options in the Area Bancária and Punta Paitilla.

Casco Viejo is the city's nightlife epicenter, with a variety of bars and clubs that rock into the wee hours on weekends. The Calzada de Amador is the place to head for a quiet drink with lovely ocean views. The streets around Calle Uruguay are packed on weekends, when a predominantly young crowd fills its bars and dance clubs. There are also a few night spots in El Cangrejo and Punta Paitilla, where a couple of hotel bars have amazing views.

The nicest casinos are in, or next to, the city's big hotels, namely the Panama Marriott, Veneto, Trump Ocean Club, and El Panamá, and often have excellent bands performing Latin music in their bars.

The city's dance clubs play a broad mix of music that includes pop, salsa, reggaetón, and house music. Cover charges run between $5 and $10, and sometimes include a drink.

There are also strip clubs, locally called "nightclubs," scattered between the Area Bancária and El Cangrejo, which have traditionally catered to business travelers, but are becoming a bit of a tourist attraction in their own right. Prostitution is legal in Panama, but streetwalking is not, so representatives of the world's oldest profession gather at a few of its bars and casinos.

CASCO VIEJO

BARS AND LOUNGES

Casablanca. Casablanca, on the ground floor of the old Hotel Colombia, has tables on beautiful Plaza Bolívar, which is a great spot for a drink and conversation at night. They have live Latin music Thursday through Saturday, when this place really hops. ⊠ *Calle 4 on Plaza Bolívar* ☎ *507/212–0040* ⊕ *www.restaurantecasablancapanama.com.*

★ **Fodor's**Choice **Ego y Narciso.** This tapas restaurant has tables on Plaza Bolívar, with views of the illuminated Iglesia de San Francisco and other historic structures, making it one of the city's most romantic spots for a drink. ⊠ *Calle 3 Este on Plaza Bolívar* ☎ *507/262–2045.*

La Rana Dorada. This popular microbrewery at the edge of Casco Viejo offers half a dozen home brews and a small menu. You can sit indoors or on the front terrace, which has a view of the modern skyline across the bay. ⊠ *Av. Eloy Alfaro and Calle 11* ☎ *507/212–2680* ⊕ *www.laranadorada.com.*

Las Bóvedas. This French restaurant on Plaza Francia has tables on the plaza and a bar inside one of the Bóvedas (arched, brick chambers dating from the colonial era) that often features live jazz on Friday night and salsa music on Saturday. Call to confirm the evening's entertainment.

2

✉ *Plaza Francia, Calle 1* ☎ *507/228–8058* ⊕ *www.lasbove-dasrestaurante.com.*

Mojitos Sin Mojitos. This funky little place on the southeast corner of Plaza Herrera looks like a construction site from the street, but at night the ancient walls and tropical foliage create a very cool atmosphere, which is complemented by the music of DJs and live bands, and the young crowd, which frequently spills out into the street and plaza. ✉ *Calle 9 and Av. A* ☎ *507/6855–4080* ⊕ *www.mojitossinmojitos.com.*

★ **Fodor's Choice Tántalo.** The rooftop bar of this hip hotel has a great view of the city's skyline beyond the ancient roofs of Casco Viejo. Weekends vibrate with the boom-boom of deafening house music, though the quality of the DJs varies. You can get a relatively quiet drink here Sunday through Wednesday. ✉ *Calle 8 and Av. B* ☎ *507/262–4030* ⊕ *www.tantalohotel.com.*

Vieja Havana. Cuban music, a massive, hardwood bar, and walls covered with photos and paintings of Cuba make it easy to imagine you're in Havana's old quarter as you sip a mojito. ✉ *Av. B and Calle 5 Este* ☎ *507/212–3873.*

DANCE CLUBS

Bora Bora Panamá. This spacious dance hall (formerly known as Habana Panamá) hosts a variety of DJs, live music, and musical styles, from rap to salsa to electronica. They also screen sports events, so call or check their Facebook page to find out what's happening. Musical groups and DJs perform on a large stage at the end of a long dance floor lined with plush booths, at the opposite end of which is a massive bar stocked with a wide variety of alcoholic refreshments. ✉ *Eloy Alfaro and Calle 12 Este* ☎ *507/212–0152.*

Platea. Platea may not have much of a dance floor, but the club—which is open only on Friday and Saturday nights—books hot salsa bands and is packed most Friday nights, when people dance in the aisles or wherever else there's room. The bartenders and waiters, dressed in black with Panama hats, are part of the show, as they dance while delivering mojitos and Cuba libres. On Saturday, Latin jazz, rock, and other types of live music are featured, so call ahead. ✉ *Calle 1, in front of the old Club Union* ☎ *507/228–8210* ⊕ *www.barplatea.com.*

EL CANGREJO

BARS AND CLUBS

El Pavo Real Panamá. El Pavo Real Panamá is an attractive, British-inspired pub on a quiet stretch of Vía Argentina. It has a long bar, indoor and outdoor seating, two pool tables, and serves bar food including fish-and-chips. They often have live music, mostly rock, on weekends, but you can always get a quiet drink on the front terrace. ⊠ *Vía Argentina and Calle José Martí, across street from Angel Restaurante* ☎ *507/394–6853* ⊕ *www.elpavoreal.net.*

The Wine Bar. The Wine Bar, located on the ground floor of the Las Vegas Hotel Suites, has live Latin music nightly, mostly mellow duos or a guitarist. They have a decent selection of wines by the glass and serve good pizza and other snacks till late. ⊠ *Calle Eusebio Morales, east of Vía Veneto* ☎ *507/265–4701.*

CASINOS

El Panamá. The Hotel El Panamá is home to a large Crown Casino that is popular with Panamanians. It includes a bar that regularly hosts live music and DJs, and also offers decent lunch specials during the day. ⊠ *Vía Veneto and Calle Eusebio Morales* ☎ *507/213–1274.*

Veneto Hotel and Casino. The Veneto Hotel and Casino has one of the city's biggest and most popular casinos, which includes craps and poker, and a sea of slot machines. Expect live music, Panamanians and foreigners who simply come to party, and lots of Colombian prostitutes. ⊠ *Vía Veneto and Calle Eusebio Morales* ☎ *507/340–8880* ⊕ *www.venetocasino.com.*

MARBELLA

BARS AND LOUNGES

Cielo. The pool bar on the roof of the Manrey Hotel is a popular weekend spot. DJs pump the crowd up and the danger of somebody falling into the pool increases with every martini served. The glowing-blue lap pool is surrounded by canopy couches, arm chairs, and tables, beyond which twinkle the city lights, making it a splendid spot for a drink any night. ⊠ *Calle Uruguay and Calle 48* ☎ *507/203–0000* ⊕ *www.manreypanama.com.*

CASINOS

Panama Marriott. The Panama Marriott has a two-story Royal Casino next door that is quite popular with locals.

It has live music most nights, and sometimes hosts concerts by the country's most popular groups. ⊠ *Calle 52 and Calle Ricardo Arias* ☎ *507/205–7777* ⊕ *www.royalcasino.com.pa.*

DANCE CLUBS

Altabar. One of Panama's hottest dance clubs, Altabar has DJs from Wednesday to Saturday and a sleek decor of white sofas and a black tile floor. There's a mezzanine for those who prefer to watch the bodies moving to the techno beat from a safe distance. ⊠ *Calle 49, half a block east of Calle Uruguay* ☎ *507/390–2582* ⊕ *www.altabarpanama.com.*

PUNTA PAITILLA

BARS AND CLUBS

Azul. This pool bar and grill on the 13th floor of the Trump Hotel is a popular weekend spot, thanks to its impressive view of the sea and the skyscrapers of Costa del Este. An elevator at the back of the building offers access to the bar for nonguests. ⊠ *Calle Punta Colón* ☎ *507/215–8800* ⊕ *www.trumphotelcollection.com.*

Martini Bar. This large lounge, located in the Radisson Decapolis hotel, was once one of the city's hottest lounges, but it's now a nice spot for a quiet drink. ⊠ *Av. Balboa, next to Multicentro* ☎ *507/215–5000* ⊕ *www.radisson.com.*

Hard Rock Hotel Panama Megalopolis. The second floor of this massive hotel has two bars that are sometimes extremely crowded: Bling, a dance club, and Stage Bar, which hosts live bands. On the 62nd floor is Bits, a bar with indoor and outdoor seating. ⊠ *Av. Balboa, behind the Radisson Decapolis Hotel* ☎ *507/380–1111* ⊕ *www.hrhpanamamega-polis.com.*

CASINOS

Trump Ocean Club. The newest major gaming venue in Panama City, Ocean Sun Casino debuted in 2014 inside the Trump Ocean Club hotel. Operated by South Africa-based Sun International, the casino features decor that is more attractive than most in Panama City, including a 75,000-square-foot main floor and a 66th-floor VIP section for big spenders. Live entertainment, 34 gaming tables, and 600 slot machines keep the excitement going. ⊠ *Trump Ocean Club International Hotel & Tower, Calle Punta Colón, Panama City* ☎ *507/215–8800* ⊕ *www.trumpho-telcollection.com.*

SHOPS AND SPAS

Panama City has more shopping options than you can shake a credit card at. Because of the country's role as an international port, manufactured goods from all over the world are cheaper in Panama than in most countries. Merchants from South and Central America regularly travel here to shop, but Americans will find that the U.S. megastores often beat the local prices for cameras and other electronic goods—plus the stores back home are more convenient in terms of warranties. Busy Vía Veneto, in El Cangrejo, and Casco Viejo have souvenir shops. The city also has several modern malls, where the selection ranges from cheap to chic.

SHOPS

A popular handicraft in Panama is the *mola,* a fabric picture sewn by Guna women and worn on their blouses as part of their traditional dress. The Guna are also known for their bead bracelets and necklaces, as well as simple jewelry made from seeds and shells. The Emberá and Wounaan are known for their animal figures carved out of dark cocobolo wood, or the seed of a rain-forest palm called *tagua.* They also produce attractive rattan baskets, bowls, and platters, which can take weeks to complete and are consequently expensive. The Ngöbe-Buglé Indians produce colorful dresses, jute shoulder bags, and intricate bead necklaces called *chaquiras.*

The city's handicraft markets are open daily from 9 to 6. The rows of stalls filled with native handicrafts are great places to browse and learn a bit about the local cultures.

DID YOU KNOW? Panama Hats are actually from Ecuador. Teddy Roosevelt wore one of the wide-brimmed white hats when he came to Panama to inspect canal construction, and the apparel became forever associated with Panama, much to Ecuador's chagrin. Any such headwear you do find for sale here should be labeled "Genuine Panama Hat Made in Ecuador."

CASCO VIEJO

HANDICRAFT MARKETS AND SHOPS

★ Fodor'sChoice **Papiro y Yo.** Many of the bags, baskets, necklaces, and other items in this colorful shop are the product of recycling, made from magazine pages, flip tops, and other trash. Others are made from natural fibers, and almost everything is the work of families in the Panamanian countryside, so they're good for the environment, and people. ✉ *Av. A, between Calle 5 and Calle 4* ☎ *507/391–3800* ⊕ *papiroyyo.com.*

JEWELRY

Reprosa. Reprosa sells elegant jewelry based on reproductions of pre-Columbian gold pieces and Spanish coins, as well as interesting modern designs in silver and high-quality indigenous chaquira beadwork, cocobolo wood carvings, paintings, and the ubiquitous molas . They have shops on Avenida A, in the heart of the Casco Viejo, and on Avenida Samuel Lewis, in Obarrio, near the Area Bancaría, as well as factory tours available weekdays at 9:30 am and 2 pm at its Parque Industrial location in Costa del Este. ✉ *Art Deco Building, Av. A and Calle 4* ☎ *507/228–4913* ⊕ *www. reprosa.com* ✉ *Av. Samuel Lewis and Calle 54, Obarrio* ☎ *507/269–0457.*

MALLS

Avenida Central pedestrian mall. The Avenida Central pedestrian mall, a short walk from Casco Viejo, is lined with shops selling cheap, imported electronics, jewelry, fabrics, and clothing. A stroll down this busy street can be quite entertaining, even if you don't buy anything. Avoid the side streets. ✉ *Between Plaza Santa Ana and Plaza Cinco de Mayo.*

SOUVENIRS

La Ronda. La Ronda is an attractive little shop in a historic building near Plaza Francia that sells a mix of handicrafts and souvenirs: molas , Carnaval masks, wood carvings, paintings, Panama hats, and assorted knickknacks. ✉ *Calle 1 and Plaza Francia* ☎ *507/211–1001.*

CERRO ANCÓN

HANDICRAFT MARKETS AND SHOPS

Centro Municipal de Artesanías Panameñas. A good place to shop for molas is the Centro Municipal de Artesanías Panameñas, a small market where most of the stands are owned by Kuna women, who are often sewing molas as they wait for customers. They also sell chaquiras , bags, hammocks, dresses, framed butterflies, T-shirts, and other souvenirs. ✉ *Av. Arnulfo Arias, three blocks up from old YMCA.*

Galería Arte Indígena. Galería Arte Indígena, just down the street from Plaza Francia, has indigenous handicrafts such as Emberá baskets, animal figures carved from *tagua* palm seeds, decorated gourds, hammocks, Panama hats (imported from Ecuador), and T-shirts. ⊠ *Calle 1, No. 844* ☎ *507/228–9557.*

DOWNTOWN

MALLS

Multicentro. This modern, four-story mall, across from Punta Paitilla, holds dozens of shops, as well as a movie theater, food court, and a casino. The location makes it convenient to many hotels, but competition from faster-growing malls like Multiplaza and Albrook have resulted in some empty retail space at Multicentro. ⊠ *Av. Balboa* ☎ *507/208–2500* ⊕ *www.multicentropanama.com.pa.*

Multiplaza. The city's largest high-end mall is just east of Punta Paitilla, on the road to ATLAPA and Panamá Viejo. Its shops include the likes of Tiffany, Cartier, Luis Vuitton, and an Apple Store (although some of these higher-end stores were expected to move to the newer, even more luxurious SOHO Mall). It also has a movie theater, several restaurants, a food court, and an adjacent hotel. ⊠ *Vía Israel* ☎ *507/302–5380* ⊕ *www.multiplaza.com.*

SOHO Panama. Panama City's newest mall, which opened its doors in 2015, is also its most upscale. Stores bearing the names of Coach, Michael Kors, Polo, Burberry, Prada, and Yves Saint Laurent are just a few of the options here, and a variety of dining venues, as well as a movie theater, were to open at this writing. ⊠ *Calle 50, between Calle 54 and Calle 56, Panama City* ☎ *507/265–8000* ⊕ *www. sohopanama.com.pa.*

SOUVENIR SHOPS

Genuine Panama Hat. This shop (formerly known as Artesanías Panamá Bahía) sells a mixture of Panamanian and Ecuadoran souvenirs, including an ample selection of Panama hats, from its new location in Bellavista, conveniently close to many hotels. ⊠ *Calle Ricardo Arias, next to Costa Sur restaurant* ☎ *507/6674–8513.*

PANAMÁ VIEJO

HANDICRAFT MARKETS AND SHOPS

Mercado de Artesanía de Panamá Viejo. The Mercado de Artesanía de Panamá Viejo, next to the *Centro de Visitantes* (Visitor Center), is packed with small shops and stalls selling everything for indigenous handicrafts—many shop owners are indigenous—to woven hats, Carnaval masks, and other artisans' works from the country's interior. A number of Guna families have shops here, making it a good place to buy molas. ✉ *Vía Cincuentenaria* ☎ *507/560–0535.*

PARQUE NATURAL METROPOLITANO AND MIRAFLORES

MALLS

Albrook Mall. Albrook Mall is the people's mall, with more discount stores than the city's other malls. That, combined with its convenient location between the city's massive bus terminal and Albrook Airport, makes it the busiest mall. Shopaholics can position themselves for multiday shopping by checking into the TRYP by Wyndham Panama Albrook Mall Hotel, which is attached to the shopping complex (and one of the closest hotels to the Miraflores Locks visitor center at the Panama Canal). ✉ *In front of Terminal de Buses* ☎ *507/303–6235* ⊕ *www.albrookmall.com.*

SPAS

Spas at most Panama City hotels are open to nonguests; there are also spas on some of the country's beaches and in the mountains, so you'll have plenty of opportunities to rejuvenate during your travels.

DOWNTOWN

Aqua Spa. One of Panama City's best spas, the Aqua Spa is located on the fourth floor of the Radisson Decapolis. If the treatments there don't leave you sufficiently relaxed, you can always top them off with a martini by the pool bar. ✉ *Radisson Decapolis, Av. Balboa, next to Multicentro* ☎ *507/215–5000* ⊕ *www.radisson.com/panamacitypan.*

Veneto Hotel and Casino. The flashy Veneto Hotel and Casino, on busy Vía Veneto, may seem like the last place you'd go to escape the hustle and bustle, but the large spa on the hotel's seventh floor is actually a very tranquil spot. ✉ *Vía Veneto and Av. Eusebio A. Morales* ☎ *507/340–8686* ⊕ *www.venetocasino.com.*

Ygia Spa. The Ygia Spa, in the Sheraton Panama, next to the ATLAPA convention center, offers an array of options ranging from the traditional massages and beauty treatments to "rejuvenation sessions" that can last anywhere from one to three hours. ✉ *Sheraton Panama, Vía Israel and Calle 77* ☎ *507/305–5100* ⊕ *www.sheratonpanama.com.pa.*

PLAYA BONITA

Sensory Spa by Clarins. Sensory Spa by Clarins is a state-of-the-art, full-service spa with 16 treatment rooms and a vast menu of treatment options as well as holistic therapies such as Shiatsu and Reiki. It employs the latest technology in relaxation therapies, including Clarins' signature "Thermal Circuit Experience," which alternates hot, cold, and hydrotherapy experiences. ⊠ *Westin Playa Bonita, Road to Veracruz, Km 6* ☎ *507/304–6600* ⊕ *www.westinplaya-bonita.com.*

SPORTS AND THE OUTDOORS

Thanks to its proximity to forest, canal, and ocean, Panama City offers plenty of options for enjoying the outdoors, which include hiking in the world's largest chunk of urban rain forest, biking down the causeway, navigating the Panama Canal, and white-water rafting in the jungle.

BEACHES

Because of the silt that the Panama Canal dumps into the ocean and the sewage from Panama City, the beaches near the city are not recommended for swimming. Some of the country's nicest Pacific beaches are on **Isla Contadora,** a 90-minute ferry ride, or 20-minute flight from the city (⇨ *Isla Contadora in "The Canal and Central Panama" chapter*). For clear water nearer to Panama City, head to **Isla Taboga,** a 60-minute ferry ride from the Calzada de Amador, which is a popular day trip (⇨ *Isla Taboga in "The Canal and Central Panama" chapter*). The closest beach to Panama City is **Playa Kobbe** (Playa Bonita), which is 8 km (5 miles) southwest of the city, across the canal. It is the site of the Dreams Buenaventura and Westin Playa Bonita resorts, where the only option for beach access for nonguests is to make lunch reservations at the hotels' beachfront restaurants.

BIKING

Bicicletas Moses. Behind Pencas Restaurant, on the mainland at the entrance to Calzada Amador, Bicicletas Moses rents an array of bikes, including kids' sizes. One hour for an individual mountain bike costs $3.50, or up to $18 for a four-seater. The shop is open Monday through Saturday 12–8 and Sunday 8–7:30. ⊠ *Behind Las Pencas, Calzada de Amador* ☎ *507/211–3671.*

BIRD-WATCHING

Panama City has world-class bird-watching as close as the **Parque Natural Metropolitano,** which is home to more than 200 avian species and is 20 minutes from most hotels (provided the traffic is agreeable). There are several spots in nearby **Parque Nacional Soberanía,** which has more than 400 bird species, within 40 minutes of downtown, including **Pipeline Road,** where the Panama Audubon Society has held several world-record Christmas bird counts (⇨ *Parque Nacional Soberanía in "The Canal and Central Panama" chapter*). Unless you're an expert, you're best off going with an experienced birding guide. Several local tour companies can set you up with a private guide or can book you onto an existing trip, which is less expensive. You may need to call several companies to find a trip for your dates, though.

Advantage Panama. This small nature tourism company offers early-morning tours of Parque Natural Metropolitano and day trips to Parque Nacional Soberanía. The company can also arrange custom trips to other protected areas. ⊠ *Calle 11 Este, No. 1040, Parque Lefevre* ☎ *507/6676–2466* ⊕ *www.advantagepanama.com.*

★ **Fodor's Choice Ancon Expeditions.** This company has excellent guides and offers day tours to protected areas near the capital, including exploration of the forest canopy of Parque Natural Metropolitano using a modified construction crane, bird-watching in Parque Nacional Soberanía, and a popular boat trip on Gatún Lake that is great for families. ⊠ *Calle Elvira Mendez, Edificio El Dorado No. 3* ☎ *507/269–9415, 888/760–3426 toll-free in U.S.* ⊕ *www.anconexpeditions.com.*

EcoCircuitos Panama. Since 1999, this ecotourism company has been offering birding tours to Parque Nacional Soberanía, near the city, and the San Lorenzo area, on the Caribbean coast, and spots in between. ⊠ *Albrook Plaza, No. 31, Urbanización Albrook* ☎ *507/315–1305, 800/830–7142 toll-free in U.S.* ⊕ *www.ecocircuitos.com.*

Panama Audubon Society. The society runs one or two inexpensive bird walks, or overnight excursions, per month. They require a bit of self-sufficiency, but can be a great way to meet local birders. ⊠ *Casa #2006-B, Llanos de Curundu* ☎ *507/232–5977* ⊕ *www.audubonpanama.org.*

Panoramic Panama. This small company offers birding tours to areas in nearby Soberanía National Park, and can set up customized trips. ⊠ *Quarry Heights, Casa #35* ☎ *507/314–1417* ⊕ *www.panoramicpanama.com.*

Rain Forest Adventures by Panama Excursions. Among this tour operator's varied offerings in Panama is an Eco Cruise on Gatún Lake, which provides the opportunity for bird-watching and viewing other wildlife. Also available is a private, custom tour to Barro Colorado Island, in conjunction with the Smithsonian Tropical Research Institute. ⊠ *Av. Roberto Chiari #722, Balboa, Panama City* ☎ *507/314–0820, 866/759–8726 toll-free in U.S.* ⊕ *www. rainforestadventure.com.*

Smithsonian Tropical Research Institute (STRI). This research institute offers full-day trips to Barro Colorado Island that combine bird-watching with general information on tropical ecology. Tours should be booked two to three months ahead of time, either through the STRI office or through one of the other tour operators, which charge more, but will pick you up at your hotel. ⊠ *Tupper Center, Av. Roosevelt* ☎ *507/228–8000* ⊕ *www.stri.org.*

FISHING

The Bay of Panama has good sportfishing, but the best fishing is around and beyond the Pearl Islands, which are best fished out of **Isla Contadora,** a short flight or ferry ride from the city (⇨ *Isla Contadora or Isla San José in "The Canal and Central Panama" chapter*). Day charters are available out of Panama City and usually head to the area around Isla Otoque and Isla Bono, which are about 90 minutes southwest of the city. You have a chance of hooking mackerel, jack, tuna, roosterfish, or wahoo in that area (billfish are less common there than in other parts of the country). A closer, less expensive option is light-tackle fishing for snook and peacock bass in **Gatún Lake,** the vast man-made lake in the middle of the Panama Canal. The lake is full of South American peacock bass, which fight like smallmouth bass but can reach 8 to 10 pounds (⇨ *Lago Gatún in "The Canal and Central Panama" chapter*).

Panama Canal Fishing. This is the premier operator for freshwater fishing on Gatún Lake, which is famous for its peacock bass. Tours can be catered to serious anglers, beginners, or families, since they also include wildlife observation and views of ships on the canal. The company offers three options for Gatún Lake fishing, for up to six people per boat: a four-hour all-inclusive tour costs $350 for two people and $50 for each additional person; the six-hour tour is priced at $495 for two and $65 for each additional person; and the nine-hour tour costs $645 for two and $65 per person after that. They also offer snook and tarpon fishing on the Bayano River, depending on tide conditions. ☎ 507/315–1905, 507/6678–2653 ⊕ www.panamacanalfishing.com.

Panama Fishing and Catching. Captain Tony offers bass and snook fishing on Gatún Lake ($460); snook and tarpon fishing on the Bayano River ($550); and deep-sea fishing charters in the Bay of Panama for mahimahi, jacks, wahoo, tuna, sailfish, and ocassionally marlin ($1,500–$2,000 per day). ☎ 507/6622–0212, 507/6505–9553 ⊕ www.panamafishingandcatching.com.

GOLF

Summit Golf Resort. The resort has an 18-hole, par-72 championship course designed by Jeff Myers that is hemmed by the rain forest of Camino de Cruces National Park. It's 30 minutes from most hotels, and is open to nonguests. Green fees are $90, golf cart included, and club rentals cost $35. The course is open 6–6, and the earlier or later you play it, the less you'll sweat. ⊠ Camino Gailard ✛ 20 km (12 miles) northwest of town on road to Gamboa ☎ 507/232–3700 ⊕ www.summitgolfpanama.com ☜ $90 ⚑ 18 holes, par 72.

HIKING

The hiking options near Panama City range from the 40-minute trek to the top of Cerro Ancón to more demanding expeditions into the vast lowland forest of Parque Nacional Soberanía. The **Parque Natural Metropolitano** has five well-marked trails covering a total of about 5 km (3 miles), which range from flat stretches to a steep road up to a viewpoint. **Parque Nacional Soberania** has several trails ranging from the historic **Camino de Cruces** to the shorter **Sendero el Charco**, which is on the right after Summit Botanical Gardens and Zoo (⇨ Parque Nacional Soberanía in "The Canal and Central Panama" chapter).

Advantage Panama. The company can arrange custom tours for hiking enthusiasts. ⊠ Llanos de Curundú, No. 2006 ☎ 507/6676–2466 ⊕ www.advantagepanama.com.

EcoCircuitos Panama. Half- and full-day tours are offered that include hiking in Parque Natural Metropolitano,

Parque Nacional Soberanía, or the hills around El Valle de Antón. ⊠ *Albrook Plaza, No. 31, Urbanización Albrook* ☎ *507/315–1305, 800/830–7142 toll-free in U.S.* ⊕ *www. ecocircuitos.com.*

WHITE-WATER RAFTING

Aventuras Panama. Aventuras Panama runs white-water rafting trips on the Chagres River (Class II–III), which flows through the rain forests. The full-day trip requires no previous rafting experience, is available from May to late March, and costs $185 per person. A shorter, more challenging trip on the Mamoní River (Class III–IV), which flows through an agricultural area, is available from early July until late February, and costs $135. They also offer kayaking tours on Lago Gatún, the Chagres River, and along the Caribbean coast near Portobelo. ⊠ *Calle 63 Oeste, No. 32, Urbanización Los Angeles* ☎ *507/260–0044, 507/6679–4404, 800/614–7214 toll-free in U.S.* ⊕ *www. aventuraspanama.com.*

THE CANAL AND CENTRAL PANAMA

Updated
by Mark
Chesnut

THE PANAMA CANAL BISECTS THE country just to the west of Panama City, which enjoys excellent views of the monumental waterway. Between the canal and the rain forest that covers its islands, banks, and adjacent national parks, there is enough to see and do to fill several days.

Central Panama stretches out from the canal across three provinces and into two oceans to comprise everything from the mountains of the Cordillera Central to the west, to the Caribbean coral reefs and colonial fortresses in the north, to the beaches of the Pearl Islands in the Bahía de Panamá (Bay of Panama) in the south. Most of this region can be visited on day trips from Panama City, but the hotels in gorgeous natural settings outside the city will make you want to do some overnights. You could easily limit your entire vacation to Central Panama; the region holds most of the nation's history and nearly all the things that draw people to the country—beaches, reefs, islands, mountains, rain forests, indigenous cultures, and, of course, the Panama Canal. Within hours of Panama City, in many cases a fraction of an hour, you can enjoy bird-watching, sportfishing, hiking, golf, scuba diving, white-water rafting, horseback riding, whale watching, or lazing on a palm-lined beach.

The Panama Canal can be explored from Panama City, Gamboa, or Colón, and its attractions range from the wildlife of Barro Colorado Island to the feisty peacock bass that abound in Gatún Lake. The coast on either side of the canal's Caribbean entrance offers the remains of colonial fortresses hemmed by jungle, half a dozen beaches, and mile upon mile of coral reef, most of it between one and two hours from Panama City. The mountains to the east of the canal hold flora and fauna that you won't find in the forests that flank it, plus there are indigenous Emberá villages and a white-water rafting route on the Chagres River. The Pacific islands offer idyllic beaches, sportfishing, decent dive sites, and seasonal whale watching, all within 90 minutes of the capital by boat or plane. The coast to the southwest of Panama City also has some nice beaches, whereas the nearby highland refuge of El Valle presents exuberant landscapes populated by a multitude of birds and an ample selection of outdoor activities.

TOP REASONS TO GO

The Engineering Marvel. History, technology, and nature combine like nowhere else in the world at the Panama Canal. The most popular way to explore is by taking one of the transit tours that ply its waters between the Calzada Amador (Amador Causeway) and Gamboa. You can get a different perspective on one of the nature or fishing tours available out of Gamboa.

The Rain Forest. Central Panama has some of the most accessible rain forest in the world, with roads, trails, and waterways leading into wilderness that's home to hundreds of bird species and other animals. Tropical nature can be experienced to the fullest in the forests along the canal, in the mountains to the east and west of it, or along the Caribbean coast.

The Oceans. With the Caribbean and Pacific just 50 miles apart at the canal, you can bathe or skin-dive in two oceans on the same day. The Caribbean coast has miles of coral reef, whereas the Pacific islands lie near good fishing, dive spots, and seasonal whale watching.

The Islands. Some of Panama's best beaches are on its islands, and Central Panama has isles where the sand is lined by coconut palms and other tropical foliage. These range from historic Isla Taboga to the uninhabited isles of the Pearl Archipelago, where three seasons of *Survivor* were based.

The Mountains. The hills of Central Panama are considerably lower than those in the country's western provinces, but they still provide a refreshing respite from the lowland heat, and their lush forests are home to hundreds of bird species.

ORIENTATION AND PLANNING

GETTING ORIENTED

Central Panama's destinations are nearly all within a two-hour drive from Panama City, or in the case of the islands to the southeast, within 90 minutes of the city by boat or plane. Most of the region's attractions can be visited on day trips from the capital, but a couple of spots require overnights. Calle Omar Torrijos leads north from Panama City's Balboa neighborhood to the canal's Pacific locks, Summit, Gamboa, and Gatún Lake. If you go straight on that road past the left turn for Gamboa, you'll reach the

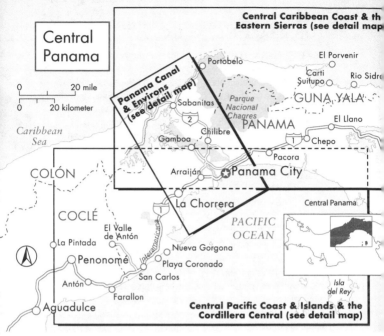

Autopista Alfredo Motta, a toll road that leads to Sabanitas—where the road east to Portobelo and Santa Isabel begins—and Colón, and the turnoff for the Gatún Locks and San Lorenzo, shortly thereafter. The westbound Carretera Interamericana is reached by taking Avenida de los Mártires over the Bridge of the Americas. It becomes a two-lane highway and veers west before Chorrera, and winds over the mountains before reaching the Central Pacific beaches and El Valle de Antón, one to two hours from the city by car. The Pacific islands of Islas Taboga, and Contadora are reached by daily ferries or flights.

The Panama Canal and Environs. A visit to the Panama Canal offers not only the chance to see—and perhaps transit—one of the world's great engineering wonders, but also to witness its 21st-century expansion. The national parks nearby provide myriad opportunities for hiking and wildlife viewing.

The Central Caribbean Coast. The historic town of Portobelo is a scenic hub for Caribbean-influenced Panamanian culture and lively events, as well as a gateway to the natural and cultural wonders that lie farther east, while the San Lorenzo protected area is great for hiking and bird-watching near a centuries-old fort.

The Eastern Sierras. The unspoiled grandeur of Chagres national park and the Sierra Llorona mountain range provide an inspiring backdrop for hiking, white-water rafting, and visiting indigenous Emberá communities.

The Central Pacific Islands. Travelers looking for a relaxed, beach-oriented getaway from bustling Panama City do well in the sun-soaked Central Pacific Islands, including Taboga, an easy day trip by ferry from Panama City, and Contadora, which once attracted the nation's rich and famous to its shores.

The Central Pacific Coast. Panama's highest concentration of large, all-inclusive beach resorts—as well as golf courses—make this a popular vacation spot for Panama City residents as well as visitors.

The Cordillera Central. This cool, verdant mountain range provides a breathaking alternative to the often-hot coastline, with stunning vistas, great hiking, and charming small hotels.

PLANNING

WHEN TO GO
Most of the canal and Central Pacific sites lie within 30 minutes to two hours of Panama City, so if you're based there, plenty of attractions can be visited on a spare morning or afternoon; others are amenable to spending an extra night or two. The best time to explore the area is the December to May dry season, or when rains let up in July and August. Note that Panamanians generally travel between Christmas and New Year's, during the weekend of Carnaval, in mid-February, or during Easter week; hotels fill up quickly at these times, and you will need to reserve rooms well in advance. Colorful Congo dances are performed in Portobelo for New Year's, Carnaval, and the Festival de Diablos y Congos (which takes place shortly after Carnaval).

PLANNING YOUR TIME
The amount of time needed to visit the Panama Canal and central Panama depends on the number of activities that you'd like to do, since several require joining guided excursions. It's easy to take in the Panama Canal itself by land in one day, making time for the visitor centers that offer up-close views. You'll want to spend at least a night or two

in the Pacific beaches and El Valle de Antón, since they're a farther drive (and you'll want time to relax and enjoy the scenery). You can easily visit Summit, Parque Nacional Soberanía, and Gamboa by taxi or rental car as a day trip, but you may also want to stay overnight at either Summit or Gamboa to have more time to enjoy those destinations. You'll need to join tours to do the canal transit, trips on Gatún Lake, visit indigenous communities, and white-water rafting in Chagres National Park. You should rent a car to explore more distant areas such as Portobelo, the Pacific beaches, and El Valle de Antón. The Panama Canal Railway is an interesting trip, but the downside is getting dumped in Colón, which is why most people take the train as part of a tour that meets them at the Colón train station and takes them to nearby sites.

GETTING HERE AND AROUND

AIR TRAVEL

The domestic airline Air Panama has daily 25-minute flights to Isla Contadora, usually in the morning, though also on Sunday afternoons. Flights depart Panama City's Marcos A. Gelabert Airport (aka Aeropuerto de Albrook).

Contacts Air Panama. ✉ *Marcos A. Gelabert Airport* ☎ *507/316–9000* ⊕ *www.airpanama.com.*

BOAT TRAVEL

Contacts Barcos Calypso Taboga. ✉ *Marina Isla Naos* ☎ *507/314–1730.*

BUS TRAVEL

Contacts Terminal de Transporte de Albrook. ✉ *Av. Gaillard* ☎ *507/303–3030.*

CAR TRAVEL

Renting a car is an easy way to visit many of the Central Pacific sites, because there are paved roads to just about everything but the islands. Cars can be rented in Panama City and Colón. Increased competition has greatly reduced the cost of rental, with prices now between about $6 and $60 a day for a car and $20 and up for 4WD vehicles, plus insurance. Most major car-rental companies have offices in Panama City (⇨ *Essentials, in "Panama City" chapter*); only Budget and Hertz have offices in Colón, both at the Colón 2000 cruise port.

TRAIN TRAVEL

The Panama Canal Railway's commuter train to Colón departs from the train station in Panama City weekdays at 7:15 am and departs from Colón at 5:15 pm. The trip costs $25 one way, $50 round-trip.

Train Station Information Atlantic Passenger Station. ✉ *Calle Mt. Hope* ⊕ *www.panarail.com.* **Corozal Passenger Station.** ✉ *Av. Omar Torrijos and Calle Corozal* ☎ 507/317–6070 ⊕ *www.panarail. com.* **Panama Canal Railway.** ✉ *Estación de Corozal, Av. Omar Torrijos and Calle Corozal* ☎ 507/317–6070 ⊕ *www.panarail.com.*

HOTELS

The accommodations in Central Panama range from big resorts to colorful bungalows in stunning natural surroundings. The region includes some comfortable nature lodges surrounded by rain forest, all-inclusive beach resorts where the bars stay open well past midnight, homey B&Bs, and boutique hotels in natural settings. Even in the cheapest hotels you can expect a private bathroom and air-conditioning. Although nearly all the hotels accept credit cards, some smaller places offer a discount if you pay in cash. Most hotels can book area tours for you, but tour companies will generally expect payment in cash. You can sometimes save a bundle (occasionally upward of $100) at some of the more expensive hotels and resorts by booking via their websites, especially for midweek or off-season stays.

Hotel reviews have been shortened. For full information visit Fodors.com.

RESTAURANTS

Though Central Panama's restaurant selection is neither as impressive nor as varied as Panama City's, the region has some fun dining options. Rather than unforgettable food, you're likely to enjoy good food in unforgettable settings, which include the ocean views on the Caribbean coast and Pacific Islands and Chagres River views in Gamboa.

WHAT IT COSTS				
	$	$$	$$$	$$$$
Restaurants	under $10	$10–$15	$16–$20	over $20
Hotels	under $100	$101–$160	$161–$220	over $220

Restaurant prices are per person for a main course at dinner. Hotel prices are for two people in a standard double room, excluding service and 10% tax.

MONEY

Credit cards are widely accepted in this region, except for at the smaller restaurants and hotels. ATM distribution is less uniform outside of Panama City, so it is often a good idea to stock up on cash before exploring the Central Pacific's rural reaches. The only ATMs near the Caribbean Coast's attractions are in and around Colón, whereas the eastern sierras and Pacific islands have no ATMs, so get cash before driving east or boarding the ferry or plane to Islas Taboga or Contadora. There are ATMs in the Albrook Airport terminal and at the Brisas de Amador shopping center, near the Taboga ferry dock, as well as in the lobby of the Gamboa Rainforest Resort, the Gatún Locks, in the Super 99 supermarket in Colón 2000, and the El Rey supermarket in Sabanitas. To the west of Panama City, you can find ATMs in the El Rey Supermarket at the entrance to Coronado, one block north of the Royal Decameron Beach Resort, in the lobby of the Playa Blanca Resort, on Avenida Principal of El Valle, and the shopping center by the JW Marriott Panama Golf & Beach Resort.

SAFETY

There are certainly safety issues in the city of Colón, which you should generally avoid exploring on foot. When hiking through the forest, always be careful where you put your hands and feet, because there are poisonous snakes and stinging insects. If you slip on a muddy trail in the rain forest, resist the temptation to grab the nearest branch, because palms with spiny trunks are relatively common. If there are big waves at any beach you visit, don't go in unless you are an expert swimmer, because waves can create dangerous currents. The sun intensity at these latitudes means sunscreen and a brimmed hat are musts.

THE PANAMA CANAL AND ENVIRONS

The Panama Canal stretches across one of the narrowest parts of the isthmus to connect the Pacific Ocean and the Caribbean Sea. For much of that route it's bordered by tropical wilderness. About half of the waterway is made up of Lago Gatún (Gatún Lake), an enormous artificial lake created by damming the Río Chagres (Chagres River). In addition to forming an integral part of the waterway, the lake is notable for its sportfishing and for the wildlife of its islands and the surrounding mainland.

As much an attraction as the canal itself are the forests that line it, which for decades were protected within the Canal Zone. The Panamanian government has turned most of those forests into national parks, whereas most of the former U.S. infrastructure has been privatized. Some of the former U.S. communities have become part of Panama City, while others, such as Gamboa, stand apart. The national parks have become increasingly important tourist attractions, and trails into the wilderness of Parque Nacional Soberanía and Monumento Natural Barro Colorado make the former Canal Zone one of the best places in the world to visit a tropical rain forest.

THE COUNTRY? NO, THE CITY. No matter where you travel in the central part of the country, you'll see highway signs directing you to "Panamá." Yes, you're already in the country of Panama, but that's the Spanish-language name for Panama City, too. In true developing-country fashion, all roads lead to the capital.

THE PANAMA CANAL

Panama's most famous landmark stretches 80 km (50 miles) from the edge of Panama City to the Caribbean port of Colón, and a paved road follows its route between the islands of the Amador Causeway and the inland port of Gamboa.

GETTING HERE AND AROUND
Since the Panama Canal runs along the western edge of Panama City, there are various spots within the metropolitan area from which to admire it (⇨ *Chapter 2*). A taxi should charge $15 to Miraflores Locks and $25 to Gamboa. Buses to Gamboa depart from the Terminal de Transporte in Albrook about every other hour *(Gamboa, below)* and can drop you off at Miraflores Locks.

TOURS
Although the canal is impressive when admired from any of Panama City's various viewing points, there's nothing quite like getting onto the water and navigating it amid the giant cargo ships. People spend thousands of dollars on cruises that include a canal crossing, but you can have the same experience for $100 to $200 and be free to spend the night in a spacious hotel room. Two companies offer partial transit tours, which travel through the canal's Pacific locks and Gaillard Cut, and full transits, which take you

Panama Canal and Environs

Caribbean Sea

Punta Toro

Fuerte San Lorenzo

Piña

Limon Bay

Colón

Cristóbal

Cativa

Esclusas de Gatún

Arco Iris

Ashiote

Gatún

Sabanitas

Puerto Pilón

COLÓN

Isla Zorra

Lago Gatún

Isla Juan Gallego

Escobal

Panama Canal

Trinidad Bay

Isla Barro Colorado

Sardinilla

Lagarterita

Gatuncito

Parque Nacional Soberanía

Porque Nacional Soberanía

Rio Chagres

Buenos Aires

Lag Alaju

La Laguna

Panama Rainforest Discovery Center

Mendoza

Gamboa

Chilibre

Santa Clara

Gaillard Cut

María Eugenia

Calzado Larga

PANAMA

Panama Canal

Summit

Parque Nacional Camino de Cruces

Alcal Díaz

Nuevo Emperador

Puente Centenario

Paraíso

Las Cumb

La Chorrera

Pedro Miguel Locks

San Isidro

Arraiján

Miraflores Locks

Interamericana

Cordoza

San Miguelito

La Mitra

Point Claimito

Veracruz

Panama City

Vacamonte

Fuerte Kobbe

Amador Causeway

Playa Leona

Isla Flamenco

KEY

--- *Panama Canal*

PACIFIC OCEAN

0   5 miles

0   5 kilometers

from one ocean to the other. All transits are accompanied by an expert guide who tells a bit of the canal's history, and include a Continental breakfast, and, on full transits, a cold box lunch. Partial transits travel between the island marinas on the Amador Causeway and the port of Gamboa, on Gatún Lake, a trip that lasts four to five hours. Transits take place every Friday and Saturday from May through December, and Thursday to Saturday (with additional days per demand) during the January through April high season. Full transits take place once or twice a month, usually on Saturday, and last eight or nine hours. ■TIP→ **Departure times are fixed, but finishing times are approximate; the Panama Canal Authority always gives priority to larger cargo and cruise ships.** Either trip is an unforgettable experience, suitable for travelers of all ages.

Canal & Bay Tours. This company offers partial and full transit tours on one of three ships: the 115-foot *Fantasía del Mar*, which has air-conditioned cabins and a large upper deck, and the 85-foot *Isla Morada*, and the 85-foot *Tuira II*, both of which have one large covered deck. Partial transits are $115 adults and $60 for children; full transits are $165 for adults and $75 for children. ⊠ *Bahia Balboa Building, next to Nunciatura* ☎ *507/209–2009* ⊕ *www. canalandbaytours.com.*

Panama Marine Adventures. Panama Marine Adventures runs canal transits on the 119-foot *Pacific Queen*, a comfortable ship with air-conditioned cabins and two large decks. Partial transits are $150 for adults and $95 for children; full transits are $195 for adults and $105 for children. ⊠ *Via Porras and Calle 66, San Francisco, No. 106* ☎ *507/226–8917* ⊕ *www.pmatours.net.*

EXPLORING

★ Fodor'sChoice **The Panama Canal.** The most interesting spot for viewing the Panama Canal is the visitor center at the **Miraflores Locks.** North of Miraflores the road to Gamboa heads inland but still passes a couple of spots with canal vistas, namely the Pedro Miguel Locks and the one-way bridge over the Chagres River. The bridge (and Gamboa in general) offers front-row views of the big ships as they pass though the canal. The Panama Canal Railway train to Colón continues north from Gamboa past other vantage points, which is much of that trip's draw. Two other spots with impressive views are the monument erected by the country's Chinese community on the Bridge of the

CANAL FACTS

More than 14,000 vessels under the flags of some 70 countries use the canal each year.

Canal administration requires captains to turn over control of their ships to canal pilots for the duration of the transit.

A boat traveling from New York to San Francisco saves 7,872 miles by using the Panama Canal instead of going around Cape Horn.

Most ships take 8–10 hours to traverse the canal, but the U.S. Navy hydrofoil *Pegasus* has the record for the fastest transit at 2 hours and 41 minutes.

Each of the canal's locks is 1,000 feet long and 110 feet wide, dimensions that have governed shipbuilding since the canal's completion in 1914. The massive Panamax ships that move most cargo through the canal are designed to carry as much as possible while still fitting into the locks.

For each large ship that passes through the canal, 52 million gallons of fresh water are used by six locks, and more than one billion gallons of water flow from the canal into the sea every day. (It's a good thing the canal was built in a rain forest.)

At this writing the highest toll paid for Panama Canal passage was $375,600, paid by the cruise ship *Norwegian Pearl* in July 2011.

The lowest toll on record was the $0.36 paid by Richard Halliburton, who swam the canal in 1928. Halliburton's record is safe for posterity, since tolls have risen considerably since then.

Shipping companies may reserve transit slots up to one year in advance and must do so a minimum of four days ahead. Tolls—it's cash only, no credit—must be paid prior to arrival.

Americas' western side, and the Esclusas de Gatún (Gatún Locks), 10 km (6 miles) south of Colón. Near Colón, the Panama Canal Expansion Visitor Center offers views of construction on the expanded canal (as long as that work continues) and will likely remain open after the new section is finished. But nothing matches the experience of getting out onto the water, which can be done on a canal transit tour or on a nature tour or fishing trip on Gatún Lake. ⊕ *www.pancanal.com.*

Panama Canal Railway. The one-hour trip on the Panama Canal Railway from Corozal, just north of Albrook, to the

Caribbean city of Colón, offers an interesting perspective of the rain forests of Soberanía National Park and the wetlands along Gatún Lake. The railway primarily moves freight, but it has a commuter service on weekdays that departs from Panama City at 7:15 am (returning from Colón at 5:15 pm), and costs $25 each way. Tourists ride in one of six air-conditioned cars with curved windows on the roof that let you see the foliage overhead. The best views are from the left side of the train, and though the train moves too fast to see much wildlife, you may spot toucans, herons, and black snail kites flying over the lake. The downside: the trip passes a garbage dump and industrial zone near the end, and leaves you just outside the slums of Colón at 8:15 am, which is why you may want to take the trip as part of a tour that picks you up in Colón and takes you to either San Lorenzo or Portobelo. It is possible to do the trip on your own, in which case you should board one of the shuttle vans that await the train in Colón and have them take you to the Colón 2000 (pronounced coh- *loan* dose- *mill)* cruise-ship port, where you can pick up a rental car and drive to Portobelo, or hire a taxi for the day ($80–$100). The trains leave promptly, and it is complicated to pre-purchase tickets, so get to the station by 6:45 am to buy your tickets. ✉ *Av. Omar Torrijos* ☎ *507/317–6070* ⊕ *www.panarail.com.*

PARQUE NACIONAL SOBERANÍA

One of the planet's most accessible rain-forest reserves, Parque Nacional Soberanía comprises 19,341 hectares (48,000 acres) of lowland rain forest along the canal's eastern edge that is home to everything from howler monkeys to chestnut-mandible toucans. Long preserved as part of the U.S. Canal Zone, Soberanía was declared a national park, after being returned to Panama, as part of an effort to protect the canal's watershed.

GETTING HERE AND AROUND

Soberanía is an easy drive from Panama City and is reached by following the same route for Summit and Gamboa. Shortly after the Summit Golf Club the road passes under the railroad and comes to an intersection where a left turn will put you on the road to Gamboa and most of the park's trails. If you want to hike the Camino Cruces trail, you should head straight at that intersection, toward Chilibre, and drive 6 km (4 miles) to a parking area with picnic

Building the Panama Canal

More than a century after its completion, the Panama Canal remains an impressive feat of engineering. It took the U.S. government more than a decade and $352 million to dig the "Big Ditch," but its inauguration was the culmination of a human drama that spanned centuries and claimed thousands of lives. As early as 1524, King Carlos V of Spain envisioned an interoceanic canal, and he had Panama surveyed for routes where it might be dug, though it soon became clear that the task was too great to attempt. It wasn't until 1880 that the French tried to make that dream a reality, but the job turned out to be tougher than they'd imagined. The Frenchman Ferdinand de Lesseps, who'd recently overseen construction of the Suez Canal, intended to build a sea-level canal similar to the Suez, which would have been almost impossible given the mountain range running through Panama. But a different obstacle thwarted the French enterprise: Panama's swampy, tropical environment. More than 20,000 workers died of tropical diseases during the French attempt, which together with mismanagement of funds drove the project bankrupt by 1889.

The United States, whose canal-building enterprise was spear-headed by President Theodore Roosevelt, purchased the French rights for $40 million, and went to work in 1904. Using recent advances in medical knowledge, the Americans began their canal effort with a sanitation campaign led by Dr. William Gorgas that included draining of swamps and puddles, construction of potable water systems, and other efforts to combat disease. Another improvement over the French strategy was the decision to build locks and create a lake 85 feet above sea level. For the biggest construction effort since the building of the Great Wall of China, tens of thousands of laborers were brought in from the Caribbean islands, Asia, and Europe to supplement the local workforce. Some 6,000 workers lost their lives to disease and accidents during the American effort, which, when added to the deaths during the French attempt, is more than 500 lives lost for each mile of canal.

The most difficult and dangerous stretch of the canal to complete was Gaillard Cut through the rocky Continental Divide. Thousands of workers spent seven years blasting and digging through that natural barrier, which consumed most of the 61 million pounds of dynamite detonated during canal construction. The countless tons of rock removed were used to build the Amador Causeway.

Building the Panama Canal

By the time the SS *Ancon* became the first ship to transit the Panama Canal in August 15, 1914, numerous records and engineering innovations had been accomplished. One of the biggest tasks was the damming of the Chagres River with the Gatún Dam, a massive earthen wall 1½ miles long and nearly a mile thick. It was the largest dam in the world when built, and the reservoir it created, Gatún Lake, was the largest man-made lake. The six sets of locks, which work like liquid elevators that raise and lower ships the 85 feet between Gatún Lake and the sea, were also major engineering feats.

Each lock chamber is 1,000 feet long and 110 feet wide—measurements that have governed shipbuilding ever since and gave the industry the term "Panamax"—and water flows in and out of them by gravity, so there are no pumps. Fears that the canal would fall into disrepair with the changing of the guard at the turn of the millennium never materialized, and experts have credited Panama for its forward-thinking administration and maintenance of the facility. Panama has also made the canal more tourist-friendly than it ever was during the U.S. administration, a boon to you, dear visitor, as you view it in action. A $5.2-billion construction of new pairs of locks to complement Miraflores and Gatún began in 2007 and will allow larger post-Panamax ships, now 7% of the world's shipping fleet, to use the canal. It remains an innovative and vital link in the global economy, and a monument to the ingenuity and industriousness of the people who built it.

tables on your left, behind which is the trail. Turn left for Plantation Road, which is on the right 3 km (2 miles) past the Parque Natural Summit, at the entrance to the Canopy Tower. The dirt Plantation Road heads left from that entrance road almost immediately. The Sendero Los Charcos is on the right 2 km (1 mile) after Plantation Road. Pipeline Road begins in Gamboa, at the end of the main road, past the dredging division and town. A taxi should charge $20–$25 to drop you off at any of these trails, and buses to Gamboa depart from the terminal in Albrook every two hours. You're better off driving here, but you'll see and understand much more if you book a tour with an ecotourism company *(Sports and the Outdoors, below)*.

EXPLORING

Parque Nacional Soberanía (*Soberanía National Park*). Trails into the Parque Nacional Soberanía wilderness can be reached by public bus, taxi, or by driving the mere 25 km (15 miles) from downtown Panama City, though you are best off visiting the park on a guided tour. Those trails wind past the trunks and buttress roots of massive kapok and strangler fig trees and the twisted stalks of lianas dangling from their high branches. Though visitors can expect to see only a small sampling of its wildlife, the park is home to more than 500 bird species and more than 100 different mammals, including such endangered species as the elusive jaguar and the ocelot.

If you hike some of the park's trails, you run a good chance of seeing white-faced capuchin monkeys, tamandua anteaters, raccoon-like coatimundi, or the large rodents called agouti. You may also see iridescent blue morpho butterflies, green iguanas, leafcutter ants, and other interesting critters. On any given morning here you might see dozens of spectacular birds, such as red-lored parrots, collared aracaris, violaceous trogons, and purple-throated fruit crows. From November to April the native bird population is augmented by the dozens of migrant species that winter in the park, among them the scarlet tanager, Kentucky warbler, and Louisiana water thrush. It is the combination of native and migrant bird species, plus the ocean birds along the nearby canal, that have enabled the Panama Audubon Society to set the Christmas bird count world record for two decades straight. ⊠ *Ranger station, Av. Omar Torrijos ✛ 25 km (15 miles) northwest of Panama City* ☎ *507/232–4192* ⊠ *$5* ⊘ *Daily 7–5.*

WHERE TO STAY

$$$$ ⊞ **Canopy Tower.** *B&B/Inn*. Occupying a former U.S. Army radar tower deep in the rain forest of Soberanía National Park, this lodge caters almost exclusively to serious bird-watchers and natural history enthusiasts. **Pros:** constant exposure to nature; excellent guides; good food; sustainable practices. **Cons:** basic rooms; lots of stairs; expensive. Ⓢ *Rooms from: $267* ⊠ *Carretera Gamboa, 25 km (15 miles) northwest of Panama City* ☎ *507/264–5720, 800/930–3397 in the U.S.* ⊕ *www.canopytower.com* ⌁ *10 rooms, 2 suites* ⊗ *All meals.*

SPORTS AND THE OUTDOORS

BIRD-WATCHING

Soberanía has world-class bird-watching, especially from November to April, when the northern migrants boost the local population. Unless you're an expert, though, you're really better off joining a tour or hiring a guide through one of Panama City's nature-tour operators. Guests at the Canopy Tower (above) enjoy almost nonstop birding and tours led by the lodge's resident guides.

Advantage Panama. Advantage Panama has a day trip to Soberanía that combines a forest hike with a boat trip on Gatún Lake. ☎507/6676–2466 ⊕www.advantagepanama. com.

Ancon Expeditions. This company has excellent guides that can take you bird-watching on Pipeline Road, or on Gatún Lake. They also have a tour that combines a hike through Soberanía National Park with a boat trip on the Chagres River. ☎507/269–9415 ⊕www.anconexpeditions.com.

EcoCircuitos Panama. A Soberanía birding tour is offered that starts with a hike and ends with a boat trip, birding on Pipeline Road, a hiking tour on the Camino de Curces trails, and a tour to Barro Colorado Island. ☎507/315–0315 ⊕www.ecocircuitos.com.

Pesantez Tours. Pesantez Tours runs a half-day tour to Soberanía. ☎507/366–9100 ⊕www.pesantez-tours.com.

HIKING

Soberanía's natural treasures can be discovered along miles and miles of trails and roads, whereas the western edge of the park can be explored on boat tours through local companies. The park also protects a significant portion of the old **Camino de las Cruces,** a cobbled road built by the Spanish that connected old Panama City with a small port on the Chagres River, near modern-day Gamboa. It's more than 10 km (6 miles) long and intersects with Plantation Road before reaching the river, but you don't have to hike far to find cobbled patches that were restored a couple of decades ago.

Plantation Road is a dirt road that heads east into the forest from the road to Gamboa for about 6 km (4 miles), to where it connects to Camino de Cruces. That wide trail follows a creek called Río Chico Masambi, and it's a great place to see waterbirds and forest birds. Two kilometers (1 mile) past the entrance to the Canopy Tower is the **Sendero el Charco** (Pool Trail), which forms a loop through the forest to the east of the road to Gamboa. The *charco* (pool) refers to a man-made pond near the beginning of the trail that was created by damming a stream. The trail follows that stream part of the way, which means you may spot waterbirds such as tiger herons, in addition to such forest birds as toucans and *chachalacas*. It is one of the park's most popular trails because it's a loop, it's short (less than a kilometer), and it's flat enough to be an easy hike.

The park's most famous trail is **Camino del Oleoducto** (Pipeline Road), a paved road that follows an oil pipeline for 17 km (11 miles) into the forest parallel to the canal. One of the country's premier bird-watching spots, it is here that the Panama Audubon Society has had record-breaking Christmas bird counts year after year. Pipeline Road is a great place to see trogons (five species have been logged there), motmots, forest falcons, and hundreds of other bird species as well as monkeys and agoutis. You can hike any of these on your own, but you'll see and learn more if you take a bird-watching tour.

KAYAKING

Aventuras Panama. This company offers kayaking tours on the Chagres River, or Gatún Lake, which allows you to watch ships navigating the canal. ☎ *507/260–0044, 800/614–7214 toll-free in U.S.* ⊕ *www.aventuraspanama. com.*

GAMBOA

32 km (20 miles) northwest of Panama City.

Though it lies only about 40 minutes from downtown Panama City, the tiny community of Gamboa feels remote, no doubt due to the fact that it is surrounded by exuberant tropical nature. Its location on the north bank of the flooded Chagres River, nestled between the Panama Canal and rain forest of Soberanía National Park, makes Gamboa a world-class bird-watching destination and the departure point for boat trips on Gatún Lake. It is also a great place to stroll, have lunch amid nature, or kick back and admire the impressive tropical scenery. It is home to a massive nature resort that offers enough diversions to fill several days, but Gamboa's proximity to the capital also makes it a convenient day-trip from Panama City.

The town of Gamboa was built by Uncle Sam in the early 20th century to house workers at the Panama Canal dredging division, which is based here. The town's tiny port is full of canal maintenance equipment, but it's also the point of departure for the boat to Barro Colorado Island and for Pacific-bound partial canal transits. Private yachts sometimes spend a night near the port on the way through the canal, and a simple marina on the other side of the Chagres River holds the boats of local fishermen and tour companies that take groups onto the canal for wildlife watching along the forest's edge.

Over the years, biologists and bird-watchers have come to realize that Gamboa's combination of forests and wetlands make it home to an inordinate diversity of birds. The Panama Audubon Society has set world records for Christmas bird counts year after year on **Camino del Oleoducto** (Pipeline Road), which heads into Parque Nacional Soberanía on the northwest end of town. That trail is the main destination for day visitors, but you can also see plenty of wildlife from the roads around town and the banks of the Chagres River.

GETTING HERE AND AROUND
Gamboa is an easy 40-minute drive from Panama City. Follow the signs from Avenida Balboa or Avenida Central to Albrook, veer right onto Avenida Omar Torrijos at the traffic circle and follow it north into the forest. Shortly after driving under a railroad bridge, turn left and stay on that road all the way to the one-lane bridge over the Chagres River. Turn right just after the bridge for the Rainforest Resort and Los Lagartos restaurant, or continue straight ahead for Pipeline Road and STRI dock. A taxi from Panama City should charge $20–$25 to drop you off here. SACSA buses depart from the Terminal de Transport in Albrook every two hours from 6 am to 6 pm.

EXPLORING
The massive **Gamboa Rainforest Resort** *(below)*, just east of town, is spread over a ridge with a panoramic view of the Chagres River. The resort has a 340-acre forest reserve that is contiguous with Soberanía National Park, within which is an aerial tram, a small orchid collection, a butterfly farm, an aquarium, and an exotic frog garden. The resort also has its own marina on the Chagres River; near it is the riverside restaurant Los Lagartos, which is a great spot for lunch and wildlife watching even if you don't stay

at the hotel. The resort's owner even convinced a small indigenous Emberá community who were living in nearby Chagres National Park to rebuild their village across the Chagres River from the hotel, where they now receive tourists. (Realize the setup is artificial; it can't compare to a visit to an Emberá community in the Darién.)

Panama Rainforest Discovery Center. Just beyond Gamboa, adjacent to the Parque Nacional Soberanía and near the start of Pipeline Road, lies the Panama Rainforest Discovery Center, operated by the local Eugene Eisenmann Avian Wildlife Foundation. Its centerpiece is a 32-meter (105-ft) steel observation tower giving ample opportunity for observation of life in the rain-forest canopy. Three other decks are positioned at about each of the quarter-way marks. A solar-powered visitors' center contains exhibits about avian life in the Panamanian rain forest. Leading from the visitors' center is 1.1 km (0.7 miles) of hiking trails. They open at 6 am, which is the best tme to see birds. Capacity is limited to 25 visitors at a time during the peak viewing hours, before 10 am, and to 50 people for the rest of the day, so you should make reservations at least a day ahead from December to April. ✉ *3 km (2 miles) northwest of Gamboa* ☎ *507/6588–0697, 507/6450–6630 in Panama City* 🌐 *www.pipelineroad.org* 🎫 *$30 before 10 am; $20 after 10 am* 🕘 *Daily 6–4.*

WHERE TO EAT

$$ ✕ **Los Lagartos.** *Latin American.* Built out over the Chagres
FAMILY River, this open-air restaurant at the Gamboa Rainforest Resort is a great place to see turtles, fish, crocodiles, and waterfowl feeding in the hyacinth-laden water. If you travel with binoculars, you'll definitely want to bring them here, so that you can watch wildlife while you wait for your lunch. A small buffet is frequently available, but the à la carte selection is usually a better deal, with choices such as peacock bass in a mustard sauce, grouper topped with an avocado sauce and cheese, or the hearty, spicy fisherman's stew. Lighter items include Caesar salad, hamburgers, and quesadillas. It isn't Panama's best food, but it's good, and the view of the forest-hemmed Chagres River populated with grebes, jacanas, turtles, and other wildlife is worth the trip out here even if you have only a cup of tea. [$] *Average main: $15* ✉ *Carretera Gamboa, right after bridge over Chagres River* ☎ *507/314–5000* 🕘 *Closed Mon. except during high season.*

WHERE TO STAY

$$$$ FAMILY 🏨 **Gamboa Rainforest Resort.** *Resort.* Panoramic views of the Chagres River and surrounding rainforest, abundant wildlife, a selection of outdoor excursions, and amenities such as a spa and massive pool make this hotel a great place to experience the rain forest without sacrificing comfort. **Pros:** amazing views; abundant wildlife; ample facilities and diversions; friendly staff. **Cons:** food can be disappointing. [$] *Rooms from: $240* ✉ *Av. Omar Torrijos, 32 km (19 miles) northwest of Panama City* ☎ *507/314–5000, 877/800–1690 in U.S.* 🌐 *www.gamboaresort.com* 🛏 *160 rooms, 4 suites* 🍴 *Breakfast.*

SPORTS AND THE OUTDOORS

BIRD-WATCHING

All the big nature tour operators offer bird-watching tours on Pipeline Road *(Parque Nacional Soberanía, above).*

HIKING

Ancon Expeditions. Ancon Expeditions has a tour that includes a nature hike on Pipeline Road in Soberanía National Park, followed by a boat trip on Gatún Lake. ✉ *Edificio Dorado #3, Calle Elvira Méndez* ☎ *507/269–9415, 888/760–3426 in U.S.* 🌐 *www.anconexpeditions.com.*

FISHING

Gatún Lake is full of feisty peacock bass and also has snook and tarpon, adding up to excellent sportfishing. Charters depart from Gamboa's two marinas.

Panama Canal Fishing. Panama Canal Fishing is the best operator for fishing on Gatún Lake. The company offers three options for Gatún Lake fishing, for up to six people per boat: a four-hour, all-inclusive tour costs $350 for two people and $50 for each additional person; the six-hour tour is priced at $495 for two and $65 for each additional person; and the nine-hour tour costs $645 for two and $65 per additional person. ☎ *507/315–1905, 507/6678–2653* 🌐 *www.panamacanalfishing.com.*

LAGO GATÚN (GATÚN LAKE)

Covering about 262 square km (163 square miles), an area about the size of the island of Barbados, Gatún Lake extends northwest from Parque Nacional Soberanía to the locks of Gatún, just south of Colón.

GETTING HERE AND AROUND

Aside from seeing the entire canal on a complete transit tour, you can see a bit of the lake during the boat trip to Barro Colorado, or on one of the nature tours or sportfishing charters that leave from the marinas at Gamboa and the Meliá Resort, near Colón. You can also see parts of it from the Panama Railway.

EXPLORING

Lago Gatún (Gatún Lake). Gatún Lake was created when the U.S. government dammed the Chagres River, between 1907 and 1910, so that boats could cross the isthmus at 85 feet above sea level. By creating the lake, the United States saved decades of digging that a sea-level canal would have required. It took several years for the rain to fill the convoluted valleys, turning hilltops into islands and killing much forest (some trunks still tower over the water nearly a century later). When it was completed, Gatún Lake was the largest man-made lake in the world. The canal route winds through its northern half, past several forest-covered islands (the largest is Barro Colorado, one of the world's first biological reserves). To the north of Barro Colorado are the Islas Brujas and Islas Tigres, which together hold a primate refuge—visitors aren't allowed. The lake itself is home to crocodiles—forgo swimming here—manatees, and peacock bass, a species introduced from South America and popular with fishermen. Fishing charters for bass, snook, and tarpon are out of Gamboa Rainforest Resort.

ISLA BARRO COLORADO

55 km (34 miles) northwest of Panama City, in the Panama Canal.

The island of Barro Colorado in Lago Gatún is a former hilltop that became an island when the Río Chagres was dammed during construction of the Panama Canal. It covers 1,500 hectares (3,700 acres) of virgin rain forest and forms part of the Barro Colorado Nature Monument, which includes five peninsulas on the mainland and protects an area several times that size.

GETTING HERE AND AROUND

Barro Colorado can only be visited on tours run by the Smithsonian Tropical Research Institute. (⇨ *See review.*) From Panama City, you can hire a taxi ($20–$30) or book through a tour operator, which will pick you up at your hotel.

TOURS

Smithsonian Tropical Research Institute (*STRI*). Barro Colorado can be visited on full-day tours run by the Smithsonian Tropical Research Institute (STRI), which depart the STRI dock in Gamboa at 7:15 on Tuesday, Wednesday, and Friday, and 8 on weekends. The $80 tour is well worth the money, since the English-speaking guides do an excellent job of pointing out flora and fauna and explaining the rain forest's complex ecology. Lunch in the research station's cafeteria and boat transportation to and from Gamboa are included. Tours should be booked and paid for a minimum of two months in advance through the STRI website. Reservations that haven't been paid for 15 days before the tour will be canceled. If you failed to reserve, they sometimes have spaces available; it's worth calling the STRI office and asking. ⊠ *Av. Roosevelt* ☎ *507/212–8951* ⊕ *www.stri.si.edu* ⊙ *Open Mon.–Fri. 8 am–1pm.*

EXPLORING

★ Fodor'sChoice **Isla Barro Colorado.** The Isla Barro Colorado reserve is home for more than 400 species of birds, 225 ant species, and 122 mammal species, including collared peccaries, ocelots, coatis, and five kinds of monkeys. Its forest has 1,200 plant species—more than are found in all of Europe—ranging from delicate orchids to massive strangler fig trees.

In 1923 the island was declared a biological reserve and a tropical research station was built there; it is now the oldest such facility in the world. The island is administered by the Smithsonian Tropical Research Institute (STRI), which facilitates research by 200 or so visiting scientists and students per year and runs several weekly educational tours. Those tours are not only one of the most informative introductions to tropical ecology you can get in Panama, they are also excellent opportunities to see wildlife; after decades of living in a protected area full of scientists, the animals are hardly afraid of people.

Bring your passport, tour receipt, bottled water, insect repellent, binoculars, and a poncho or raincoat (May through December). Wear long pants, hiking shoes, and socks to protect against chiggers. You should be in decent shape, since the tour includes several hours of hiking on trails that are steep in places and can be slippery; children under 10 are not allowed, students pay a discounted rate. You can reserve and pay for tours at the STRI website, or through one of the city's tour companies that specialize in nature tours; the tour companies will charge extra to book the STRI tour and provide transportation between your hotel and the dock in Gamboa. ⊕ *www.stri.si.edu.*

THE CENTRAL CARIBBEAN COAST

Coral reefs, rain forests, colonial ruins, and a predominant Afro-Caribbean culture make Panama's Caribbean coast a fascinating place to visit. People from Panama City head to the Costa Arriba, the coast northeast of Colón, to enjoy its beaches and feast on fresh lobster, conch, or king crab. Scuba divers flock to Portobelo, a colonial town guarded by ancient fortresses and surrounded by rain forest, but the diving is even better northeast of there. The bird-watching is excellent around the colonial fortresses of San Lorenzo and Portobelo, and on the slopes of the Sierra Llorona.

COLÓN

79 km (49 miles) northwest of Panama City.

The provincial capital of Colón, beside the canal's Atlantic entrance, is named for the Spanish-language surname of Christopher Columbus, though the Americans called it Aspinwall in the 19th century. It was once a prosperous city, as the architecture of its older buildings attests, but it spent the second half of the 20th century in steady decay. Though the 21st century brought relief to the city's chronic unemployment problems, much of it remains a slum, and crime is endemic.

GETTING HERE AND AROUND

The easiest way to get to Colón from Panama City is to take the Panama Canal Railway commuter train that departs from Panama City at 7:15 am and returns at 5:15 pm. If you start your railway journey in Colón, you will need to purchase tickets from the conductor. Buses depart from Panama City's Albrook Terminal de Buses every 20 minutes, and the trip takes from 90 minutes to two hours. Get directly into a taxi upon arrival at either the train or bus station; both are in unsafe neighborhoods. ■TIP→ **Take only licensed taxis in Colón—the license plate and number on the door should match. Robberies have been committed by unofficial cabbies.** You can rent a car at the Colón 2000 cruise center. A spiffy, four-lane toll highway opened in 2009 and puts Colón less than an hour from Panama City. Take Avenida

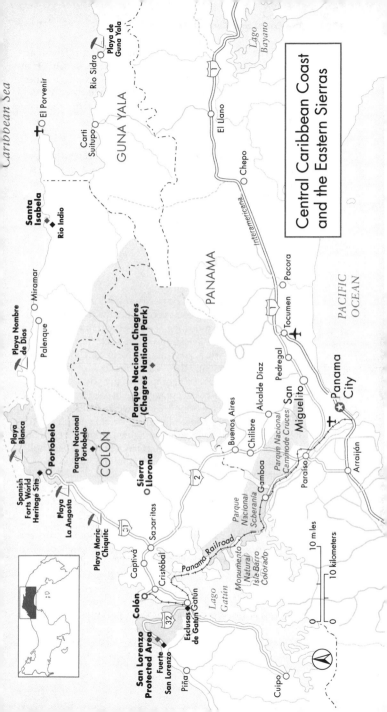

Caribbean Sea

Lago Bayano

Playa de Guna Yala

Río Sidra

El Porvenir

Santa Isabela

Río Indio

Playa Nombre de Dios

Miramar

Palenque

Carti Suitupo

GUNA YALA

El Llano

Chepo

Pacora

Playa Blanca

Portobelo

Parque Nacional Chagres
(Chagres National Park)

Parque Nacional Portobelo

Spanish Forts World Heritage Site

COLÓN

Sierra Llorona

PANAMA

Interamericana

Tocumen

PACIFIC OCEAN

Playa La Angosta

Playa Maria Chiquita

Sabanitas

Buenos Aires

Chilibre

Alcalde Díaz

San Miguelito

Pedregal

Panama City

Arraiján

Captiva

Cristóbal

Colón

Parque Nacional Soberanía

Parque Camino de Cruces

Gamboa

Paraíso

Panama Railroad

Esclusas de Gatún Gatún

Monumento Natural Isla Barro Colorado

Lago Gatún

San Lorenzo Protected Area

Fuerte San Lorenzo

Piña

Cuipo

10 miles

10 kilometers

Central Caribbean Coast and the Eastern Sierras

Omar Torrijo to the Autopista Alfredo Motta. If you are headed for the Gatún Locks, or San Lorenzo, turn left at the Centro Comercial Cuatro Altos, about 8 km (5 miles) before Colón, and follow the signs to Esclusas de Gatún. ⇨ *See By Car and By Train, above, for rental car and train travel information.*

SAFETY

■TIP➔ Travelers who explore Colón on foot risk being mugged, and the route between the train station and the bus terminal is especially notorious. Do all your traveling in a taxi, rental car, or on a guided tour. If you do the Panama Railway trip on your own, take one of the shuttle vans to the Colón 2000 (pronounced coh- *loan* dose- *mill*) cruise-ship terminal, where you can rent a car or hire a taxi to see the sights near town.

EXPLORING

TOP ATTRACTIONS

Esclusas de Gatún (*Gatún Locks*). Twelve kilometers (7 miles) south of Colón are the Esclusas de Gatún, a triple-lock complex that's nearly a mile long and raises and lowers ships the 85 feet between sea level and Gatún Lake. There's a small visitor center with a viewing platform and information about the boats passing through is broadcast over speakers. The visitor center doesn't compare to the one at Miraflores Locks, but given the sheer magnitude of the Gatún Locks—three sets of locks, as opposed to two at Miraflores—it is an impressive sight, especially when packed with ships. You have to cross the locks on a swinging bridge to get to San Lorenzo and the **Represa Gatún** (Gatún Dam), which holds the water in Gatún Lake. At 2½ km (1½ miles) long, it was the largest dam in the world when it was built, a title it held for several decades. Get there by taking the first left after crossing the locks. ✉ *12 km (7 miles) south of Colón* ⊕ *visitcanaldepanama.com* ✆ *$5* ⊙ *Daily 8–4.*

Panama Canal Expansion Observation Center. Not far from the Gatún Locks, this visitor center offers the best view of work on the new part of the Panama Canal. A video presentation provides an introduction to the canal's history and expansion, but the open-air observation area is the most interesting part, since it offers hilltop views of the work (when construction is complete, supposedly in 2016, this will become a good place to view the finished work). The facility has a playground and gift shop, as well as a pleasant, open-air restaurant operated by El Panamá hotel, which is open daily 12–4 for lunch (call *507–215–9927* for reservations). The restaurant offers great views of Gatún Lake. ✢ *From the Gatún Visitor Center, turn right just before the railroad tracks and make the first right* ☎ *507/276–8325* 🌐 *visitcanaldepanama.com/expansion-observation-center* 🎟 *$15, $10 for children ages 6–17* 🕒 *Daily 8–4.*

WORTH NOTING

Colón 2000. Two blocks from the Zona Libre is the city's cruise-ship port, Colón 2000, which is basically a two-story strip mall next to the dock where ships tie up and passengers load onto buses for day trips. It has a supermarket, restaurants, two rental-car offices, and English-speaking taxi drivers who can take you on sightseeing excursions ($70–$100 for a full day). A second terminal opened in 2008 and briefly served as the home port for Royal Caribbean's *Enchantment of the Seas*; the Panamanian government is aggressively courting other cruise companies to set up shop here. ✉ *Calle El Paseo Gorgas* ☎ *507/447–3197.*

WHERE TO STAY

$$ 🏨 **Radisson Colón 2000.** *Hotel.* If you have to spend a night in Colón, this is your best option, since it's next to the Colón 2000 cruise port, with its shops and restaurants, in one of the safest parts of town. **Pros:** quiet; safe; business amenities. **Cons:** facilities can be overrun with cruise-ship passengers when ships are in port. [$] *Rooms from: $109* ✉ *Paseo Gorgas, Calle 13* ☎ *507/446–2000, 800/830–5222 in U.S. and Canada* 🌐 *www.radisson.com* 🛏 *98 rooms, 4 suites* 🍴 *Breakfast.*

SPORTS AND THE OUTDOORS

FISHING

Meliá Panama Canal. The Meliá Panama Canal runs inexpensive fishing tours on Gatún Lake that are open to nonguests. The fishing gear is basic, but you are pretty much guaranteed to catch some peacock bass. Prices start at $50, and you should reserve the tours at least two days in advance. ✉ *Calle Principal* ☎ *507/470–1100* 🌐 *www.melia.com.*

SAN LORENZO PROTECTED AREA

40 km (25 miles) west of Colón.

The San Lorenzo region, on Panama's Pacific coast near the city of Colón, combines picturesque natural beauty and historic significance. The ruins of San Lorenzo fort, built by the Spanish to protect the entry to the Chagres

River, offers impressive views from its UNESCO-recognized lookout points, while the surrounding Parque Nacional San Lorenzo is graced with lush vegetation and excellent bird-watching. For more information about San Lorenzo's park, fort, tours, and accommodations, visit ⊕ *www. sanlorenzo.org.pa*.

GETTING HERE AND AROUND

It usually takes two hours to drive to San Lorenzo from Panama City and 40 minutes from Colón, if it doesn't take too long to cross the Gatún Locks. Follow directions for Colón, but turn left at the Centro Comercial Cuatro Altos, 8 km (5 miles) before Colón, and follow the signs to Esclusas de Gatún. After crossing the locks, veer right and drive 12 km (7 miles) to Fort Sherman. Turn left onto a dirt road after the entrance to Fort Sherman and drive another 11 km (6 miles) to the fort. The Achiote Road is reached by turning left after crossing the locks and driving 12 km (7 miles)—over the Gatún Dam—to the second road on the right. The town of Achiote is 10 km (6 miles) up that dirt road.

EXPLORING

WORTH NOTING

Fuerte San Lorenzo (*San Lorenzo Fort*). Perched on a cliff overlooking the mouth of the Chagres River are the ruins of the ancient Spanish Fuerte San Lorenzo, destroyed by pirate Henry Morgan in 1671 and rebuilt shortly after, then bombarded a century later. The Spaniards built Fort San Lorenzo in 1595 in an effort to protect the South American gold they were shipping down the Chagres River, which was first carried along the Camino de Cruces from Panamá Viejo. The gold was then shipped up the coast to the fortified city of Portobelo, where it was stored until the Spanish armada arrived to carry it to Spain. The fortress's commanding position and abundant cannons weren't enough of a deterrent for Morgan, whose men managed to shoot flaming arrows into the fort, causing a fire that set off stored gunpowder and forced the Spanish troops to surrender. Morgan then led his men up the river and across the isthmus to sack Panamá Viejo.

In the 1980s UNESCO restored the fort to its current condition, which is pretty sparse—it hardly compares to the extensive colonial ruins of Portobelo. Nevertheless, the setting is gorgeous, and the view from that promontory of the blue-green Caribbean, the coast, and the vast jungle behind it is breathtaking. Be careful walking around the edge outside the fort; there are some treacherous precipices, and guardrails are almost nonexistent. One visitor did have a fatal fall several years ago. ⊠ *23 km (14 miles) northwest of Gatún Locks* ☎*Free* ☉ *Daily 8–4.*

Parque Nacional San Lorenzo. The wilderness just behind the Fuerte San Lorenzo is part of Parque Nacional San Lorenzo, a 23,843-acre (9,653-hectare) protected area that includes rain forest, wetlands, rivers, and coastline. For decades this was the U.S. Army's jungle training area, where tens of thousands of troops trained for warfare in the tropics. The army used parts of the park as a bombing range, and there may still be unexploded ordnance in its interior, though far from the roads and fortress. Today the park is the haunt of bird-watchers, who hope to focus their binoculars on some of the more than 400 bird species. Mammalian residents include spider monkey, armadillo, tamarin, and coatimundi. The lush forest here gets nearly twice as much rain as Panama City, and it doesn't lose as much of its foliage during the dry season. Most of that rain falls at night, so mornings are often sunny, even during the rainy season.

The most famous bird-watching area in Parque Nacional San Lorenzo is **Achiote Road** (Camino a Achiote), which is about 25 km (15 miles) south of the fort. To reach it, turn left after crossing the locks and drive 15 km (9 miles) south. Members of the Panama Audubon Society once counted 340 bird species in one day on Achiote Road during their Christmas bird count. The community of Achiote, about 4 km (2½ miles) northwest of the park on Achiote Road, has trained birding guides and a visitor center, the Centro del Tucan, with rustic shared, dormitory-style accommodations for $12 a night, as well as private cabins at prices that vary according to the season. ⊠ *15 km (9 miles) west of Gatún Locks* ☎*507/226–4529* ⊕ *www.sanlorenzo.org. pa* ☎*Free* ☉ *Daily 9–6:30.*

SPORTS AND THE OUTDOORS

BIRD-WATCHING

Ancon Expeditions. Panama City–based operator Ancon Expeditions offers a tour that combines bird-watching and forest exploration in San Lorenzo with a visit to the Panama Canal Expansion Visitors Center. ☎*507/269–9415, 888/760–3426 in U.S.* ⊕ *www.anconexpeditions.com.*

EcoCircuitos Panama. Located in Panama City, this company offers a half-day birding tour to Achiote Road, in San Lorenzo National Park, and a general interest tour that combines visits to the fortress and Gatún Locks. ☎ 507/315–1305 ⊕ www.ecocircuitos.com.

Nattur Panama. Colón-based Nattur Panama can put together à la carte birding tours of San Lorenzo, Portobelo National Park, and other areas. ☎ 507/442–1340 ⊕ www.natturpanama.com.

PORTOBELO

99 km (62 miles) north of Panama City, 48 km (30 miles) northeast of Colón.

Portobelo has an inspiring mix of colonial fortresses, placid waters, and lushly forested hills. Christopher Columbus named it "beautiful port" in 1502 during his fourth and final voyage to the Americas. Unfortunately, cement-block houses crowded higgledy-piggledy amid the ancient walls detract from an otherwise lovely setting. Portobelo contains some of Panama's most interesting colonial ruins, with rusty cannons still lying in wait for an enemy assault, and is a UNESCO World Heritage Site, together with San Lorenzo. Depending on your timing, you could see congo dancing, or the annual Festival del Cristo Negro *(Black Christ Festival, below)*. Between the history, turquoise sea, jungle, coral reefs (great for scuba diving or snorkeling), beaches, and local culture, it's an enticing spot to spend a few days.

Once the sister city of Panamá Viejo, Portobelo was an affluent trading center during the 17th century, when countless tons of Spanish treasure passed through its customs house, and shiploads of European goods were unloaded on their way to South America. The Spaniards moved their Atlantic port in Panama from Nombre de Dios to Portobelo in 1597, since the deep bay was deemed an easier place to defend against pirates, who had raided Nombre de Dios repeatedly. During the next two centuries Portobelo was one of the most important ports in the Caribbean. Gold from South America was stored here after crossing the isthmus via Camino de Cruces and Chagres River, awaiting semiannual *ferias*, or trade fairs, in which a fleet of galleons and merchant ships loaded with European goods arrived for several weeks of business and revelry before sailing home laden with gold and silver. That wealth attracted pirates, who repeatedly attacked Portobelo, despite the

Spanish fortresses flanking the entrance to the bay and a larger fortress near the customs house. After a century and a half of attacks, Spain began shipping its South American gold around Cape Horn in 1740, marking the end of Portobelo's ferias, and turning the town into an insignificant Caribbean port. What remains today is a mix of historic and tacky, twentieth-century structures surrounded by spectacular natural scenery that looks much the same as it did in Columbus's day.

GETTING HERE AND AROUND

Portobelo is a 90-minute drive from Panama City and a mere 40 minutes from Colón. To drive there from Panama City, follow the directions to Colón but turn right after 60 km (37 miles), at the town of Sabanitas; from there it's 39 km (24 miles) to Portobelo. From Colón, head south toward Panama City for 15 km (9 miles) and turn left at Sabanitas. There's not much reason to go to Colón on your way to Portobelo, unless you take the Panama Canal Railway, in which case hire a taxi or rent a car and drive to Portobelo.

EXPLORING

TOP ATTRACTIONS

Parque Nacional Portobelo (*Portobelo National Park*). Parque Nacional Portobelo is a vast marine and rain-forest reserve contiguous with Chagres National Park that protects both natural and cultural treasures. It extends from the cloud forest atop 3,212-foot Cerro Brujo down to offshore islands and coral reefs, and comprises the bay and fortresses of Portobelo. It holds an array of ecosystems and a wealth of biodiversity that ranges from nurse sharks and sea turtles along the coast to toucans and spider monkeys in the mountains. There is no proper park entrance, but you can explore the rain forest and mangrove estuaries along the coast on hiking or boat trips from Portobelo.

You can't miss the remains of the three Spanish fortresses that once guarded Portobelo Bay. The first is **Fuerte Santiago de la Gloria,** which is on the left as you arrive at the bay. It has about a dozen cannons and sturdy battlements that were built out of blocks of coral, which were cut from the platform reefs that line the coast. Coral was more abundant and easier to cut than the igneous rock found inland, so the Spaniards used it for most construction in Portobelo.

Portobelo's largest and most impressive fort is **Fuerte San Jerónimo,** at the end of the bay. Surrounded by the "modern" town, it was built in the 1600s but was destroyed by Vernon and rebuilt to its current state in 1758. Its large interior courtyard was once a parade ground, but it's now the venue for annual celebrations such as New Year's, Carnaval, the Festival de Diablos y Congos (shortly after Carnaval), and the town's patron saint's day (March 20).

Fuerte San Fernando, across the bay from Fuerte Santiago, consists of two battlements—one near the water and one on the hill above. The upper fortress affords a great view of the bay and is a good place to see birds because of the surrounding forest.

Local boatmen who dock their boats next to Fuerte Santiago or Fuerte San Jerónimo can take you across the bay to explore Fuerte San Fernando for a few dollars. They also offer tours to local beaches, or a trip into the estuary at the end of the bay, which is a good place to see birds. ⊠ *Surrounding Portobelo* ☎ *507/442–8348 park office* ✉ *Free* ☾ *24 hrs daily.*

WORTH NOTING

Iglesia de San Felipe. One block east of Real Aduana is the Iglesia de San Felipe, a large white church dating from 1814 that's home to the country's most venerated religious figure: the Cristo Negro (Black Christ). According to legend, that statue of a dark-skinned Jesus carrying a cross arrived in Portobelo in the 17th century on a Spanish ship bound for Cartagena, Colombia. Each time the ship tried to leave, it encountered storms and had to return to port, convincing the captain to leave the statue in Portobelo. Another legend has it that in the midst of a cholera epidemic in 1821 parishioners prayed to the Cristo Negro, and the community was spared. The statue spends most of the year to the left of the church's altar, but once a year it's paraded through town in the Festival del Cristo Negro. Each year the Cristo Negro is clothed in a new purple robe, donated by somebody who's earned the honor. Behind San Felipe is the Iglesia de San Juan, a smaller, 17th-century church that is closed indefinitely for renovation. ⊠ *Calle Principal* ☾ *Daily 8–6.*

Real Aduana (*Royal Customs House*). Near the entrance to Fuerte San Jerónimo is Real Aduana, where servants of the Spanish crown made sure that the king and queen got their cut from every ingot that rolled through town. Built in 1630, Real Aduana was damaged during pirate attacks and then destroyed by an earthquake in 1882, only to be rebuilt in 1998. It is an interesting example of colonial architecture—note the carved coral columns on the ground floor—and it houses a simple museum with some old coins, cannonballs, and displays on Panamanian folklore. ✉ *Calle de la Aduana* ☎ *507/448–2024* 🌐 *www.inac.gob.pa* 🎟 *$5* 🕘 *Daily 8–4.*

BEACHES

Playa Blanca. Playa Blanca is a small, white-sand beach about 30 minutes by boat east of Portobelo. It has the nicest sand of any beach in the area, some shade trees, and there are reefs off shore for snorkelling. There are no roads there, nor are there restaurants or stores. The water is almost always calm, but if there are waves, don't go in deep. Amenities: none. Best for: solitude; snorkeling; swimming.

Playa La Angosta. The easiest beach to visit in the vicinity is Playa La Angosta, which is about 8 km (5 miles) south of Portobelo. The long, beige beach backed by coconut palms and other trees is quiet during the week, but on weekends and holidays, it can get packed with visitors from Colón and Panama City. There is a small charge for parking a car and renting tables on the beach with thatched sombrillas; you can also rent Bali-style daybeds for $15-$20 for the day. Restaurant Mamani, on the beach, serves a small selection of seafood and cool drinks, and has the only bathrooms. Amenities: food and drink; parking; toilets. Best for: partiers; swimming; walking.

WHERE TO EAT

$$ ✕ **Restaurante Los Cañones.** *Seafood.* This rambling restaurant with tables among palm trees and Caribbean views is one of Panama's most attractive lunch spots. The food and service fall a little short of the setting, but not so far that you'd want to scratch it from your list. In good weather, dine at tables edging the sea surrounded by dark boulders and lush foliage. The other option is the open-air restaurant, decorated with shells, buoys, and driftwood, with a decent view of the bay and forested hills. House specialties include *pescado entero* (whole fried snapper), *langosta al ajillo* (lobster scampi), and *centolla al jengibre* (king crab in a ginger sauce). [$] *Average main: $12* ✉ *2 km (1 mile) before Portobelo on left* 💳 *No credit cards* 🕘 *Closes at 7 pm.*

WHERE TO STAY

$ 🏨 **Casa Congo.** *B&B/Inn.* This simple-but-comfortable small hotel, located in downtown Portobelo, is part of a small complex that includes a restaurant, art gallery, and active art workshop with artists who specialize in the region's Congo artwork. **Pros:** cheery decor; reasonable room rates; easy access to local art scene and central location for exploring the town of Portobelo. **Cons:** no pool; limited services nearby; few options for dining other than the hotel's own restaurant. [$] *Rooms from: $80* ✉ *on the waterfront in downtown Portobelo* ☎ *507/202–0111* 🌐 *www.fundacionbp.org* 🕑 *Closes at 7 pm.* 🛏 *4 rooms* 🍴 *Breakfast.*

★ $$$$ **Fodor's Choice** 🏨 **El Otro Lado.** *B&B/Inn.* This private retreat across the bay from Portobelo offers a splendid mix of ocean views, tropical nature, abundant art, friendly service, and fine dining. **Pros:** gorgeous atmosphere; intimate; great service. **Cons:** expensive. [$] *Rooms from: $490* ✉ *Across bay from town, Bocas del Toro* ☎ *507/202–0111* 🌐 *www.elotrolado.com.pa* 💳 *No credit cards* 🛏 *3 suites, 4 houses* 🍴 *Breakfast.*

$ 🏨 **Sunset Cabins.** *Hotel.* This dive resort owned by Scuba Panama, the country's biggest dive company, has decent rooms in a lovely coastal setting at very low rates, making it a good option for budget travelers who can do without a lot of service. **Pros:** great location; inexpensive; scuba diving and snorkeling. **Cons:** basic rooms; limited service. [$] *Rooms from: $50* ✉ *6 km (4 miles) south of Portobelo on left* ☎ *507/448–2147, 507/261–3841 in Panama* 🌐 *www.scubapanama.com* 🛏 *6 rooms, 5 cabañas* 🍴 *No meals.*

SPORTS AND THE OUTDOORS

BIRD-WATCHING

The bird-watching is quite good at the edge of town and around the ruins. Bird-watchers may want to hire one of the boatmen who hang out around the docks near Batería Santiago and Fuerte San Jerónimo to take them into the estuary behind town, which should cost $20.

SCUBA DIVING AND SNORKELING

Miles of coral reefs awash in rainbows of underwater wildlife lie within the northern reaches of **Portobelo National Park,** and dive centers on the road to Portobelo provide easy access to those marine wonders. Though they've suffered damage from fishermen, erosion, and climate change, the reefs in the Portobelo area consist of nearly 50 coral species and are inhabited by more than 250 fish species.

The underwater fauna ranges from moray eels to colorful butterfly fish, damselfish, trumpet fish, and other reef dwellers. Popular spots include Buffet Reef, a plane wreck, a shipwreck, and the distant Escribano Bank, east of Isla Grande. Visibility varies according to the sea conditions, but tends to be low from December to April, when high seas can hamper dives. The best conditions are between July and December. PADI certification courses are also available.

Aventuras Panama. The Panama City-based outfitter Aventuras Panama runs a day tour to Portobelo that combines kayaking and snorkeling for $165 per person. ☎ 507/260–0044 ⊕ www.aventuraspanama.com.

Panama Divers. Panama Divers, a small American-owned company, offers various boat dives, tours, and courses; the average cost for an excursion is about $100 per person. ✉ Coco Plum Ecolodge ⊹ 5 km (3 miles) before Portobelo on left ☎ 314–0817 ⊕ www.panamadivers.com.

Scuba Panama. The country's oldest dive operator, Scuba Panama has a dive center at the Sunset Cabins hotel, where it operates day and overnight dive tours to reefs near Portobelo. ✉ 6 km (4 miles) before Portobelo on the left ☎ 507/448–2147, 507/261–3841 ⊕ www.scubapanama. com.

SANTA ISABELA

44 km (27 miles) east of Isla Grande, 26 km (16 miles) west of El Porvenir (Guna Yala).

To the east of Portobelo, the coast becomes wilder, and the ocean more pristine. About two-thirds of the way between Isla Grande and the Guna enclave of El Porvenir (⇨ *Chapter 6*), near the Coral Lodge eco-lodge, which is currently closed for renovation, you'll find access to miles of coral reefs that few divers have seen. Nearby is the fishing village of Santa Isabela, which is 16 km (10 miles) from the nearest road, in Miramar, and 29 km (18 miles) by water from the island of El Porvenir.

THE EASTERN SIERRAS

A large mass of mountains rises up to the northeast of the Panama Canal, which collects much of the rainwater used by the locks. The Panamanian government consequently protected that vast watershed within Parque Nacional

Chagres. Chagres is contiguous with Portobelo National Park—the relatively small Sierra Llorona defines the border between the two parks.

PARQUE NACIONAL CHAGRES (CHAGRES NATIONAL PARK)

40 km (24 miles) north of Panama City.

The mountains to the northeast of the canal form a vast watershed that feeds the Chagres River, which was one of the country's principal waterways until it was damned to create the canal, and is now the source of nearly half of the water used in the locks. To protect the forests that help water percolate into the ground and keep the river running through the dry season, the Panamanian government declared the entire watershed a national park in 1985.

GETTING HERE AND AROUND

There is no easy access to Parque Nacional Chagres, so you have to take a tour—hiking, white-water rafting—to visit it.

EXPLORING

Parque Nacional Chagres (*Chagres National Park*). Covering more than 320,000 acres, Parque Nacional Chagres is one of Panama's largest parks. It holds an array of ecosystems and expanses of inaccessible wilderness that are home to spider monkeys, harpy eagles, toucans, tapirs, and other endangered species. The park's northern border, defined by Sierra Llorona, and its southern extreme, in Cerro Azul, are the easiest areas to visit, thanks to paved roads. Most people visit the national park on day tours from Panama City to one of several Emberá villages, but you can see more of its forests on a white-water rafting trip down the Chagres River or by hiking on the trails of Cerro Azul.

All the major tour operators in Panama City offer day trips to **Emberá villages** in the park. Visiting the villages—relocated here from Alto Bayano three decades ago, when their land was flooded by a hydroelectric project—is an interesting cultural experience, but most itineraries aren't great for seeing wildlife. The Emberá's traditional territory stretches from eastern Panama to northwest Colombia, but the relocated communities live much as their relatives to the east do, in thatched huts with elevated floors. They wear their traditional dress for tour groups—men wear loincloths and women wrap themselves in bright-color cloth skirts, with no tops, sometimes covering their breasts with large necklaces. Men and women paint their upper bodies with a dye made from mixing the sap of the *jagua* fruit with ashes. The tours are a bit of a show, but they provide an interesting introduction to Emberá culture. Tours usually include demonstrations of how the Emberá live, a traditional dance, handicraft sales, and optional painting of visitors' arms with *jagua*. (Note the *jagua* tattoos take more than a week to wash off.) Communities that receive visitors include Parara Puru and San Juan de Pequiní, but the best trip for nature lovers or adventurers is to Emberá Drua, since it entails a boat trip deep into the park and a tough hike. ✉ *Transístmica, Km. 40* ☎ *507/260–8575* 💲*$5* 🕙 *Daily 7–5.*

SHOPPING

A big part of a visit to an Emberá village is the opportunity to buy authentic indigenous handicrafts from the artisans themselves. Among the items usually sold are tightly woven baskets and platters, and animal figures carved from *tagua* palm seeds, or *cocobolo* wood.

SPORTS AND THE OUTDOORS

HIKING

Camino Real. Serious hikers can trek deep into the jungles of Parque Nacional Chagres by following the old Camino Real across the mountains to the Caribbean coast. Spanish colonists built the "Royal Road" in the 16th century to carry gold and other goods between Panamá Viejo and the Caribbean port of Nombre de Dios, and most of that route remains surrounded by lush rain forest. Weeklong trips organized by **Ancon Expeditions** include visits to colonial ruins and an Emberá village and several nights in tent camps in the national park.

WHITE-WATER RAFTING

Aventuras Panama. Aventuras Panama runs white-water rafting trips on the Chagres River (class II–III), which flows through the heart of Parque Nacional Chagres. The full-day trip requires no previous rafting experience, but is available only from early July to late February; it costs $185, which includes lunch and breakfast. ☎ *507/260–0044* 🌐 *www.aventuraspanama.com.*

THE CENTRAL PACIFIC ISLANDS

The Gulf of Panama holds more than a dozen islands and countless rocky islets, which include Isla Taboga, a mere 20 km (12 miles) south of Panama City, and the Archipelago de las Perlas (Pearl Islands), which are scattered across the gulf between 60 and 90 km (about 40 to 60 miles) southeast of the city. Isla Taboga has a historic town lined with vacation homes, whereas the Pearl Islands remain largely undeveloped, with a few fishing villages and vast expanses of rain forest. The aquamarine waters that wash against the islands hold varied and abundant marine life, providing opportunities for sportfishing, scuba diving, and whale watching (June to October).

The islands were inhabited when the Spaniards arrived in Panama, Isla Taboga became a Spanish stronghold from the start due to its deep bay, ideal for mooring ships close to shore. The Spanish conquistador Francisco Pizarro defeated the indigenous leader of the Pearl Islands, King Toe, in 1515. Pizarro stole plenty of pearls from Toe's people, and the Spanish government continued to exploit the archipelago's pearl beds for the next two centuries, first with indigenous labor, and later with African slaves, after disease decimated the indigenous population. Overexploitation exhausted the pearl supply in the 19th century, and since then the archipelago's inhabitants have survived on fishing, tourism, and building vacation homes.

Because the Pearl Archipelago is so extensive, its islands were often the haunt of pirates, who used them as bases from which to attack Spanish galleons carrying South American gold to Panama during the 16th and 17th centuries. More recently, the archipelago has been exploited by a new breed of opportunist: the producers of the *Survivor* reality television series, who based three seasons here (2003, 2004, and 2006). Modern-day invaders have discovered that the islands' true treasures are their beaches and ocean views.

ISLA TABOGA

20 km (12 miles) south of Panama City.

Isla Taboga is known as the "Island of Flowers" for the abundant gardens of its small town, San Pedro, spread along the steep hillside of its eastern shore. The traditional celebrations on Isla Taboga are on June 29, when the

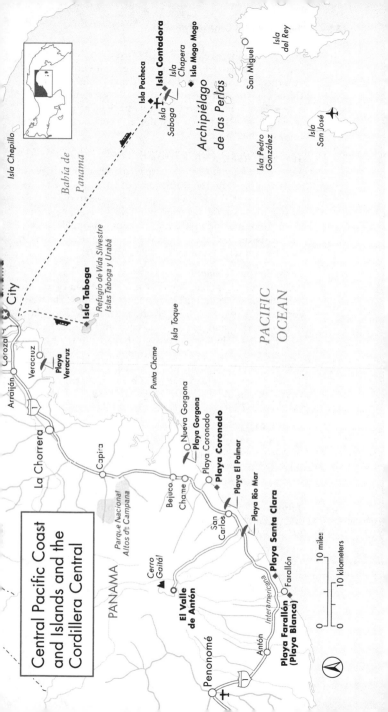

Central Pacific Coast and Islands and the Cordillera Central

PANAMA

Parque Nacional Altos de Campana

Cerro Gaital ▲

El Valle de Antón

Penonomé

Antón

Playa Farallón (Playa Blanca) ◆ Farallón

Playa Santa Clara ◆

Interamericana

San Carlos

Chame

Bejuco

Capira

La Chorrera

Arraiján

Corozal

Playa Río Mar ◣

Playa El Palmar ◆

Playa Coronado

Nueva Gorgona

Playa Gorgona ◣

Punta Chame

Playa Coronado

△ Isla Toque

City

Veracruz

Playa Veracruz ◣

Bahía de Panamá

Isla Chepillo

Isla Taboga ◆
Refugio de Vida Silvestre Islas Taboga y Urabá

PACIFIC OCEAN

Isla Pacheca ◆

Isla Contadora ◆

Isla Saboga

Isla Chapera

◆ **Isla Mogo Mogo**

Archipiélago de las Perlas

San Miguel ○

Isla del Rey

Isla San José

Isla Pedro González

Isla San José

10 miles

10 kilometers

local parishioners celebrate San Pedro's day, and July 16, when the Virgen del Carmen is celebrated with a procession through town and a boat caravan around the island. Taboga has no pharmacy, and only a very small clinic. ■TIP→ **There is no ATM on Taboga, so stock up on cash before heading there—Isla Perico, near the ferry dock on the Amador Causeway, has ATMs.**

GETTING HERE AND AROUND

A pleasant 60-minute ferry ride from the Amador Causeway takes you far from the traffic jams of Panama City to the tranquil isle of Taboga. The island lies close to the city, so most people visit on day trips, but it does have hotels. Due to its proximity and easy ferry access at reasonable prices, weekends and holidays can make the main beach areas a bit crowded with families from Panama City.

Barcos Calypso Taboga. Barcos Calypso Taboga has a daily ferry service to Taboga from the marina on Isla Naos, on the Calzada de Amador. The trip takes one hour. The ferry departs Isla Naos at 8:30, Monday through Thursday; Friday at 8:30 and 3; and weekends and holidays at 8, 10:30, and 4. The ferry departs Taboga from the pier on the west end of town at 4:30, Monday through Thursday; Friday at 9:30 and 4:30; and weekends and holidays at 9, 3, and 5. Arrive at least one hour before departure to buy your ticket, and be sure to bring ID. ✉ *Marina Isla Naos* ☎ *507/314–1730.*

EXPLORING

San Pedro. One of the country's oldest towns, San Pedro was founded in 1524, though its whitewashed church is the only surviving structure from the colonial era; folks here claim it is the second-oldest still-operating church in the Americas. The conquistador Francisco Pizarro embarked from Taboga in 1530 on his voyage to crush the Inca Empire, and it remained an important port until the 20th century. Because of the extreme variation of Panama's Pacific tides, ships were unable to moor near the coast of Panama, so the deep bay on Taboga's eastern shore was the perfect alternative. The Spanish built a fortress on Taboga in an attempt to defend the bay from pirates, the Pacific Steamship Company was based there during the 19th century, and the French built a sanatorium on the island during their attempt to build a canal. Upon completion of the canal, with its various docks and marinas, Taboga became what it is today, a sleepy fishing village that wakes up on weekends and holidays, when visitors from the capital arrive en masse.

There are few vehicles on the island, and most of its streets resemble extra-wide sidewalks. The main road runs along the town beach, Playa Honda, which lines a small bay holding dozens of fishing boats. Many of the bougainvillea-lined streets pass shrines to the Virgen del Carmen, considered the protector of fishermen throughout Latin America, who is celebrated every July 16 here.

3

BEACHES

Isla Taboga has two beaches: Playa Honda, an unattractive, rocky, and dirty—you are as likely to see vultures on it as seagulls—beach in front of town, and Playa Restinga, a spit of sand that connects Taboga with the tiny island of El Morro, just north of town.⚠ *San Pedro's sewage flows untreated into the bay, so swimming at Playa Honda, or even on the south side of Playa Restinga, is not recommended.*

Playa Restinga. At low- or mid-tide, Playa Restinga is a gorgeous swath of golden sand flanked by calm waters, but at high tide, it disappears. It's often packed on weekends and holidays, when the radios and screaming kids can be a bit too much, but it is practically deserted on most weekdays. The barely visible ruins of the Hotel Taboga, which was demolished in 2005, stand behind the beach. Swimming here is not recommended because of nearby untreated sewage from San Pedro. **Amenities:** food and drink. **Best for:** quick, midweek sunbathing getaways from Panama City.

WHERE TO STAY

$ 🏨 **Hotel Vereda Tropical.** *B&B/Inn.* Isla Taboga's best hotel, the Vereda Tropical is perched on the hillside overlooking the Bay of Panama. **Pros:** great views; decent restaurant; short walk to beach. **Cons:** inconsistent service; noisy neighborhood. [$] *Rooms from: $72* ✉ *Calle Francisco Pizarro* ✣ *100 meters south of ferry dock* ☎ *507/250–2154* 🌐 *www.hotelveredatropical.com* 🛏 *10 rooms* 🍴 *Breakfast.*

SPORTS AND THE OUTDOORS

Aside from swimming and sunbathing, Taboga's outdoor options include snorkeling, hiking, fishing, or a boat trip around the island. Trails lead to the island's two highest points: Cerro de la Cruz, a hill south of town that is topped with a 20-foot cross, and Cerro Vigia, the mountain behind town. A **wildlife refuge** covers the western half of

Isla Taboga and the nearby island of Urabá, which is the best dive spot in the area. One of the best parts of going to Isla Taboga is actually the trip itself, since the ferry passes dozens of massive ships and provides great views of the islands and the city.

SNORKELING

The snorkeling is pretty good around El Morro, where the visibility is best when the tide is high. Serious divers head to Isla Urubá, a protected island just south of Taboga.

Hotel Vereda Tropical. The Hotel Vereda Tropical rents snorkeling equipment to guests (only) and can arrange a boat ride around the island for about $60 that includes snorkeling. ☎ 507/250–2154.

Scuba Panama. Taboga lacks a dive center, but the Panama City–based operator Scuba Panama offers diving day trips to Isla Taboquilla, which include a stop at Isla Taboga. ☎ 507/261–3841 ⊕ www.scubapanama.com.

ISLA CONTADORA

70 km (43 miles) southeast of Panama City.

The island of Contadora, a mere 20 minutes from Panama City by plane, has some of the country's loveliest beaches. Half a dozen swaths of beige sand backed by exuberant foliage line Contadora's coves, and they lie within walking distance of affordable accommodations. It is a small island, covering less than a square mile, but it can serve as a base for day trips to nearby isles with deserted beaches and snorkeling sites, as well as deep-sea fishing, scuba diving, and whale watching.

The Pearl Archipelago's indigenous inhabitants undoubtedly had another name for Isla Contadora, but its current name, which translates as "counting isle," was given to it nearly five centuries ago, when it held the offices of the Spanish crown's pearl-diving enterprise. The island was deserted for years after the pearl harvest diminished. Contadora gained its current status as a vacation destination in the 1970s, when wealthy Panamanians began to buy coastal property here. The government built the massive Hotel Contadora—now in ruins—and the island developed a vibrant weekend party scene. The island's most famous temporary resident was the deposed Shah of Iran, on the heels of the Tehran embassy takeover in 1979, who recovered from heart surgery here. Contadora's star has since faded, and it isn't the haunt of the glitterati it once was, but it can be a fun, mid-range place for a vacation.

The island's tiny town center is just to the west of the airstrip, next to which sits its largest hotel. Nearly everything to the west is residential. A series of narrow roads winds through the forests that cover most of the island to the stately vacation homes scattered along its coastline, and an inland neighborhood that has some smaller houses. In the center of the island are a soccer field, a pond, and a small church; to the north lies Playa Ejecutiva, and to the south, Playa Cacique, two of the island's nicest beaches. Contadora is small enough to walk everywhere, but given the heat you may want to rent a golf cart or scooter.

Isla Contadora's main attraction is its selection of beaches, but there is decent snorkeling around its many rocky points, and better snorkeling at several nearby islands. Though the water is warm most of the year, high winds from December to April cool it down and decrease visibility.

GETTING HERE AND AROUND
Sea Las Perlas runs a daily ferry between Panama City and Contadora, departing the Calzada de Amador at 8 am, and returning at 2:45. The trip takes 90 minutes. Panama's domestic airline, Air Panama, has daily flights to Contadora (OTD) from Aeropuerto Marcos A. Gelabert (Aeropuerto Albrook). The flight takes 25 minutes.

Contacts Air Panama. ☎ 507/316–9000 ⊕ www.airpanama.com. **Sea Las Perlas.** ✉ Brisas de Amador, Isla Perico ☎ 507/391–1424 ⊕ www.sealasperlas.com.

EXPLORING
Boat tours to Isla Contadora's surrounding islands are recommended, and from June to October, you may see humpback whales. The Contadora Welcome Center, across from the airstrip, can arrange boat tours.

Isla Mogo Mogo (*Isla Pájaros*). Isla Mogo Mogo, 6 km (4 miles) south of Contadora, on the other side of Isla Chapera, has a sugar-sand beach in a deep cove where snorkelers may find sea stars. Tiny **Isla Boyarena,** just to the south, has a pale sandbar that becomes a beach at low tide.

Isla Pacheca. Isla Pacheca, 5 km (3 miles) north of Contadora, has a lovely white-sand beach and a brown pelican rookery where about 8,000 birds nest, whereas the nearby islets of Pachequilla and Bartolomé have good scuba-diving and snorkeling spots.

BEACHES

Because Panama's Pacific tides are extreme, beaches change considerably through the course of the day; what is a wide swath of sand at low tide is reduced to a sliver at high tide. All beaches in Panama are public property, so you can use any of them, no matter what hotel you stay in.

Playa Cacique. Stretched along a small cove on the south side of the island, Playa Cacique is Contadora's loveliest beach, with pale beige sand backed by tropical trees and vacation homes. The water is calm and clear, making it a decent snorkeling spot, and a popular area for people to moor their boats. You can see Isla Chapera beyond those boats. The Villa Romántica hotel sits on the ridge behind the beach, and its restaurant is a good spot for lunch or a sunset drink. At low tide, you can walk west, around a small bluff, to a smaller beach called **Playa Camarón. Ameni-ties:** food and drink. **Best for:** snorkeling; swimming; sunset.

Playa Ejecutiva. One of Contadora's quietest beaches is Playa Ejecutiva, a few hundred yards north of the church and soccer field. It's a tiny beach that practically disappears at high tide, but the water is calm and safe for swimming, and you can snorkel around the point to the west of it. Its backed by a small forest, which provides convenient shade, and several vacation homes, the owners of which have built a attractive shelter behind the beach for parties. If you visit Contadora on a busy weekend, or holiday, this is a good spot to escape the crowd. **Amenities:** none. **Best for:** solitude; swimming.

FAMILY **Playa Galeón.** Just north of the airstrip and east of the Hotel Punta Galeón, this small beach is one of Contadora's most popular spots. It's where the ferry arrives and departs from, so it can get crowded during the high season. But it's a good swimming beach, with calm, blue-green water, and it has decent snorkeling. This is a pretty convenient spot to hang out: the hotel's restaurant is next to the beach, Gerald's is just up the hill, and the welcome center, across from the airstrip, rents everything from towels and beach umbrellas to Jet Skis. **Amenities:** food and drink; toilets; water sports. **Best for:** snorkeling; swimming.

Playa Larga. Contadora's longest beach, Playa Larga, stretches along the island's eastern end, in front of the long-vacant Hotel Contadora—the island's original resort. It's a lovely strip of ivory sand, backed by coconut palms, Indian almonds, and other trees, but the ruins of the hotel and the abandoned ferry boat at one end give it a forlorn feel. At high tide, it's a mere sliver of sand, whereas at low tide, massive black rocks are exposed. The water can be murky, so it usually isn't good for snorkeling. **Amenities:** none. **Best for:** solitude; swimming; walking.

Playa Suecas. Hidden in the island's southeast corner, at the end of the road that runs east from Villa Romantica, Playa Sueca (Swedish Beach) is Contadora's officially sanctioned nude beach. It is relatively small, backed by forest, with tan sand sloping into calm, aquamarine waters. At low tide, there are some exposed rocks in front of the beach. Be sure to use plenty of sunscreen on those pale parts! **Amenities:** none. **Best for:** solitude; nudists; swimming.

WHERE TO EAT

$$ ✕ **Gerald's.** *Eclectic.* This restaurant is a short walk from the beach, serves some of the best food on the island, and rents basic rooms. The eight rooms are in a two-story building behind the restaurant, with high ceilings, TVs, and air-conditioning. The restaurant is a rustic, open-air affair under a high-thatched roof, which means it picks up the breeze, if one is blowing. The menu is a mix of fresh fish and seafood dishes, and German standards such as Wiener schnitzel and goulash. They also make a decent pizza. Food is tasty, but service can be very slow. Ⓢ *Average main: $15* ✉ *Contadora Island* ⊕ *on ridge above landing strip* ☎ *507/250–4159* ⊕ *www.island-contadora.com* ▭ *No credit cards.*

$$ ✕ **Pimienta y Sal.** *Latin American.* Located in the small downtown area of Isla Contadora, this pleasant, open-air restaurant (formerly known as Hot Stone Rincón) has an ample menu of seafood, beef, and sandwiches. Ⓢ *Average main: $15* ☎ *507/250–4251* ▭ *No credit cards.*

WHERE TO STAY

$$ ▥ **Contadora Island Inn.** *B&B/Inn.* This small B&B occupies a ranch house in a quiet residential neighborhood, just a 10-minute walk from the beach. **Pros:** affordable; quiet; clean. **Cons:** not on the beach. Ⓢ *Rooms from: $100* ✉ *Paseo Urraca 50* ☎ *507/6699–4614* ⊕ *www.contadoraislandinn. com* ⇌ *5 rooms* ⊠ *Breakfast.*

$$ ▥ **Perla Real Inn.** *B&B/Inn.* This attractive B&B was designed to resemble a Spanish mission, and the owners paid great attention to the details, importing hand-painted tiles and sinks and getting a local carpenter to make replicas of furniture found in southern California missions. **Pros:** tasteful; friendly staff. **Cons:** not on the beach. [$] *Rooms from: $127* ✉ *Paseo Urraca 50* ☎ *507/250–4095, 949/228–8851 in North America* 🌐 *www.perlareal.com* 🛏 *4 rooms, 2 suites, 1 villa* 🍴 *Breakfast.*

SPORTS AND THE OUTDOORS

Contadora Welcome Center. The welcome center across from the airstrip rents golf carts, scooters, and bikes for getting around the island. They also rent Jet Skis, kayaks, and snorkeling equipment, and can arrange boat tours to explore the marine surroundings. ✉ *Across from airstrip, next to Playa Galeón* ☎ *507/250–4081* 🌐 *www.contadorapanama.com.*

SCUBA DIVING

The reefs around Contadora have much less coral than you find in the Caribbean, but you can see a lot of fish there, some of which gather in big schools. Isla Pachequilla is one of the area's best dive spots, where you might see rays, moray eels, white-tipped reef sharks, and large schools of jacks. The only problem is visibility, which averages 15 to 30 feet, but sometimes tops 45 feet, especially from June to August, though there is less marine life in the area then. The best diving is in December and January, when there is decent visibility and large numbers of fish; the worst visibility is from February to April.

Coral Dreams. Coral Dreams offers scuba diving at various dive spots, as well as certification courses and snorkeling excursions. ✉ *Main road* ✛ *across from airstrip* ☎ *507/6536–1776* 🌐 *coral-dreams.com.*

FISHING

The fishing around Contadora is quite good, which means you can go out for half a day and stand a decent chance of hooking something. The most common fish in the area are dolphin, jack, tuna, wahoo, roosterfish, and—in deeper water—snapper and grouper. The Contadora Welcome Center can arrange light-tackle fishing charters.

THE CENTRAL PACIFIC COAST

The Central Pacific Coast has Panama's most popular beaches, if not its most beautiful. Due to the organic matter that washes out of rivers along the coast, its beaches tend to have salt-and-pepper sand. The sea is usually calm, but in the rare event that there are significant waves, swimming can be dangerous. The beaches are popular weekend destinations for city folk from December to May, but you may have them to yourself if you visit during the week, especially between May and November.

The Central Pacific beaches range from Coronado, lined with vacation homes and with little access for tourists, to Farallón (aka Playa Blanca), which has the country's largest beach resorts.

PLAYA CORONADO

84 km (52 miles) southwest of Panama City.

Playa Coronado began to develop as a weekend destination for wealthy Panamanians decades ago, and today the coast is almost completely lined with condos and weekend homes, leaving few spots for nonresidents to get onto the beach. The sand here is pale gray with swaths of fine black dirt, which gives it a sort of marbled appearance. It is usually safe for swimming. The big attraction is the 18-hole golf course that is part of the BlueBay Coronado Golf & Beach Club *(below)*. One of the country's best golf destinations, the resort gets packed with Panamanian families on weekends and holidays, but is practically dead most weekdays.

GETTING HERE AND AROUND

Public buses from Panama City's Albrook bus terminal take about an hour to reach Coronado. It is also an easy drive; take the Carretera Interamericana west from Panama City one hour, and look for the turnoff next to a large shopping center on the left, just after the town of Chame. You'll have to stop at a guardhouse, then look for the golf resort on the left.

WHERE TO EAT

$$ ✕**El Rincón del Chef.** *Latin American.* In a colonial-style building on the road to Playa Coronado, this attractive restaurant serves a good variety of quality dishes. The menu changes daily, but always offers a good mix of meat and seafood dishes that feature a mix of Panamanian and

international fare. There is invariably *corvina* (sea bass), *langostinos* (prawns), and grilled (rather expensive) USDA-certified beef, including a good burger. The ambiance—terra-cotta floors, ocher walls, and a high wooden-beams ceiling—is right out of the 19th century, except for the TV and ceiling fans. $ *Average main: $12* ✉ *Beginning of road to Playa Coronado, on right* ☎ *507/345–2072.*

SPORTS AND THE OUTDOORS

GOLF

Coronado Golf Course. This 18-hole, par-72 golf course was designed by Tom and George Fazio. Hotel guests at Blue-Bay Coronado Golf & Beach Resort (formerly Coronado Beach Resort) pay $75 plus tax on weekend mornings and $55 on weekend afternoons, and $65 weekdays, golf cart rental included (green fees are sometimes waived for hotel guests during special promotions). The course is only open to nonguests when invited by a hotel guest or club member. Clubs can be rented and there is a 9-hole, par-27 course for beginners and younger golfers. ✉ *BueBay Coronado Golf & Beach Resort, Av. Punta Prieta Coronado* ☎ *507/240–3137* 🌐 *www.bluebayresorts.com* 🎫 *$75 weekend mornings, $55 on weekend afternoons, $65 weekdays* ⛳ *18 holes, par 72; 9 holes, par 27.*

HORSEBACK RIDING

Club Ecuestre Coronado. The Equestrian Club offers guided rides on several breeds of horses. Horseback tours cost $26.75 per half hour or $48.15 per hour; the same rate is charged for the services of a guide. ✉ *Av. Punta Prieta* ☎ *507/6155–7947.*

PLAYA SANTA CLARA

115 km (71 miles) southwest of Panama City.

The small beach town of Santa Clara lies just to the east of Playa Blanca. For years, it consisted of a tiny fishing enclave, a handful of vacation homes, and a few budget hotels. It now has the large Sheraton Bijao Beach Resort and surrounding residential development, just to the east of town.

BEACHES

Playa Santa Clara. Playa Santa Clara has the same pale sand with swaths of gray dirt as the adjacent, and more famous, Playa Blanca. The sea here is usually calm enough for swimming, but isn't a good spot for snorkeling. On those rare occasions when there are waves, you shouldn't go in any deeper than your waist, due to the danger of rip currents. Much of the beach is lined with vacation homes, but the Sheraton Bijao Beach Resort towers sits over its eastern end and the rambling Las Veraneras Restaurant sits behind its western end. The western end can get packed, and littered, on holidays and dry-season weekends, but this beach is quiet most of the year. **Amenities:** food and drink; parking (fee); toilets. **Best for:** partiers; swimming; walking. ✉ *CA 1* ✣ *111 km (69 miles) west of Panama City.*

WHERE TO STAY

$$$$ 🏨 **Sheraton Bijao Beach Resort.** *Resort.* Rooms in the upper floors of this stately resort are steps away from the beach, and have great views of a cascading series of pools and the glistening Pacific. **Pros:** nice rooms; on beach. **Cons:** inconsistent service; food may disappoint. [$] *Rooms from: $250* ✉ *Carretera Interamericana* ✣ *109 km (68 miles) west of Panama City* ☎ *507/908–3600* 🌐 *www.starwoodhotels.com* 🛏 *275 rooms, 18 suites* 🍴 *All-inclusive.*

PLAYA FARALLÓN (PLAYA BLANCA)

115 km (71 miles) southwest of Panama City.

For years, few people visited this lovely, long stretch of white beach because it lay behind a military base used by Panama's national guard and was restricted. The base saw heavy fighting during the 1989 U.S. invasion, and for much of the 1990s its buildings, pockmarked with bullet holes, were slowly being covered with jungle. Everything changed at the beginning of the 21st century, when the Colombian hotel chain Decameron opened a massive resort here and began promoting it as "Playa Blanca" (White Beach). Panamanians still use the Farallón (*fahr-ah-YOHN*) name. Now the area is the epicenter of beach development in Panama, with several new resorts, two 18-hole golf courses, and a growing number of homes and condos.

GETTING HERE AND AROUND

To drive to Playa Blanca, take the Carretera Interamericana west from Panama City for about 90 minutes and look for the hotel entrances on the left after Santa Clara—the entrance to the Playa Blanca Beach Resort is 2 km (1 mile) after the entrance to the Royal Decameron, and the Buenaventura Beach Resort is several kilometers farther down the same road. All resorts provide shuttle services from Tocumen Airport and Panama City hotels. Scarlett

Martinez International Airport (RIH) opened at Farallón in 2013, offering the chance to skip the long trip from Tocumen airport, but as of this writing was only served by charter flights from Canada.

WHERE TO STAY

$$$$ **JW Marriott Panama Golf & Beach Resort.** *Resort.* Formerly the Bristol Buenaventura, Panama's loveliest beach resort combines elegant rooms and Spanish colonial architecture with an 18-hole golf course and a splendid stretch of sand. **Pros:** gorgeous design and beach; golf course; good restaurants. **Cons:** inconsistent service; pricey. [$] *Rooms from: $329* ✉ *CA 1* ✣ *121 km (75 miles) west of Panama City* ☎ *507/908–3333* 🌐 *www.marriott.com* 🛏 *118 rooms, 5 suites, 4 villas* 🍴 *No meals.*

$$$$ FAMILY **Royal Decameron Beach Resort, Golf and Casino.** *Resort.* Panama's largest, and one of its most attractive, beach resorts offers good deals outside of the peak season, but also the food and service problems typical of all-inclusive resorts. **Pros:** great beach and grounds; lots of activities; competitive rates. **Cons:** droves of guests; inconsistent service and food. [$] *Rooms from: $234* ✉ *Road to Farallón, 155 km (96 miles) west of Panama City on Carr. Panamericana (CA 1)* ☎ *507/993–2255, 507/294–1900 Panama City sales office* 🌐 *www.decameron.com* 🛏 *852 rooms* 🍴 *All-inclusive.*

SPORTS AND THE OUTDOORS

GOLF

Mantarraya Golf Club. The club is near the Royal Decameron Beach Resort, but guests at any hotel can play its 18-hole, par-72 golf course, which was designed by Randall Thompson. Cart rental costs $16 for 9 holes and $26 for 18. Club rentals range from $15 to $25, according to their condition. ☎ *507/986–1915* 🌐 *www.decameron.com* 🎟 *Hotel guests $53 weekdays, $74 weekends and holidays for 18 holes; $37 weekdays, $47 weekends and holidays for 9 holes. Non-hotel guests $58 weekdays, $79 weekends and holidays for 18 holes; $42 weekdays, $53 weekends and holidays for 9 holes* ⛳ *18 holes, par 72.*

WATER SPORTS

Xtreme Adventures. Farallón-based Xtreme Adventures offers all manner of guided beachy activities here and at adjoining Playa Coronado, including horseback riding, jet skiing, parasailing, and waterskiing. ☎ *507/993–2823* 🌐 *www.xtremepanama.com.*

THE CORDILLERA CENTRAL

Mountains to the north of the Central Pacific coast offer a refreshing alternative to the hot and deforested lowlands a short drive from the beaches. The massif to the southwest of Panama City, an extinct volcano that was in eruption 5 million years ago, forms the eastern extreme of the Cordillera Central, the country's longest mountain range. On the eastern slope of that verdant mountain is Parque Nacional Altos de Campana; its western slope holds Cerro de la Vieja. The highest point of the range is Cerro Gaital, a forested hill more than 3,500 feet above sea level that towers over El Valle de Antón. Both Cerro de la Vieja and El Valle de Antón are cool and verdant refuges where you can take a break from the lowland heat, explore the mountain forests, and do a bit of bird-watching and hiking. El Valle is a well-established destination with an array of hotels and restaurants, but Cerro la Vieja, to the northeast of Penonomé, has just one eco-lodge.

EL VALLE DE ANTÓN

125 km (78 miles) southwest of Panama City, 28 km (17 miles) north of Las Uvas: the turnoff from Carretera Interamericana.

A serpentine road winds north from the town of Las Uvas, on the Carretera Interamericana between Playa Coronado and Playa Farallón, to a small, lush mountain valley and the town that is sheltered in it, both called El Valle de Antón, commonly referred to as El Valle (The Valley). That verdant valley has a refreshing climate, an abundance of trees and birds, and an array of outdoor activities. Thanks to its altitude of approximately 2,000 feet above sea level, the temperature usually hovers in the 70s °F, and at night it often dips down into the 60s. El Valle has long been a popular weekend and holiday destination for Panama City's wealthier citizens, and its roads are lined with comfortable vacation homes with large lawns and gardens. In fact, one of those streets is called *Calle de los Millionarios* (Millionaires' Row).

The town's Avenida Principal belies the beauty of El Valle's remote corners, with ugly supermarkets and other uninspiring cement-block structures. The attractions for travelers are the flora and fauna of the protected forests north and west of town center, the varied hiking and horseback-riding routes, and the Sunday handicraft market. Since El Valle has long been popular with Panamanian tourists, it has developed some touted but tepid attractions that can be skipped, such as its tiny hot springs, Pozos Termales, and the "square trees," or *arboles cuadrados,* behind the old Hotel Campestre.

GETTING HERE AND AROUND

El Valle is 125 km (75 miles) southwest from Panama City, about two hours by car, on good roads. To drive, take the Carretera Interamericana west for 98 km (59 miles) to Las Uvas, where you turn right and drive 28 km (17 miles) north on a narrow, winding road. Buses to El Valle depart from the Terminal de Buses in Albrook every hour and cost $4, but they take almost three hours. Taxis hang out at the Mercado during the day, and charge $1–$2 for most trips within the valley.

EXPLORING

IN TOWN

FAMILY **El Nispero.** El Nispero (named after a native fruit tree) is a private zoo and plant nursery hidden at the end of a rough dirt road. It covers nearly seven acres at the foot of Cerro Gaital, and its forested grounds are attractive, but most of the animals are in small cages. This is one of the only places you can see the extremely rare golden toad, which has been wiped out in the wild by a fungal disease. Those little yellow-and-black anurans—often mistakenly called frogs—are on display at the **El Valle Amphibian Research Center,** funded by several U.S. zoos. Biologists at the center are studying the fungus that is killing the species (*Batrachochytrium dendrobatidis*), while facilitating the toad's reproduction in a fungus-free environment. The zoo has many other Panamanian species that you are unlikely to see in the wild, such as jaguars, tapirs, collared peccaries (wild pigs), white-faced capuchin monkeys, and various macaw species. Exotic species such as Asian golden pheasants and white peacocks run the grounds. Most of the animals at El Nispero are former pets that were donated, or confiscated from their owners by government authorities. The tapirs, for example, belonged to former dictator Manuel Noriega. ⊠ *Calle Carlos Arosemena ⊕ 1½ km (1 mile) north of cell tower on Av. Principal* ☎ *507/983–6142, 507/6615–9690 cell* ⊠ *$5, kids $2 (ages 1–12)* ⊙ *Daily 7–5.*

Mercado. One traditional tourist attraction worth checking out is the Mercado, an open–air bazaar under a high red roof on the left side of Avenida Principal, two blocks before the church. The market is most interesting on weekends, especially Sunday morning, when vendors and shoppers arrive from far and wide. Locals go to the market to buy fresh fruit, vegetables, baked goods, and plants. Handicrafts sold here include the *sombrero pintao* (a traditional straw hat), handmade jewelry, soapstone sculptures, and knickknacks such as the various renditions of El Valle's emblematic golden toad. Even if you don't want to buy anything, it's a colorful, festive affair. Some Panama City tour operators offer a day trip—a long day trip—to the market on Sunday. ⊠ *Av. Princpal* ✛ *on left two blocks before church* ⊡ *Free* ☉ *Daily 8–6.*

NORTH AND WEST OF TOWN

Monumento Natural Cerro Gaital (*Cerro Gaital Natural Monument*). El Valle's northern edge is protected within the 827-acre (335-hectare) nature reserve Monumento Natural Cerro Gaital, which covers the hills of Cerro Gaital, Cerro Pajita, and Cerro Caracoral. Cerro Gaital is a steep, forest-draped hill that towers over the valley's northern edge, rising to a summit of more than 3,500 feet above sea level. The lush wilderness that covers it is home to more than 300 bird species, including such spectacular creatures as the red-legged honeycreeper, bay-headed tanager, and blue-crowned motmot. It also protects the habitat of the rare golden toad (*Atelopus zeteki*). The bird-watching is best along the edges of that protected area, since its lush foliage provides too many hiding places for those feathered creatures, and the terrain is dangerously steep. The areas around El Nispero, Los Mandarinos hotel, and the old Hotel Campestre are also excellent for bird-watching. There is a trail into the forest by the ranger post on the right, above the Refugio Ecológico Chorro Macho, approximately 10 km (6 miles) from the church. It requires good shoes and decent physical condition and is best done with a guide. ✛ *Turn right at end of Av. Principal, continue past Canopy Tour, trail on the right* ☎ *507/983–6411* ⊴ *$5* ☉ *Weekdays 8.30–3:30, weekends 8:30–2.*

Piedra Pintada. A short drive to the west of the Mercado, at the end of a rough road and trail, is a simple remnant of El Valle's pre-Columbian culture called Piedra Pintada, a 15-foot boulder, the underside of which is covered with a bizarre collection of ancient petroglyphs. To get there, turn right at the end of Avenida Principal and left onto the second road after the bridge, then drive to the end of that road, where a foot path heads to the nearby boulder. Cars left at the trailhead have been broken into, so don't leave any valuables in your vehicle, and leave the doors unlocked to avoid broken windows. ✉ *End of Calle La Pintada* 🎟 *Free* ⏲ *24 hrs.*

★ FodorsChoice **Refugio Ecológico del Chorro Macho** (*Chorro el*
FAMILY *Macho Ecological Reserve*). El Valle's most user-friendly forest experience is available at the small, private Refugio Ecológico del Chorro Macho, west of Cerro Gaital. The reserve has well-kept trails, walking sticks, and the option of hiring a guide at the gate. It belongs to Raúl Arias, who also owns the adjacent Canopy Lodge, and it contains one of El Valle's major landmarks, **El Chorro Macho,** a 115-foot cascade surrounded by lush foliage. You're not allowed to swim beneath the waterfall, but there is a lovely swimming pool fed by river water to the left upon entering the reserve, so bring your bathing suit and a towel. Enter the gate to the left of the main entrance to reach the pool. The refuge has a tour called **Canopy Adventure**, which can take you flying through the treetops and over the waterfall on zip lines strung between platforms high in trees. Most visitors are happy simply to explore the trails that loop through the lush forest past the waterfall and over a small suspension bridge that spans a rocky stream. ✣ *2½ km (1½ miles) northwest of church, at west end of Av. Principal, on left* ☎ *507/983–6547* 🎟 *$5, guided hike $65* ⏲ *Daily 8–5.*

WHERE TO EAT

$ 🍴 **Bruchetta.** *Italian.* This small Italian restaurant next to the lobby of the Anton Valley Hotel has a covered terrace where you can watch the townsfolk roll by. The food is quite good and the menu includes an ample selection of salads and pastas, half a dozen different bruschetta, *corvina* (sea bass), salmon, and beef tenderloin. The nicest seating is on the front terrace, which has a view of the main road and the church, and access to Wi-Fi. [$] *Average main: $9* ✉ *Av. Prinicpal* ☎ *507/983–5118* ▭ *No credit cards* ⏲ *Closed Thurs.*

★ FodorsChoice 🍴 **La Casa de Lourdes.** *Eclectic.* After years of
$$$ running one of Panama City's most popular restaurants, Lourdes Fabrega de Ward built this elegant place across from her retirement home so that she wouldn't get bored. It now seems unlikely that she'll ever retire, since old clients and a growing list of new fans pack the place on weekends, drawn by Lourdes' inventive menu and the magical ambience of her Tuscan-style *casa*. Meals are served on a back

terrace with views of her garden and Cerro Gaital framed by high columns, arches, and an elegant pool. It is truly a house, and you enter through a spacious living room with couches, a piano, and family photos. She changes her menu frequently, but it always has a good mix of seafood and meat dishes, as well as amazing desserts. Reservations are essential on weekends. [$] *Average main: $17* ✉ *Calle El Ciclo* ✣ *behind Hotel Los Mandarinos, 1.2 km (½ mile) north and 800 meters west of Supermercado Hong Kong* ☎ *507/983–6450* 🌐 *www.lacasadelourdes.com.*

$$ 🍴 **Restaurante Rincón Vallero.** *Latin American.* This open-air restaurant, a short drive from the main road, is like something out of a fairy tale. There are stone floors, plants everywhere, goldfish ponds and a stream running between the tables; the food is pretty good, too. The ample menu ranges from traditional Panamanian dishes such as *sancocho* (chicken soup with tropical tubers) and *corvina* (sea bass) prepared various ways, to filet mignon and chicken cordon bleu—they spell it "gordon blue." There's a playground and a tiny menagerie in the back garden. They also rent rooms, but they're cramped, dark, and musty. [$] *Average main: $10* ✉ *Calle Espavel* ✣ *1 km (½ mile) south of main road, near Park Eden B&B* ☎ *507/397–1393* 💳 *No credit cards.*

FAMILY

WHERE TO STAY

$$$$ 🏨 **Canopy Lodge.** *B&B/Inn.* Nestled in the forest overlooking the boulder-strewn Guayabo River, this lovely lodge is a mecca for bird-watchers and other nature enthusiasts. **Pros:** gorgeous setting; abundant birds; good guides; friendly staff; quiet setting. **Cons:** expensive; most tours not included; free Wi-Fi only in lobby. [$] *Rooms from: $534* ✣ *2 km (1 mile) past church, turn right on road to El Chorro Macho, on left* ☎ *507/264–5720 Panama City, 507/983–6837, 800/930–3397 in U.S.* 🌐 *www.canopylodge.com* 🛏 *12 rooms* 🍽 *All meals.*

$ 🏨 **The Golden Frog Inn.** *Rental.* One of the best deals in El Valle, this vacation rental near Cerro Gaital consists of just three suites with kitchenettes and two standard rooms surrounded by 2½ acres of gardens and lovely views. **Pros:** friendly owners; lovely grounds; great views; quiet. **Cons:** no bar or restaurant; 2 km (1 mile) from town. [$] *Rooms from: $90* ✉ *Calle Central* ✣ *1½ km (1 mile) north of Texaco Station, dirt road on right* ☎ *507/983–6117* 🌐 *www.goldenfroginn.com* 🛏 *2 rooms, 3 suites* 🍽 *No meals.*

$$ 🏨 **Los Mandarinos Boutique Spa and Hotel.** *Hotel.* This attractive hotel and spa, built in the Tuscan style—stone walls, arched doorways, and barrel-tile roofs—has some of the nicest rooms in El Valle. **Pros:** great location; lovely architecture; well-equipped rooms; friendly staff. **Cons:** standard rooms lack views. [$] *Rooms from: $155* ✉ *Calle El Ciclo* ☎ *888/281–8413 toll-free in U.S.* 🌐 *www.losmandarinos.com* 🛏 *64 rooms, 6 suites* 🍴 *Breakfast.*

$$ 🏨 **Park Eden.** *B&B/Inn.* This lovely collection of houses
FAMILY and rooms surrounded by manicured gardens, great trees, and a babbling brook has a tranquil, homey feel. **Pros:** friendly owners; nice gardens. **Cons:** far from center of town. [$] *Rooms from: $100* ✉ *Calle Espave* ✥ *100 meters south of Rincón Vallero* ☎ *507/983–6167, 507/6695–6190 cell* 🌐 *www.parkeden.com* 🛏 *3 rooms, 2 suites, 1 cottage* 🍴 *Breakfast.*

SHOPPING

Artesanía Don Pedro. A handicrafts selection to rival that at the weekly Mercado is available at Artesanía Don Pedro, open seven days a week. ✉ *Av. Principal* ✥ *on left 1 block before Mercado* ☎ *507/983–6425.*

Mercado. El Valle is known for its Sunday-morning handicrafts market at the Mercado, a festive affair that brings together vendors and shoppers from far and wide. ✉ *Av. Principal* ✥ *on left two blocks before church.*

SPORTS AND THE OUTDOORS

BIRD-WATCHING

From tiny green hermits to elegant swallow-tailed kites, a remarkable diversity of birds inhabits El Valle's sky and forests. More than 350 bird species have been spotted in the area—compared with 426 species in all of Canada. The best viewing season is October to March, when northern migrants such as the yellow warbler and northern waterthrush boost El Valle's bird diversity. The migrants are especially common in the gardens of the valley's hotels and homes, whereas the forests of Cerro Gaital and surroundings hold such tropical species as the tody motmot and sun bittern. El Valle's avian rainbow includes five kinds of toucans, six parrot species, and 25 hummingbird species. Though you can only hope to see a fraction of those birds, your chances will be greatly increased if you hire an experienced guide.

Canopy Lodge. Guests at the Canopy Lodge enjoy the services of the area's best birding guides (one tour is included free with a minimum three-night stay; all other tours cost extra). ☎ *507/983–6837* ⊕ *www.canopytower.com.*

Mario Bernal. El Valle's most experienced guide is Mario Bernal, who has written a guide to the birds of El Valle. But he is often on the road guiding groups during the dry season. ☎ *507/6693–8213.*

Mario Urriola. The nature guide Mario Urriola, a biologist who owns the Serpentario (a reptile zoo), has trained a cadre of local guides and can arrange bird-watching, general nature, or hiking tours, for surprisingly low rates. ✉ *Serpentario, Calle el Hato* ☎ *507/6569–2676.*

CANOPY TOUR
Canopy Adventure. Adventure seekers will want to try the Canopy Adventure, an installation affiliated with the Canopy Tower Ecolodge in Parque Nacional Soberanía. It takes you—you're strapped in with a very secure harness—flying through the forest canopy and over a 115-foot waterfall via zip-line cables strung between four platforms high in trees. The tour ($65) is in the **Refugio Ecológico del Chorro Macho,** a private reserve a few kilometers northwest of El Valle. This is more adrenaline rush than nature tour, though you do pass through some gorgeous rain forest scenery. The tour takes about 90 minutes and begins with a 30-minute hike to the first platform. ☎ *507/983–6547* ⊕ *www.canopytower.com.*

HIKING
El Valle has enough hiking routes to keep you trekking for days. ■TIP→ **Hikes are best done early in the morning, when the air is clearer and the birds are more active.** One of the best hiking trips in El Valle is the two- to three-hour hike up **Cerro Gaital,** which passes through lush forest and includes a *mirador* (lookout point) affording a view of the valley, the Pacific coast, and, on clear days, the Caribbean coast. Another impressive view of El Valle is the one from the **Monte de la Cruz,** a deforested mountain ridge topped by a cement cross on the northwest end of the valley. Both of these trails are reached by heading up the road to El Chorro Macho, with the Cerro Gaital trail on the right, and the Monte de la Cruz trail a continuation of the road itself.

The popular hiking route up and along the **India Dormida** ridge, on the western end of the valley, combines treks through patches of forest with scenic views. The trail up the ridge is reached by heading west of town, turning right after the baseball stadium, and left again at the first road.

Because El Valle's trails are not well marked, you should hire a guide for these hikes. Nature guide Mario Urriola (*507/6569–2676*) is the contact person for a group of local guides who can lead you up Cerro Gaital, the India Dormida, and other hiking routes.

HORSEBACK RIDING
Alquiler de Caballos Mitzila. An inexpensive horseback adventure is available from Alquiler de Caballos Mitzila, across from the small church on Calle El Hato, a few blocks before the Hotel Campestre. A horse costs $15 per hour, and each group has to pay an additional $15 per hour for the guide. The most popular ride is around the back of Cerro Gaital, a loop that takes about four hours to complete, though you can also ride for an hour and then come back on the same route. English-speaking guides are available. ⊠ *Calle El Hato* ☎ *507/6646–5813*.

CHIRIQUÍ
PROVINCE

Updated
by Marlise
Kast-Myers**PANAMA'S SOUTHWEST PROVINCE OF CHIRIQUÍ** contains the country's most varied scenery. Landscapes that
evoke different continents—from alpine peaks to palm-
lined beaches—lie mere hours apart. The diverse envi-
ronments provide conditions for world-class sportfishing,
bird-watching, scuba diving, river rafting, horseback riding,
hiking, and surfing, making Chiriquí an ideal destination
for nature lovers.

Lush cloud forest covers the northern sector of the province.
The valleys that flank Volcán Barú—an extinct volcano and
Panama's highest peak—have cool mountain climates and
unforgettable scenery. Boquete, Bambito, and Cerro Punta
are popular with bird-watchers, rafters, and hikers, and have
captivating landscapes and charming restaurants and inns.
The southern lowlands are less impressive—hot and mostly
deforested—and become brown and dusty in the dry season.
To the south lies the Golfo de Chiriquí, with dozens of pristine
islands and countless acres of coral reef awash with rainbows
of marine life, and an opportunity to sample world-class, but
little-known, surfing and sportfishing.

ORIENTATION AND PLANNING

GETTING ORIENTED

The provincial capital of David sits centrally located in
the lowlands and is no more than two hours from most of
Chiriquí's attractions. The Carretera Interamericana skirts
David's northern edge, as a four-lane highway. It becomes
a two-lane road east of town, where it leads to the town of
Chiriquí and to the turnoff for Boca Chica, the gateway to
Parque Nacional Marino Golfo de Chiriquí. A 30-minute
drive southwest of David takes you to Playa Barqueta; a
40-minute drive north takes you to Boquete. Concepción
is a short drive west of David on the Interamericana, and
there the road veers north to Volcán, Bambito, and Cerro
Punta, bases from which to explore the Barú Volcano. The
Costa Rican border at Paso Canoas lies about 20 minutes
west on the Interamericana.

The Lowlands and Gulf. From the city life of bustling David to
the tranquil beaches of the pristine coastline, the Lowlands
and Gulf pack enough variety to satisfy nearly any traveler's
vacation desires. Less than an hour from the province's
capital are the black-sand beaches of Playa La Barqueta,
fading into greys and eventually snow-white strands along

the Gulf of Chiriquí. In Boca Chica, where freestanding bungalows are perched on peninsulas accessible by boat, you'll find a haven for sportfishing. The region has plenty of activities if the fish aren't biting, too—kayaking, snorkeling, horseback riding, and hiking (with Howler monkeys overhead). For world-class surfing, Playa Santa Catalina consistently delivers epic waves, and is the closest port to Isla Coiba, Panama's top dive destination.

The Mountains. The mountains offer unspoiled splendor where travelers enjoy a scenic landscape with diverse ecology and wildlife. In the small towns of Volcan, Bambito, and Cerra Punta, wild rivers frame farm roads where rusty tractors are parked under tin-roof shacks. Patchwork fields cover hillsides, with clouds rolling in fast and low as if on the verge of swallowing mountains whole. Famous for its coffee farms, hiking trails, and bird population, Boquete's greatest attraction is the town itself, where tiny wooden houses are draped in pink-and-purple bougainvillea as common as weeds. An added bonus are the two highland national parks, La Amistad and Volcan Baru.

4

PLANNING

WHEN TO GO

The December-to-May dry season is the most popular time to visit Chiriquí since days tend to be sunny in the lowlands. From December to March the valleys of Cerro Punta and Boquete can be cool and windy and may get light rain.

In March and April the mountain valleys are warm and sunny, whereas the lowlands become increasingly dry and brown. It rains just about every day from May to mid-July and from mid-September to mid-December, but from mid-July to mid-September you can get several sunny days in a row.

The water in the Golfo de Chiriquí is clearest for scuba diving and snorkeling from December to July, whereas the surf is best from July to December.

PLANNING YOUR TIME

Unless you need a day to unwind, or would like to experience the province's sweltering capital, David is a city you could bypass for an immediate visit to the coast. Dedicate three to four days to the Lowlands and Gulf, selecting your destination based on your agenda. Although Boca Chica and Isla Boca Brava have subpar beaches, they both have

TOP REASONS TO GO

Misty Mountains. The upper slopes of the Cordillera de Talamanca are draped with lush cloud forest and are usually enveloped in mist. Much of that forest is protected within La Amistad and Barú Volcano National Parks, home to a wealth of wildlife, which can be explored via hiking trails.

Teeming Sea. The Golfo de Chiriquí is home to an amazing array of fish, ranging from colorful king angelfish to the mighty black marlin, making the province an ideal destination for scuba divers and sport fishers alike.

Birds in the Bush. The mountains of Chiriquí are a must-visit for bird-watchers because they hold species found nowhere else in Panama, such as the resplendent quetzal and long-tailed silky flycatcher. From November to April, northern migrants push the bird count to more than 500 species.

Pristine Islands. Between Parque Nacional Marino Golfo de Chiriquí and the Islas Secas, the sea here brims with uninhabited islands: think palm-lined beaches, crystalline waters, and coral reefs a short swim from shore.

Farming Communities. The mountain communities of Boquete, Bambito, and Cerro Punta are surrounded by gorgeous scenery and are distinguished by charming wooden houses, exuberant flower gardens, cozy restaurants, and hotels that combine all of the above.

excellent sportfishing and are close to the Gulf of Chiriquí. Set aside a full day for fishing, diving, or kayaking, with a second day reserved for island exploration of Chiriquí Marine National Park. Since this area inspires relaxation, spend a third (and even fourth) day just soaking in the setting. For serious divers and surfers, make Playa Santa Catalina your priority. It's home to the country's best surf spots and is near Isla Coiba, a true diver's paradise. From beaches to mountains, unpack those fleeces for the four or five days ahead. Depending on your wish list, three days in Boquete should be enough to experience a coffee tour, bird-watching, hiking, and river rafting or zip-lining. For a trip within your trip, drive one hour to the picturesque valley near Reserva Forestal Fortuna. Within this area are hot springs, waterfalls, rivers, and trails. Carve out your final days for Cerro Punta and Bambito, the bowl-shaped highland valley excellent for spotting wildlife. If you have the time and energy, you could easily spend several days exploring the trails of the two national parks, La Amistad and Volcan Baru.

GETTING HERE AND AROUND

AIR TRAVEL

Air Panama flies daily between Panama City and David's Aeropuerto Enrique Malek (DAV). Air Panama has direct flights between David and San José, Costa Rica, three days a week. The airport underwent a major expansion in 2012. There are no direct flights between Bocas and David, meaning you have to return to Panama City if you want to travel by air.

Contacts Aeropuerto Enrique Malek. ⊠ *Av. Reed Gray* ✛ *5 km (3 miles) south of David* ☎ *507/721-1072.* **Air Panama.** ☎ *507/316-9000* ⊕ *www.airpanama.com.*

BUS TRAVEL

Padafront has hourly buses between Panama City's Albrook Terminal and David from 6 am to 8 pm and direct buses at 10:45 pm and midnight. The trip takes about eight hours, with a meal stop in Santiago. Small buses to Boquete, Volcán, Cerro Punta, and Paso Canoas (the border post with Costa Rica) depart every 30 minutes during the day.

Contacts Padafront. ☎ *507/774-9205, 507/775-8853.* **Terminal de Buses.** ⊠ *Av. del Estudiante* ✛ *one block east of Av. Obaldía* ☎ *507/775-2974.*

CAR TRAVEL

A car is the best way to explore Chiriquí as roads are in good shape and well-marked. Avenida Obaldía heads straight north out of David to Boquete as a four-lane highway, no turns required. All other areas are reached via the Carretera Interamericana, which skirts David to the north and east.

Most major rental agencies have offices in David and offer 4WD vehicles as well as less expensive standards (sufficient for most trips).

TAXI TRAVEL

It is possible, if a little less convenient, to explore this region without a car. Yellow taxis ply the streets of major tourist centers. Your hotel or restaurant will be happy to arrange transportation for you. In fact, if you want to hike the Sendero los Quetzales, it's best to hire a taxi in Cerro Punta to take you to the trailhead. It only takes about 90 minutes to drive from David to Boca Chica. If you spend a few nights there, you may want to have your hotel arrange a taxi transfer from David.

HOTELS

Accommodation in Chiriquí ranges from Boquete's affordable B&Bs to the luxurious bungalows on Isla Boca Brava. The province has some of Panama's best small lodges, many surrounded by tropical nature.

Hotel reviews have been shortened. For full information, visit Fodors.com.

RESTAURANTS

You can get a good meal almost anywhere in the province, but Boquete has the best restaurant selection. The specialty in the mountains is local farm-raised trout, but because the Gulf of Chiriquí has such great fishing, seafood is also a good bet. Chiriquí is cattle country, so you'll also find plenty of beef on the menu.

WHAT IT COSTS				
	$	$$	$$$	$$$$
Restaurants	under $10	$10–$15	$16–$20	over $20
Hotels	under $100	$100–$160	$161–$220	over $220

Restaurant prices are per person for a main course at dinner. Hotel prices are for two people in a standard double room, excluding service and 10% tax.

MONEY

There are ATMs all over David, in front of banks and in the big supermarkets, pharmacies, and gas stations, though they tend to be concentrated around the central plaza and along the Interamericana. There are also ATMs at the banks in the centers of Boquete and Volcán.

SAFETY

Aside from the usual dangers associated with scuba diving and surfing, the province's biggest health concerns are sunburn and hypothermia on the heights of Volcán Barú. If you hike to the summit of Barú, take warm, waterproof clothing, even in the dry season, because the weather can change radically near the peak.

ESSENTIALS

VISITOR INFORMATION

People at the ATP's regional office (open weekdays 8:30–4:30) in David are amiable but not very helpful. The

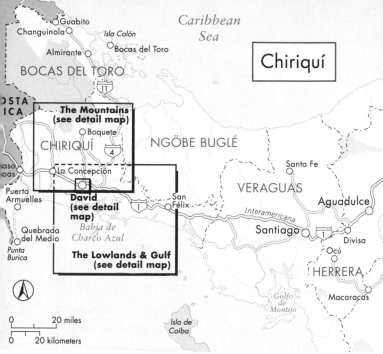

CEFATI Visitor Center (open daily 8:30–3:30), on the southern end of Boquete, does a better job. ANAM (the Autoridad Nacional del Ambiente, or the National Environment Authority) is the government entity charged with administering Panama's national parks. Individual park offices are helpful in providing information for your visit.

Tourist Information ANAM (*National Environment Authority*). ☎ 507/500–0855 *in Panama City* ⊕ *www.miambiente.gob.pa.* **ATP.** ✉ *Av. Domingo Díaz ✛ across from Cable and Wireless* ☎ *507/775-2839* ⊕ *www.visitpanama.com.* **CEFATI.** ✉ *Av. Central, at south entrance to town* ☎ *507/720–4060* ⊕ *www.atp.gob.pa.*

THE LOWLANDS AND GULF

The torrid lowlands that spread out around David are almost all pasture, and the small towns there are home to the province's traditional Chiricano cowboy culture. The vast Golfo de Chiriquí holds dozens of islands, coral reefs, and world-class surf breaks and sportfishing. Although David can serve as a base for gulf trips, it's more easily explored from Boca Chica, Boca Brava, the Islas Secas, or Morro Negrito.

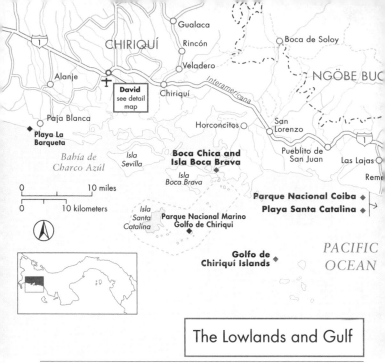

DAVID

440 km (274 miles) west of Panama City, 53 km (33 miles) east of Paso Canoas.

The province's bustling, sweltering capital won't be the Chiriquí you came to see. All services are here, however—at 144,000 inhabitants, lowland David clocks in as Panama's third largest city. With the vagaries of transportation in this region, you may find yourself spending the night here, so we list a few lodgings and services. Whether staying or just passing through, pronounce the city's name the Spanish way (Dah-VEED), so that people understand what you're talking about.

GETTING HERE AND AROUND

The 440-km (274-mile) drive between David and Panama City takes about six hours—an easy trip on the Carretera Interamericana that can be done in a day. However, because there are plenty of flights and rental-car companies in David, it isn't worth doing unless you visit destinations such as Santa Catalina en route, because the scenery consists primarily of pastures and unattractive towns.

BEACHES

Playa La Barqueta. The closest beach to David, Playa La Barqueta is a long ribbon of dark-gray sand that's popular with local surfers. The area behind the beach is deforested, and the sea is often murky due to a nearby mangrove estuary. Nonetheless, it's a pleasant spot to spend the day, and you can stroll for miles without seeing a soul (except during holidays). The beach is public, but a day pass ($10) from the resort, Hotel Las Olas, includes pool, gym, and bar access. There are also several simple restaurants with inexpensive Panamanian fare. ■TIP➔ **La Barqueta's sand can get hot enough to burn your feet. If the sea is rough there's a risk of rip currents, so don't go in any farther than waist-deep.** ⊹ *Take Av. 9 de Enero south, across Calle F Sur, and follow the signs.*

WHERE TO EAT

$$ ✕**Pizzería Gran Hotel Nacional.** *Italian.* This simple restaurant serves 17 varieties of good pizza, as well as mediocre pastas, many meat and seafood dishes, and inexpensive, three-course lunch specials. The decor is limited to vibrant tablecloths and tacky art, but the place is clean, bright, air-conditioned, and very popular. Ⓢ *Average main: $12* ⊠ *Gran Hotel Nacional, Calle Pérez Balladares (Calle Central) at Av. 9 de Enero (Av. Central)* ☎ *507/775–1042.*

WHERE TO STAY

$$ ⊡**Gran Hotel Nacional.** *Hotel.* Rooms are spacious at this central landmark hotel, popular for its facilities complete with a pool, gardens, casino, movie theater, three restaurants, and two bars. **Pros:** pool; spacious rooms; central location; decent restaurants. **Cons:** brusque receptionists at times; rooms facing the street have poor views. Ⓢ *Rooms from: $110* ⊠ *Calle Pérez Balladares (Calle Central) and Av. 9 de Enero (Av. Central)* ☎ *507/775–2222* ⊕ *www.hotelnacionalpanama.com* ⤳ *106 rooms, 13 suites* ⦿*Breakfast.*

$ ⊡**Hotel Castilla.** *Hotel.* This three-story building located kitty-corner from Parque Cervantes has basic rooms with good beds and small desks at reasonable prices. **Pros:** central location; competitive rates; elevator access. **Cons:** interior rooms dark; junior suites can be noisy; few amenities. Ⓢ *Rooms from: $75* ⊠ *Calle Aristides Romero (Calle A Norte) at Calle Bolívar (Calle 3 Este), Diagonal from Parque de Cervantes* ☎ *507/774–5260* ⊕ *www.hotel-castilla. net* ⤳ *67 rooms, 2 suites* ⦿*No meals.*

★ **Fodor$Choice** ⊡ **Hotel Ciudad de David.** *Hotel.* Escape the
$$$ honking horns and city bustle at David's most upscale property, complete with a pool, gym, spa, and parking

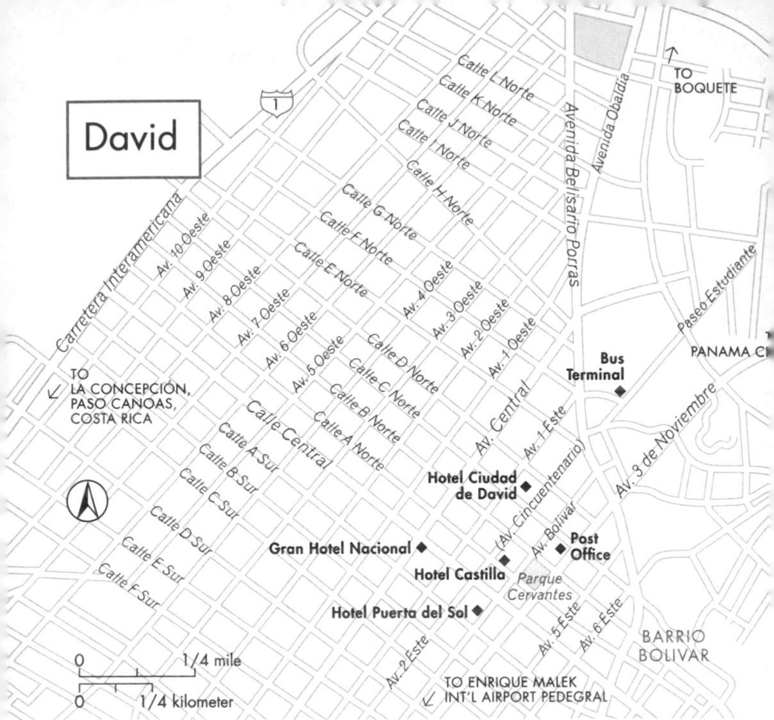

garage. **Pros:** central location; good restaurant; clean and modern property. **Cons:** shaded pool; no views; somewhat pricey. [$] *Rooms from: $175* ✉ *Calle D Norte, Av. 2 Este* ☎ *507/774–3333* 🌐 *www.hotelciudaddedavid.com* 🛏 *94 rooms, 9 suites* 🍴 *Breakfast.*

$ 🏨 **Hotel Puerta del Sol.** *Hotel.* Just a five-minute drive from David's Enrique Malek Airport, this clean hotel has rooms that sleep up to four people, each with cable TV and private bath. **Pros:** large rooms; central location. **Cons:** poor views. [$] *Rooms from: $54* ✉ *Between Av. 3 and Calle Central* ☎ *507/774–8422* 🌐 *www.hotelpuertadelsol.com.pa* 🛏 *84 rooms, 2 suites* 🍴 *No meals.*

BOCA CHICA AND ISLA BOCA BRAVA

54 km (32 miles) southeast of David.

Long a sleepy fishing port at the end of a long, paved road, Boca Chica has a small selection of hotels that serve the islands of Parque Nacional Marino Golfo de Chiriquí. The town is on a peninsula overlooking the nearby island of Boca Brava. Together, they define the eastern edge of a mangrove estuary that extends all the way to Playa La

Barqueta. Neither the island nor the mainland has great beaches. The attractions are beyond Boca Brava on the uninhabited islands of the Parque Nacional Marino Golfo de Chiriquí *(below)*, a 40-minute boat ride away. Beyond them lie world-class sportfishing and diving around the Islas Ladrones and Islas Secas.

GETTING HERE AND AROUND

The Panama Big Game Fishing Club and Cala Mia provide boat transport to Isla Boca Brava (20 minutes) for guests from the port in Boca Chica. It's located at the end of the road past the small town of Horconcitos. It takes about 90 minutes to drive from David to Boca Chica; go east on the Carretera Interamericana for 39 km (24 miles), then turn right at the intersection for Horconcitos.

Most hotels arrange transfers from the David airport.

WHERE TO EAT

$$$ 🍴 **Restaurant Bocas Del Mar.** *International.* This poolside restaurant on the lower level of Hotel Bocas Del Mar has ocean views and an elegant yet relaxed dining area. Each morning, local fishermen deliver the daily catch that transforms into beautifully prepared plates of ceviche, garlic shrimp, grilled lobster, and seared tuna with linguine. The chilled salmorejo soup topped with serrano is an excellent starter, as is the Greek salad, which is large enough to share. The filet mignon with mushroom sauce comes with shoestring fries, and the grilled fish is served with a side of rice and vegetables. Vegetarians will appreciate the pasta primavera or the veggie tower stacked with eggplant, zucchini, tomato, and mozzarella. Save room for the crêpe suzette filled with vanilla ice cream. [$] *Average main: $16* ✉ *Hotel Bocas del Mar, Boca Chica* ✣ *2 km (1 mile) before Boca Chica* ☎ *507/6395–8757* 🌐 *www.bocasdelmar.com* 🕒 *Closed 2 pm–6 pm.*

WHERE TO STAY

★ $$$ Fodor's Choice 🏨 **Bocas del Mar.** *Hotel.* Stark white buildings housing modern rooms have water views and are just a short kayak trip away from Boca Brava. **Pros:** every room has ocean view; filtered tap water; plenty of activities; excellent restaurant. **Cons:** early meal times; bugs in jungle setting; hotel often full. [$] *Rooms from: $185* ✉ *2 km (1 mile) before Boca Chica, Boca Chica* ✣ *Pass Horconcitos town, take right fork by the church to access Boca Chica Rd.* ☎ *507/395–8757* 🌐 *www.bocasdelmar.com* 🛏 *20 rooms* 🍽 *Breakfast.*

$$$$ 🏨 **Cala Mia Boutique Resort.** *Resort.* After a 2014 remodel, Cala Mia's new owner has upgraded this Boca Brava island property with tastefully decorated bungalows, each with air-conditioning, Wi-Fi, and sunken terraces with couches, hammocks, and tree-shrouded water views. **Pros:** gorgeous design and location; rate includes boat transport, breakfast, and kayaks; friendly staff. **Cons:** isolated; no-see-ums can be a problem. [$] *Rooms from: $300* ✉ *Isla Boca Brava, Boca Chica* ☎ *507/851–0025 in Panama, 361/537–7456 in U.S.* 🌐 *www.boutiquehotelcalamia.com* 🕓 *Closed Oct.* 🛏 *7 bungalows, 2 villas* 🍴 *Breakfast.*

$$ 🏨 **Gone Fishing.** *Resort.* Though fishing is an option here, this is really a waterfront hotel that offers various activities. **Pros:** great view; nice pool; huge rooms. **Cons:** bugs can be a problem; occasional noise and smell of smoke in common areas. [$] *Rooms from: $130* ✉ *On left before town, Boca Chica* ☎ *786/393–5882 in U.S., 507/6930–4215* 🌐 *www.gonefishingpanama.com* 🛏 *4 rooms* 🍴 *No meals.*

$$$$ 🏨 **Panama Big Game Fishing Club.** *Hotel.* This small lodge on Boca Brava, just across the channel from Boca Chica, is all about sportfishing, and it has some of the country's best. **Pros:** small and intimate setting; great fishing; good food. **Cons:** no pool; nothing for nonfishers, although get break in rates; bugs can be a problem; four-night minimum. [$] *Rooms from: $1420* ✉ *Isla Boca Brava, Boca Chica* ☎ *507/6627–5431, 786/600–1672 in U.S.* 🌐 *www.panamabiggamefishingclub.com* 🛏 *4 bungalows* 🍴 *All-inclusive* ☞ *Price for 2 based on starting price of five-night packages of $3,553.*

$$$ 🏨 **Seagullcove Lodge.** *B&B/Inn.* This hillside hotel sports Mediterranean decor with its arched doorways, terra-cotta flooring, and manicured gardens. **Pros:** great views of the bay; good food; friendly service. **Cons:** steep stairs; small grounds; bugs can be a problem. [$] *Rooms from: $180* ✉ *Camino por la playa piedrita, Calle Gone Fishing, on left just before town, Boca Chica* ☎ *507/851–0036, 786/735–1475 in U.S.* 🌐 *www.seagullcovelodge.com* 🛏 *5 bungalows* 🍴 *Breakfast.*

SPORTS AND THE OUTDOORS

SCUBA DIVING AND SNORKELING

Boca Chica is the most convenient base for scuba-diving and snorkeling trips to Parque Nacional Marino Golfo de Chiriquí *(below)* and to Islas Ladrones and Islas Secas *(below)*.

FISHING

The Gulf has superb fishing, especially around the Islas Montuosos and Hannibal Bank. The best fishing is for black marlin and sailfish from January to April. Find huge yellowfin tuna from March to May; dolphin (the fish, not the mammal) abound from November to January. From July to January it's roosterfish and wahoo; catch amberjacks, mackerel, snapper, and grouper year-round.

Gone Fishing. Gone Fishing offers deep-sea charters for $1,200, or less-expensive inshore fishing that starts at $700. ⊠ *Boca Chica* ☎ *507/6930–4215* ⊕ *www.gonefishingpanama. com* ⌷ *From $700.*

Panama Big Game Fishing Club. Panama Big Game Fishing Club includes daily fishing trips to the gulf's best spots in their rates. ⊠ *Boca Chica* ⊕ *www.panamabiggamefishingclub. com* ⌷ *From $650.*

GOLFO DE CHIRIQUÍ ISLANDS

The vast Gulf of Chiriquí holds dozens of uninhabited islands surrounded by healthy coral formations and excellent conditions for surfing, diving, and fishing. You can base yourself in the Boca Chica/Boca Brava area *(above)* to explore these islands. Isla Ensenada, in the gulf's northeast corner, is near five of the country's best and most remote breaks. The beautiful, remote **Islas Secas** (Dry Islands), a 16-isle archipelago 35 km (21 miles) from the coast, can be visited from Boca Chica or Boca Brava.

GETTING HERE AND AROUND

Transportation to Golfo de Chiriquí lodges is provided by the lodges. The Parque Nacional Marino Golfo de Chiriquí, Islas Secas, and Islas Ladrones can be visited on day trips from Boca Chica and Boca Brava via boat.

EXPLORING

Parque Nacional Marino Golfo de Chiriquí (*Chiriquí Marino National Park*). The 36,400 acres of the Parque Nacional Marino Golfo de Chiriquí include more than 20 islands— all but one of which are uninhabited. The islands' beaches are the nicest in Chiriquí Province, with pale sand, clear waters, tropical dry forest, and colorful reef fish just a shell's toss from shore. The loveliest are the palm-lined strands of **Isla Parida** (the largest in the archipelago), **Isla San José, Isla Gamez,** and **Isla Bolaños,** where the sand is snow-white. Various species of sea turtle nest on the islands' beaches, and the water holds hundreds of species including lobsters, moray eels, and schools of parrot fish. You may also see frigate birds, brown pelicans, and green iguanas. Dolphins sometimes cruise the park's waters, and from August to October you may spot humpback whales. There are no lodging facilities; visit on day trips from Boca Chica, 30 to 60 minutes away, depending on the island. ✉ *12 km (7 miles) southwest of Boca Chica* ☎ *507/775–3163 in David* ✉ *$5* ⊙ *Daily 8–6.*

SPORTS AND THE OUTDOORS

SCUBA DIVING AND SNORKELING

The Islas Secas and Islas Ladrones are surrounded by more than 50 excellent dive sites, with visibility averaging 70 feet and healthy coral formations surrounded by hundreds of fish species and comparable invertebrate diversity. You might see various species of sea stars and angelfish, elegant Moorish idols, frog fish, and sea turtles.

Closed for renovations at the time of writing, the **Islas Secas Resort** lies in the middle of the archipelago's coral gardens. Those islands can also be visited on day trips from the Boca Chica/Boca Brava lodges.

PLAYA SANTA CATALINA

190 km (114 miles) east of David, 360 km (223 miles) southwest of Panama City.

Literally at the end of the road, the tiny fishing village of Santa Catalina sits near some of the best surfing spots in the country and is the closest port to Isla Coiba, Panama's top dive destination. For years, the only people who visited Playa Santa Catalina, technically outside Chiriquí in the province of Veraguas, were adventurous surfers who made the long trip here on rough roads and slept in rustic rooms for the pleasure of riding La Punta, a right point break. The roads and accommodations are better now, and two dive centers have opened. Never fear: This is still a quiet beach town, and you come here to enjoy ocean views through the palm fronds, friendly locals, cheap seafood, and amazing surf and diving.

Santa Catalina virtually shuts down in early fall, with some businesses closed in September or October. Call businesses you plan to visit in advance if you go at this time of year. The town's limited night scene is hampered by a fairly well-respected 10 pm closing time for bars and restaurants,

GOLFO DE CHIRIQUÍ SURFING

The Golfo de Chiriquí has some undervisited, remote surf breaks. Surfing is best from June to December when waves consistently break overhead, and faces sometimes reach 20 feet. Here's a list of some of the island's best surf breaks.

Emily. The most convenient wave for guests at the Morro Negrito Surf Camp is Emily, a left that breaks over the reef right in front of the camp.

Nestles. Advanced surfers enjoy the rush of Nestles, a big reef break in front of Isla Silva de Afuera. The quick peak, big barrels, and reef bottom make this a challenging wave.

P Land. Intermediate and advanced surfers enjoy P Land, a left reef break on Isla Silva de Afuera, year-round. It's one of the few waves that can hold huge swells without closing out, even at 20+ feet.

The Point. The most impressive wave in the gulf is The Point, a tubular reef break that has surfers booking several weeks at the Morro Negrito Surf Camp year after year. The left-hand wave breaks on a lava rock bottom, and can hold huge swells.

The Sandbar. This long break, which has both lefts and rights, is popular with intermediate surfers and beginners. Named for the sandbar where it breaks, it is located near a river mouth accessible by boat.

which is only flaunted during the busiest times of year like Easter. Most of the area's dirt roads are passable in a basic car, but a truck or 4x4 is a safer bet.

GETTING HERE AND AROUND

It takes about six hours to drive to Santa Catalina from Panama City, driving west on the Carretera Interamericana to Santiago, and then southwest, via Soná, the 110 km (68 miles) to Playa Santa Catalina.

WHERE TO EAT

$ ✕**Jammin Pizza.** *Italian.* Surprisingly good pizza is served at this small, Italian-owned open-air restaurant a short walk from the beach. The thin pies baked in a wood-burning brick oven would be popular in Panama City, but they taste that much better served at the edge of civilization. On holidays and dry-season weekends the place can get packed, and it stays open late as locals and visitors top off their dinners with cold beers and good music. Service is relatively slow, so if your stomach is grumbling, get there by 6:30 pm if you don't want to wait longer than an hour for your food. [$] *Average main: $6* ✉ *Via Catalina Farms, Road to El Estero, first right* 💳 *No credit cards* ⏲ *Closed Sun. No lunch.*

$$ 🍴 **Pinguino Cafe.** *Italian.* Smack at the end of the main road to Santa Catalina, this beachside restaurant has a fine selection of seafood and Italian dishes, with recipes for pollo a la scalopina and filete de pescado a la mediterránea taken straight from the cookbook of the Italian owner's mother. With a great sunset view of the bay at Playa Santa Catalina, finer dining in a more sandals-optional location won't be found. [$] *Average main: $10* ✉ *End of Carretera Nacional, right side facing the beach* 💳 *No credit cards.*

WHERE TO STAY

$ 🏨 **Hotel Hibiscus Garden.** *Hotel.* Ten kilometers (6 miles) before Santa Catalina is this simple but comfortable and affordable lodge at Playa Lagartero on the Gulf of Montijo. **Pros:** relaxed location; good restaurant; great value. **Cons:** many mosquitoes on beach; resident dogs and cats might be a problem for those with allergies ; breakfast not included. [$] *Rooms from: $66* ✉ *Playa Lagartero, 10 km (6 miles) northeast of Santa Catalina* ☎ *6615–6097* 🌐 *www.hibiscusgarden.com* 💳 *No credit cards* 🛏 *8 rooms, 1 dorm* 🍽 *No meals.*

$ 🏨 **La Buena Vida.** *B&B/Inn.* Charming fauna-themed villas showcase the U.S. owners' attention to detail at this small lodge. **Pros:** central location close to dive shops, beach, and restaurants; great value; good and healthy food. **Cons:** often booked full; slow Wi-Fi. [$] *Rooms from: $66* ✉ *Carretera Nacional, on left in front of school* ☎ *507/6635–1895* 🌐 *www.labuenavidahotel.com* 💳 *No credit cards* 🛏 *4 rooms* 🍽 *No meals.*

SPORTS AND THE OUTDOORS

SCUBA DIVING AND SNORKELING

Playa Santa Catalina is the closest embarkation point to Isla Coiba, which has Panama's best scuba diving, but there are numerous other spots nearby. Visibility and sea conditions can change from one day to the next, but in general the diving is better during the rainy season than during the dry season. Many of the dive spots around Isla Coiba require ocean-diving experience, but some closer to town are appropriate for novices or for snorkeling. Within an hour of Santa Catalina are dive sites such as **Punta Pargo** and **Palo Grande,** where you might see moray eels, parrot fish, various types of puffers, and big schools of jacks, among other things.

Coiba Dive Center. Coiba Dive Center offers the complete slate of PADI courses, as well as multiday diving excursions to Isla Coiba with overnight stays in the National Environment Authority (ANAM) cabins. ✉ *Calle Principal, on right before beach* ☎ *507/6780–1141, 507/6774–0808* ⊕ *www.coibadivecenter.com.*

Scuba Coiba. Santa Catalina's first dive center offers boat dives at dozens of nearby spots and multiday trips to Isla Coiba with overnights in the ANAM cabins there. They also offer PADI certification courses and snorkeling/beach trips to other nearby islands as well. ✉ *Calle Principal, on left before beach* ☎ *507/6980–7122* ⊕ *www.scubacoiba. com* ✇ *From $90.*

SURFING

Isla Cebaco. An excellent alternative to the coastal breaks is Isla Cebaco, a 90-minute boat ride from Santa Catalina, which has both a beach break and point break.

La Punta. Santa Catalina's legendary point break, known simply as La Punta, is one of the country's best. The waves break over a rock platform in front of a point just east of town, forming both lefts and rights, though the rights are more hollow and longer. It is best surfed from mid- to high tide and usually needs a four- to five-foot swell to break. When a good swell rolls in, the faces can get as big as 15 to 20 feet.

Panama Surf Tours. Panama Surf Tours offers surf packages that include a guide and transportation to and from Playa Santa Catalina, with overnight stays at Hotel Santa Catalina. The company also offers lessons and surf tours in other parts of Panama. ☎ *507/6571–4387* ⊕ *www. panamasurftours.com.*

Playa Santa Catalina. An easier alternative to La Punta is the nearby exposed point break at Playa Santa Catalina, which is usually smaller and less treacherous. This consistent wave is best with offshore winds blowing in from the north.

Punta Brava. If La Punta is too small or crowded, a 30-minute hike west of town takes you to Punta Brava, where a fast hollow left barrels over a rocky bottom. The waves here are often bigger than at La Punta, but it can only be surfed from low to mid-tide.

PARQUE NACIONAL COIBA

50 km (31 miles) southwest of Santa Catalina.

Remote and wild, Panama's largest island and one of the world's largest marine parks offers the country's best scuba diving, world-class fishing, and palm-lined beaches. About 80% of the island is covered with tropical dry forest, home to an array of wildlife.

GETTING HERE AND AROUND

Most people visit Isla Coiba on fishing, diving, or nature tours offered by the companies listed here. It is possible to organize your own trip, in which case you would hire a boat in Playa Santa Catalina. Most fishermen there charge about $200 for a day trip to Isla Coiba, and more if they must stay overnight on the island.

EXPLORING

★ Fodor'sChoice **Parque Nacional Coiba.** Isla Coiba began its human history as a penal colony—it was Panama's version of Devil's Island—where 3,000 convicts toiled on farms carved out of the dry forest, growing food for the country's entire prison system. The Panamanian government declared the island a national park in 1991, but it took more than a decade to relocate the prisoners. Parque Nacional Coiba now protects 667,000 acres of sea and islands, of which Isla Coiba itself constitutes about 120,000 acres.

The marine life of the park is as impressive as that of the Galápagos. The extensive and healthy reefs are home to comical frog fish, sleek rays, and massive groupers. The national park holds more than 4,000 acres of reef, composed of two-dozen different types of coral and 760 fish species. The park's waters are also visited by 22 species of whale and dolphin, including killer whales and humpback whales, fairly common there from July to September.

The wildlife on Coiba doesn't compare to that on the Galápagos, but its forests are home to howler monkeys, agoutis (large rodents), and 150 bird species, including the endemic Coiba spinetail, the rare crested eagle, and the country's biggest population of endangered scarlet macaws. Several trails wind through the island's forests; the **Sendero de los Monos** (Monkey Trail), a short boat trip from the ranger station, is the most popular. Crocodiles inhabit the island's extensive mangrove swamps, and sea turtles nest on some beaches from April to September. The most popular beach in the park is on the tiny **Granito de Oro** (Gold Nugget) island, where lush foliage backs white sand, and good snorkeling lies a short swim away.

Options for visiting Isla Coiba range from a day trip out of Playa Santa Catalina to one-week tours, or small-ship cruises that include on-board lodging. The National Environment Authority (ANAM) offers accommodations ($20 per bed; five beds per building) in air-conditioned cement buildings with communal kitchen—you have to bring your own food—near the ranger station. There is also space for 15 campers ($10 per two-person tent). Reserve at least a month ahead of time during the dry season. ☎507/998–4271 *Park office in Santiago, 507/ 998–0615 ANAM* ⊕*www.coibanationalpark.com* ⌸*$20.*

SPORTS AND THE OUTDOORS

SCUBA DIVING AND SNORKELING

Isla Coiba has Panama's best scuba diving, and some of the best diving in Central America, with vast reefs inhabited by hundreds of species of fish. On any given dive there you may see spotted eagle rays, white-tip reef sharks, sea turtles, giant snapper and grouper, moray eels, stargazers, frog fish, pipefish, angelfish, and Moorish idols. The reefs hold plenty of invertebrates, whereas offshore pinnacles attract big schools of jacks, Pacific spadefish, and other species.

Among the park's best dive spots are **Santa Cruz,** a vast coral garden teeming with reef fish; **Mali Mali,** a submerged rock formation that is a cleaning station for large fish; **La Viuda,** a massive rock between Islas de Coiba and Canales that attracts major schools of fish; and **Frijoles,** submerged rocks where divers often see sharks, large eels, and manta rays. Many of the dive spots around Isla Coiba require a bit of ocean-diving experience, but there are also dive spots that are appropriate for novices and good snorkeling areas.

EcoCircuitos. EcoCircuitos, based in Panama City, has a four-day snorkeling and hiking tour to Isla de Coiba with overnights in the ANAM cabins and in Santa Catalina. ☎507/315–1305, 800/830–7142 in U.S. ⊕*www. ecocircuitos.com* ⌸*From $975.*

Scuba Coiba. Santa Catalina's Scuba Coiba are the local experts, offering boat dives at dozens of spots in the park on trips with overnights in the ANAM cabins. ☎507/6980–7122 ⊕*www.scubacoiba.com* ⌸*From $90.*

FISHING

Catch-and-release fishing is permitted inside Coiba National Park, but the fishing is just as good outside the park. Blue marlin, black marlin, and Pacific sailfish run here in significant numbers from December to April, with January to March being the peak months. The area also holds legions of wahoo, dolphin (mahimahi), and tuna, which often run bigger than 200 pounds. The fishing is less spectacular from April to December, but there are still plenty of roosterfish, mackerel, amberjack, snapper, and grouper. Some of the area's best fishing is around **Isla Montousa** and the **Hannibal Banks,** 65 to 80 km (40 to 50 miles) west of Isla Coiba.

Coiba Adventure Sport Fishing. Captain Tom Yust's Coiba Adventure Sportfishing runs fishing tours around Isla Coiba on a 31-foot Bertram, or a 22-foot Mako, with overnights at the ANAM cabins. ☎ *800/800–0907 in U.S., 507/998–1338 in Panama* ⊕ *www.coibadventure.com* ⌖ *From $1,250.*

Pesca Panama. Pesca Panama offers one-week fishing tours to the waters west of Isla Coiba with overnights on a barge near David. ☎ *800/946–3474* ⊕ *www.pescapanama.com.*

THE MOUNTAINS

Nestled in the Cordillera de Talamanca, which towers along the province's northern edge, are the lush mountain valleys of Boquete, Cerro Punta, and Bambito, each with unique scenery. The mountain range's upper slopes are covered with lush cloud forest, which is kept wet by the mist that the trade winds regularly push over the continental divide. That mist not only keeps the landscape green, it also creates the perfect conditions for rainbows, commonly sighted during the afternoon. Mountain streams feed half a dozen rafting rivers up here, and abundant forests are excellent areas for bird-watching, hiking, horseback riding, or canopy tours. The area's captivating beauty and charming restaurants and inns make it a favorite among many visitors to Panama.

BOQUETE

38 km (24 miles) north of David.

This pleasant town sits at 3,878 feet above sea level in the always springlike valley of the Río Caldera. The surrounding mountains are covered with forest and shade coffee farms, where coffee bushes grow amidst tropical trees. It's

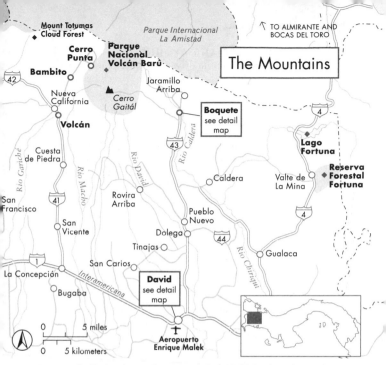

superb for bird-watching, and the roads and trails can be explored on foot, horseback, mountain bike, or four wheels.

Though the surrounding countryside holds most of Boquete's attractions, the town itself is quite appealing, with tidy wooden houses and prolific flower gardens. Around 30,000 people live here, most of them scattered around the valley. The town center holds a simple *parque central* (central park), officially the Parque de las Madres, surrounded by shops, the town hall, and roads lined with patches of pink impatiens and the pale trumpetlike flowers of the Datura, also known as jimson weed or devil's trumpet. Streams meander through town, and the Río Caldera flows through a wide swath of boulders along its eastern edge.

Among the population are now several thousand foreigners who have chosen to make the town their new (or second) home. With a four-lane highway heading out from David and the 2012 expansion of that city's airport, growth has steadily continued.

GETTING HERE AND AROUND
It's an easy 45-minute drive to Boquete from David, where you follow Avenida Obaldía north, which becomes a four-lane highway.

Buses depart from David's terminal every 30 minutes and take about 45 minutes to reach Boquete.

Boquete's local transportation is via vans that depart regularly from Avenida Central by Supermercado Bruna, just north of the parque central for either the Alto Quiel/Bajo Mono loop or the Alto Lino/Palo Alto loop. They pick up and drop off passengers anywhere en route for $1. Taxis wait around the parque central and charge $1–$5 for valley trips. Private shuttles charge $45 for up to two people and $15 for each additional person.

Contacts Boquete Tree Trek. ☎ *507/720–1635* ⊕ *www.boquete-treetrek.com.* **Daniel Higgins.** ☎ *507/6617–0570.*

TOURS
Kotowa Coffee Tour. In the hills of Palo Alto, this farm produces one of Boquete's best coffees, available at a small chain of coffee shops. The farm still has the original coffee mill from 1920. Today the Kotowa Estate is recognized for its innovations such as burning coffee bean husks for fuel. Tours provide a close look at the cultivation, harvest, and processing of coffee. Go during the October-to-May harvest and reserve your tour a day in advance for free transport from your hotel. ☎ *507/720–3852* ⊕ *www.coffeeadventures. net* 🖃 *Tour $35* ☉ *Tour daily at 2 pm by reservation.*

EXPLORING
Unlike most Panamanian towns, Boquete was settled by European and North American immigrants at the beginning of the 20th century. This lineage is apparent in everything from the architecture to the faces of many residents. Plenty of Ngöbe people migrate to Boquete from the northeast of Chiriquí to work in the orange and coffee harvests. The valley is popular with foreign retirees, drawn by the climate and beauty of the area.

TOP ATTRACTIONS
Bajo Mono Road. The road, near San Ramón, leads to the trailhead for the **Sendero Los Quetzales**, which winds its way through the forest between Cerro Punta and Boquete. Start that hike in Cerro Punta, though; it's all uphill from Boquete. Head to Bajo Mono to look for quetzals and hun-

The Quetzal and the Cloud Forest

Central American cloud forests remain the natural habitat of the resplendent quetzal (Pharomachrus mocinno), one of six quetzal species, and the forests above Boquete are some of the best places in the world to see this elusive creature. The quetzal has been revered since the days of the ancient Maya, who called it the winged serpent. The female quetzal is attractive, but the male, with its distinctive crimson belly, blue-green back, and long tail, is spectacular. Though a mature bird stands just 14 inches tall (think "robin" for body size), male quetzals have two- to three-foot tail feathers that float behind them and more than double their length. Its unforgettable appearance notwithstanding, the quetzal can be difficult to spot in the lush foliage of the cloud forest. You might want to hire a local birding guide who can take you to spots where they commonly feed, or reproduce during the February to June nesting season. (In the spirit of equality between the sexes, male and female take turns incubating the eggs.) Even if you have little interest in bird-watching, taking a tour to Finca Lérida or one of the other spots above Boquete where quetzals are common, is highly recommended. Though you may not catch a glimpse of the legendary resplendent quetzal, you're bound to see dozens of other spectacular birds, and the quetzal's cloud-forest habitat is a magically beautiful ecosystem. If you do catch a glimpse of this bird-watcher's Holy Grail, consider yourself fortunate.

dreds of other bird species; the best area for bird-watching is the beginning of the Sendero Los Quetzales, above the Alto Chiquero ranger station. Two other good hiking trails head off of the Bajo Mono Road: the **Sendero Culebra**, on the right 1½ km (1 mile) up the road to Alto Chiquero, and **Pipeline Road**, a gravel track on the left that leads to a canyon and waterfall. ⌗*$3 to access Pipeline Road.*

★ **Fodor's**Choice **Finca Lérida.** On the eastern slope of Volcán Barú, this coffee farm encompasses 370 acres of bird-filled cloud forest. The farm is recommended in *A Guide to the Birds of Panama* as the place to see quetzals, and that's practically a guarantee between January and April. You may also see silver-throated tanagers, collared trogons, clorophonias, and about 230 other species. The farm's resident guide can take you along its 10 km (6 miles) of hiking trails, one leading to a small waterfall, or you can explore them on your own. The guide is invaluable if you're looking for quetzals. The coffee tour here gives insight into the harvesting and processing of Boquete's most famous product. The farm has a great view and a moderately priced café serving homemade desserts and fresh-roasted coffee. ✉ *7 km (4 miles) northwest of second Y, via Callejón Seco* ☏ *507/720–2285* ⊕ *www.fincalerida.com* 💵 *$10, coffee tour $35, guided hike $50, bird-watching $75 (includes lunch)* ⊗ *Daily 7 am–8 pm.*

WORTH NOTING

Café Ruiz. The Ruiz family has been growing coffee in Boquete since the late 1800s, and their coffee-roasting and packaging plant is just south of Mi Jardín Es Su Jardín. A full three-hour tour visits the family farm and processing plant in the mountains above town. Because it has plenty of trees and uses few chemicals, the farm is a good place to see birds. Do the tour in the morning between October and May, during harvest. Reserve a tour by phone or via the website. ✉ *Av. Central, ½ km (¼ mile) south of park, on right* ☏ *507/6672–3786* ⊕ *www.caferuiz-boquete.com* 💵 *Tour $30* ⊗ *Mon.–Sat. 8–6; tours at 9 and 1.*

CEFATI Information Center. If you're driving, stop at the town's official visitor center, on the right at the south entrance to town. The center offers free information on local sights and services, but the main reason to stop is to admire the view of the Boquete Valley. The building also has a small café. Beware of any businesses that advertise themselves as a "Tourist Center" or "Visitor Center" near the main park on Avenida Central. Unlike CEFATI, they operate solely on commission and generally steer travelers toward operations for which they can increase service rates. Additionally, their information and prices are not always reliable. ✉ *Av. Central/Calle Principal, at south entrance to town* ☏ *507/720–4060* ⊗ *Jan.–Apr., daily 8:30–3:30; May–Dec., daily 8–4.*

Mi Jardín Es Su Jardín (*My Garden Is Your Garden*). A few blocks north of the parque central, Avenida Central veers left at a "y" in the road. Just past the junction is a garden surrounding an eccentric Panamanian's vacation home. Cement paths wind past vibrant flower beds and bizarre statues of animals and cartoon characters, which make this place a minor monument to kitsch. The coffee bar overlooking a koi pond is a pleasant spot to relax. ✉ *Av. Central* ⊹ *½ km (¼ mile) north of park, on right* ☏ *507/730–8267 coffee bar* 💵 *Free* ⊗ *Gardens, daily 9–5; coffee bar, Tues.–Sun.*

WHERE TO EAT

$$ ✕**El Oasis.** *International.* Perched on the banks of Caldera River, this pleasant restaurant is Boquete's go-to place for an intimate meal. The smoked trout and pasta with prawns are delicious, but it's the rack of lamb in a rosemary crust that is a local favorite. For a romantic dinner, the fireside gazebo has the best view. A more social setting can be found at the bar, appropriately named "La Roca" (The Rock) for a boulder that washed onto the property during a rainstorm in 1970; the boulder remains. There's often live music, which can be enjoyed with a glass of wine or the tres leches dessert. Lighter fare of soups, salads, and sandwiches is also on the menu. ⓢ *Average main: $14* ✉ *From Av. Central, over Caldera River bridge, 50 meters to the right* ☎ *507/720–1586* ⊕ *www.oasisboquete.com.*

$$ ✕**Il Pianista.** *Italian.* There is something European about the stone building that houses this restaurant a short drive northeast of town, which is made complete with authentic Italian cuisine. The small dining room is on the ground floor overlooking a stream surrounded by trees and impatiens; an outdoor patio sits beside a small waterfall. The menu includes fresh pastas such as vegetable lasagna and fettuccine *del Chef* (with prawn-and-mushroom cream sauce) or *napolitano* (with tomato-clam sauce). You can also build your own pizza or calzone or grab a pizza to go. ⓢ *Average main: $15* ✉ *Right at first Y north of town, left after the bridge, 3½ km (2 miles) north on right* ☎ *507/720–2728* ⊘ *Closed Mon., Tues., and Oct.*

$$$$ ✕**La Brulerie.** *Latin American.* Led by Michelin star Chef Andrés Madrigal, this sophisticated restaurant at Finca Lerida is based on the "Kilómetro Cero" (Zero Kilometer) concept: Only local ingredients from nearby farms are used to create a menu of authentic Panamanian flavors. Beet carpaccio with caramelized cashews is an excellent starter, as is the signature tree-tomato soup made from a sweet tomato-like fruit grown on-site. Elegant entrées range from tender lamb and seared trout to roasted skirt steak and homemade ravioli. The hydroponic greens add a colorful and healthy touch, right before the rich and savory dessert, *Pan Perdido* (black chocolate custard with rum). If the weather cooperates, request a table on the outside deck overlooking the gardens. ⓢ *Average main: $25* ✉ *At Finca Lerida, Vía Boquete ⊹ 7 km (4 miles) northwest of town, turn left at second Y, entrance on left* ☎ *507/720–1111* ⊕ *www.fincalerida.com.*

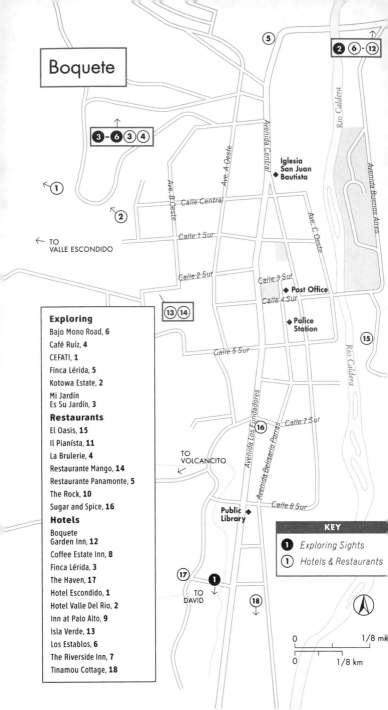

Boquete

Exploring
Bajo Mono Road, **6**
Café Ruíz, **4**
CEFATI, **1**
Finca Lérida, **5**
Kotowa Estate, **2**
Mi Jardín
Es Su Jardín, **3**

Restaurants
El Oasis, **15**
Il Pianísta, **11**
La Brulerie, **4**
Restaurante Mango, **14**
Restaurante Panamonte, **5**
The Rock, **10**
Sugar and Spice, **16**

Hotels
Boquete
Garden Inn, **12**
Coffee Estate Inn, **8**
Finca Lérida, **3**
The Haven, **17**
Hotel Escondido, **1**
Hotel Valle Del Rio, **2**
Inn at Palo Alto, **9**
Isla Verde, **13**
Los Establos, **6**
The Riverside Inn, **7**
Tinamou Cottage, **18**

Iglesia
San Juan
Bautista

Post Office

Police
Station

Public
Library

TO
VALLE ESCONDIDO

TO
VOLCANCITO

TO
DAVID

Rio Caldera

Avenida Central

Avenida Buenos Aires

Ave. A Oeste

Ave. B Oeste

Ave. C Oeste

Calle Central

Calle 1 Sur

Calle 2 Sur

Calle 3 Sur

Calle 4 Sur

Calle 5 Sur

Calle 7 Sur

Calle 8 Sur

Avenida Los Fundadores

Avenida Belisario Porras

KEY
① Exploring Sights
① Hotels & Restaurants

0   1/8 mi
0   1/8 km

★ Fodor's Choice ✕ **Restaurante Mango.** *Eclectic.* Inspired by his
$$$ travels, Chef Craig Miller delivers an ethnic blend of bites
from around the world. Thai shrimp cakes with ginger aioli
and chili vinaigrette, chicken pâté with a hint of calvados
and thyme, beef medallions with fig demi-glace, and arrow-
head spinach with feta and lemon—the organic dishes are a
mélange of international flavors all on one creative menu.
Vegetarians have a field day with veggie-tapas like cauli-
flower masala, house-marinated olives, artichoke hearts,
curried carrots, and smoked eggplant. Brick-oven pizzas
are topped with local goat cheese, homemade sausage, and
fresh pesto. The greatest draw is Mango's support of local
farmers and sustainable practices—well, that and the divine
white chocolate crème brûlée topped with mint. Ⓢ *Average
main: $16* ⊠ *Hotel Isla Verde , Calle 2 Suroeste ✛ at turn
to Valle Escondido* ☎ *507/ 720–1539* ⊕ *www.restaurante-
mango.com* ⊘ *Closed Mon. No dinner Sun.*

★ Fodor's Choice ✕ **Restaurante Panamonte.** *Latin American.*
$$$ Though Boquete's first hotel now faces stiff competition,
its stately restaurant remains one of the best in town. Cre-
ated by award-winning Executive Chef Charlie Collins,
inventive dishes are based on traditional Panamanian
cuisine and might include pumpkin soup, shrimp-and-
plantain croquettes, butter-poached trout, wild boar with
chocolate demi-glace, and grilled beef tenderloin topped
with a three-pepper sauce. Service is flawless in a historic
European atmosphere that's hardly changed over the past
century. Sunday breakfast is popular. Ⓢ *Average main: $18*
⊠ *Hotel Panamonte, Av. 11 de Abril ✛ right at first Y north
of town, on left* ☎ *507/720–1324* ⊕ *www.panamonte.com.*

$$$ ✕ **The Rock.** *Eclectic.* Next to The Riverside Inn, this place's
greatest asset is its view of the Palo Alto River and the forest
beyond it. If the weather is nice, you may want to sit outside
near the riverbank, though the large picture windows also
let you enjoy the scenery from inside. The food is tasty and
inventive, though service can be slow. Starters range from
corvina (sea bass) ceviche to hydroponic salads. Entrées
worth sinking your teeth into include pork ribs with sugar-
cane and papaya sauce and a sesame-crusted salmon filet on
a creamy risotto. The grilled portobello burger with cream
cheese and cranberry filling makes for a unique vegetarian
option. Monday night features live jazz and two-for-one
cocktails from 6 to 7. Ⓢ *Average main: $17* ⊠ *Right at first
Y north of town, left after bridge, then 1½ km (1 mile) on
left* ☎ *507/720–2516* ⊕ *www.therockboquete.com* ⊘ *Closed
Tues. and mid-May–Oct.*

★ $ **Fodor'sChoice 🍴 Sugar and Spice Dulces Gourmet.** *Bakery.* Owned by master pastry chef Richard Meyer, this colorful café is perhaps the most popular place in town, meaning guests wait in line, all while being tempted by the glass case displaying strawberry cream cake, chunky brownie muffins, walnut cranberry pie, and coconut mousse cake. Travelers on a budget come for the $1 empanadas or the lunch specials of wraps, soups, sandwiches, and salads. The Italian melt with prosciutto and provolone is perfectly toasted, and the hot pressed pastrami on rye or roast beef on ciabatta makes it clear why Sugar & Spice supplies most Boquete hotels and restaurants with breads, all made from natural starters. [$] *Average main: $6* ✉ *7th at Main Bajo Boquete* ☎ *507/730–9376* 🌐 *www.sugarandspiceboquete.com* 🕒 *Closed Wed.* 💳 *No credit cards.*

WHERE TO STAY

Hotels in Boquete don't need air-conditioning. Theft has been a problem at some Boquete hotels, so lock your valuables in a safe if you can.

$$ 🏨 **Boquete Garden Inn.** *B&B/Inn.* As the name suggests, this small hotel's grounds hold plenty of flowers, as well as trees, a few boulders, and a nature path. **Pros:** lovely grounds on river; friendly staff; spacious rooms; excellent breakfast. **Cons:** limited views; 30 minute walk to town; no phones in rooms. [$] *Rooms from: $119* ✉ *Av. Buenos Aires* ✥ *Right at first Y north of town, 1½ km (1 mile) north of bridge over Río Caldera* ☎ *507/720–2376* 🌐 *www.boquetegardeninn.com* 🛏 *10 rooms* 🍽 *Breakfast.*

$$$ 🏨 **The Coffee Estate Inn.** *B&B/Inn.* Three charming bungalows on a six-acre shade-coffee farm offer peace, privacy, plentiful bird life, and one of Boquete's best views. **Pros:** great views; lovely grounds; helpful owners; heated bathroom floors; gourmet dinners. **Cons:** often full; two-night minimum stay; no kids under 14. [$] *Rooms from: $180* ✥ *1½ km (1 mile) northeast of town; right at first Y, first right north of bridge* ☎ *507/720–2211* 🌐 *www.coffeeestateinn.com* 🛏 *3 bungalows* 🍽 *Breakfast.*

★ $$$$ **Fodor'sChoice 🏨 Finca Lérida.** *Hotel.* This working coffee farm on the eastern slope of Volcán Barú above Boquete has almost 150 acres of bird-replete cloud forest, and birders and naturalists make up the bulk of the clientele here. **Pros:** gorgeous views of the cloud forest; guided bird-watching and coffee tours; elegant decor. **Cons:** fireplaces tend to smoke up rooms; remote; expensive restaurant. [$] *Rooms from: $225* ✉ *Via Boquete* ✥ *7 km (4 miles) northwest* *of town, turn left at second Y, entrance on left, Callejón Seco* ☎ *507/720–1111* 🌐 *www.fincalerida.com* 🛏 *7 suites, 4 standard, and 11 deluxe* 🍴 *Breakfast.*

$$ 🏨 **The Haven.** *Hotel.* With a focus on wellness, relaxation, pampering, and fitness, this tranquil hotel oozes feng shui from the water features at the entrance to the garden terraces off each room. **Pros:** discounted spa treatments for hotel guests; peaceful setting; only wellness hotel in Boquete; great value. **Cons:** no restaurant; no children under 18; tiny pool; 15 minute walk from town. [$] *Rooms from: $129* ✉ *Av. A Oeste, Bajo Boquete* ☎ *507/730–9245, 507/6491–5568* 🌐 *www.boquetespa.com* 🛏 *7 rooms, 1 suite* 🍴 *Breakfast.*

$$ 🏨 **Hotel Isla Verde.** *Hotel.* Three minutes from the center of town, this garden property has six spacious "roundhouses" and seven enchanting suites. **Pros:** creative design; beautiful gardens; good location. **Cons:** minimal parking spaces; inconsistent water temperature in the showers; no screens on the windows. [$] *Rooms from: $110* ✉ *Calle 2 Sur Bajo Boquete* ⊕ *left at Delta Gas, two blocks up the hill on the right* ☎ *507/720–2533* 🌐 *www.islaverdepanama.com* 🛏 *13 rooms* 🍴 *No meals.*

★ **$$$** **Fodor'sChoice** 🏨 **Hotel Panamonte.** *Hotel.* Opened in 1914, the Panamonte was long Boquete's only tourist hotel, and a century later, this landmark historical inn is still doing things right. **Pros:** old-world charm; award-winning chef Charlie Collins; lovely gardens. **Cons:** some rooms are small; not all rooms have garden views; no spa or gym. [$] *Rooms from: $200* ✉ *Av. 11 de Abril* ⊕ *Right at first Y north of town, on left* ☎ *507/720–1324, 800/525–4800 in U.S.* 🌐 *www.panamonte.com* 🛏 *15 rooms, 6 suites, 1 house* 🍴 *No meals.*

$$ 🏨 **The Inn At Palo Alto.** *B&B/Inn.* Formerly Boquete Paradise Hotel, this small collection of two-story buildings changed hands in 2014 but still lures guests with its lush gardens, tall trees, and the rocky Río Palo Alto nearby. **Pros:** lush grounds; nice terraces; good breakfast. **Cons:** some rooms lack river views; 3 km (2 miles) from town. [$] *Rooms from: $105* ✉ *Av. Buenos Aires* ⊕ *Left at first Y, 2½ km (1½ miles) north of bridge, on left* ☎ *507/720–1563 cell* 🌐 *www.theinnatpaloalto.com* 🛏 *8 rooms, 3 suites* 🍴 *Breakfast.*

$$$ 🏨 **Los Establos Boutique Hotel.** *Hotel.* This small, Spanish-style inn with a stirring view of Volcán Barú started out as a horse stable, hence its name, and each room is named after a horse. **Pros:** volcano view from some rooms; nice decor; ample grounds; lovely lounge and porch. **Cons:** most standard rooms lack views; fairly expensive. [$] *Rooms from: $215* ✥ *2 km (1 mile) northeast of town, right at first Y north of town, left after bridge, then first right* ☎ *888/481–0656 in U.S.* 🌐 *www.losestablos.net* 🛏 *5 rooms, 2 suites, 5 cottages* 🍴 *Breakfast.*

$$ 🏨 **The Riverside Inn.** *B&B/Inn.* This large white house with six luxurious suites, cozy lounge, and stone fireplace seems to come right out of New England. **Pros:** luxurious rooms; lovely lounge; nice riverside location; great restaurant. **Cons:** grounds a bit barren; basic breakfast. [$] *Rooms from: $150* ✥ *Right at first Y north of town, left after bridge, then 1½ km (1 mile) on the left* ☎ *507/720–1076* 🌐 *www.riversideinnboquete.com* 🛏 *5 rooms, 1 master suite* 🍴 *Breakfast.*

$$ 🏨 **Tinamou Cottage.** *B&B/Inn.* Although lacking the amenities of a full-service hotel, each cottage is privately situated in a dense forest where monkeys, sloths, and plenty of birds can be found. **Pros:** jungle setting; knowledgeable managers; good beds; organized tours. **Cons:** no restaurant; one-hour walk from town; low water pressure; no kids under 8. [$] *Rooms from: $125* ✥ *Near the school, 300 meters up the road on the right* ☎ *507/720–3852* 🌐 *www.coffeeadventures.net* 🛏 *1 studio cottage, 2 2-bedroom cottages* 🍴 *Breakfast.*

$$$$ 🏨 **Valle Escondido.** *Resort.* The main attractions of this lavish resort are its 9-hole golf course and luxury spa. **Pros:** good food; reasonably priced spa treatments; excellent amenities. **Cons:** gaudy decor; slow service in restaurant; only two rooms have AC. [$] *Rooms from: $280* ✉ *Calle Costarica, just beyond Valle Del Rio Inn, entrance through private gate* ☎ *507/720–2454* 🌐 *www.veresort.com* 🛏 *36 rooms, 2 suites* 🍴 *Breakfast.*

NIGHTLIFE

Hotel Panamonte. A pleasant place for a quiet cocktail is the bar in the Panamonte, which has a terrace hemmed by gardens, a big fireplace, and lots of couches and cane chairs. ✥ *Right at first Y north of town, on left* ☎ *507/720–1324* 🌐 *www.panamonte.com.*

SHOPPING

Casa Colonial. On the road to Alto Boquete, Casa Colonial sells pottery, ceramics, furniture, and accessories, most of which are imported from Mexico and India. ✉ *Calle Principal* ✥ *main road entering Alto Boquete, on left* ☎ *507/720–3271, 507/6832–5550 cell.*

SPORTS AND THE OUTDOORS

BIRD-WATCHING

Boquete is a bird-watcher's heaven, and its avian diversity tops 400 species during the dry season. The mountain forests shelter emerald toucanets, collared redstarts, sulfur-winged parakeets, a dozen hummingbird species, and the resplendent quetzal. Even the gardens of homes and hotels offer decent birding; they're the best places to see migrant birds wintering in Boquete, from the Tennessee warbler to the Baltimore oriole. The less accessible upper slopes of Volcán Barú are home to rare species like the volcano junco and volcano hummingbird.

One of the best places to see the quetzal and other cloud-forest birds is **Finca Lérida.** Another good place to see quetzal is along the **Bajo Mono Road,** just up the road from Finca Lérida.

Even experienced birders should hire a local guide, at least for the first day.

Hans and Terry van der Vooren. Hans and Terry van der Vooren, who run coffee tours at the Kotowa Estate, also offer half- to full-day bird-watching and hiking tours. ☎ *507/720–3852* ⊕ *www.coffeeadventures.net* ☜ *From $65.*

Santiago (Chago) Caballero. Boquete's best birding guide is scaling back his excursions a bit these days, but a trip with "Chago," as everyone knows him, is sure to check off new birds on your life list. His son, César A. Caballero Quiel, is equally talented as the resident birding guide at Finca Lérida. ☎ *507/6626–2200 Chago, 507/6581–2416 César* ☜ *From $60.*

HIKING

Boquete is a great place for hiking, with countless farm roads and footpaths in and around the valley.

Boquete Tree Trek. Boquete Tree Trek has a four-hour hike to see waterfalls and wildlife in its private reserve. ⊠ *Plaza Los Establos, Av. Central* ☎ *507/720–1635* ⊕ *www.boquete-treetrek.com* ☜ *$30.*

Feliciano González. Feliciano González has been guiding hikers through Boquete's mountains for two decades. In addition to tours of the Sendero Los Quetzales and to Volcán Barú's summit, he leads a six-hour hike through primary forest on the Sendero El Pianista. ☎ *507/6624–9940* ☜ *$35–$80 per person.*

HORSEBACK RIDING

Some excellent horseback-riding routes in the mountains around Boquete include panoramic views and exposure to abundant birdlife.

Boquete Tours. Eduardo Cano at Boquete Tours can arrange inexpensive horseback tours, as well as guided hikes down the Sendero Los Quetzales or a Volcán Barú ascent. ☎ *507/720–1750* ✑ *$15 per hour.*

WHITE-WATER RAFTING

Chiriquí has Panama's best white-water rafting, with many rivers to choose from during the rainy season (June to November). ■TIP➜ **Only one river—Río Chiriquí Viejo—is navigable during the December to May dry season.**

The **Río Chiriquí Viejo** is considered Panama's best whitewater river. Of its two rafting routes, the harder is the Class III–IV Palón section, which requires previous experience and can become too dangerous to navigate during the rainiest months. The easier, Class II–III Sabo section is good for beginners. Chiriquí Viejo is a 90-minute drive from Boquete each way, which makes for a long day. Unfortunately, it's threatened by government plans to dam it for a hydroelectric project. The **Río Estí** is a Class II–III river fit for beginners that is closer to Boquete and doubles as a good wildlife-watching trip. The **Río Chiriquí** is a fun Class III river with one Class IV rapids; it's a 90-minute drive from Boquete and appropriate for beginners. The **Río Gariche** and **Río Dolega** are Class II–III rivers nearer Boquete and suitable for beginners.

Boquete Outdoor Adventures. Boquete Outdoor Adventures offers multisport trips that combine rafting, kayaking, island tours, hiking, and tree trekking. They also have horseback riding, coffee tours, bird-watching, and whale watching near Boca Chica. ✉ *Plaza Los Establos, Av. Central* ☎ *507/720–2284* ⊕ *www.boqueteoutdooradventures. com* ✑ *From $35.*

Chiriquí River Rafting. Chiriquí River Rafting makes safety and eco-friendliness a priority. The company offers trips on all area rivers including the popular Río Chiriquí Viejo. They also offer rafting trips on Rio Grande near the City of Penonome. This river, 2½ hours from Panama City, is excellent for beginnners and families with small children. ✉ *Finca El Bajareque in Palmira* ✦ *12 minutes from Boquete* ☎ *507/6879–4382* ⊕ *www.panama-rafting.com* ✑ *From $65.*

CANOPY TOURS

Boquete Tree Trek. A canopy tour involves gliding along zip-line cables (to which you're attached via a harness), strung between platforms in the high branches of tropical trees. It gives both the sensation of flying through the treetops and a bird's-eye view of the cloud forest. Boquete Tree Trek has trained guides that provide instruction and accompany groups through the tour, which lasts about four hours. Prohibited from the tours are children under six and those weighing more than 250 pounds. ⊠ *Office, Plaza Los Establos, Av. Central* ☎ *507/720–1635* ⊕ *www. boquetetreektrek.com* ✆ *$65* ☉ *Tours depart office at 8 am, 10:30 am, and 1 pm.*

4

PARQUE NACIONAL VOLCÁN BARÚ

Towering 11,450 feet above sea level, Barú Volcano is literally Chiriquí's biggest attraction, and Panama's highest peak. The massive dormant volcano is visible from David and is the predominant landmark in Boquete and Volcán, but Bambito and Cerro Punta are tucked so tightly into its slopes that you can hardly see it from there. The upper slopes, summit, and northern side of the volcano are protected within Barú Volcano National Park, which covers some 35,000 acres and extends northward to connect with the larger Parque Internacional La Amistad, shared by Panama and Costa Rica.

GETTING HERE AND AROUND

You can drive to the park's entrances in a 4WD vehicle or hire a 4WD taxi to drop you off and pick you up.

For information about hiking in Parque Nacional Volcán Barú, see Hiking in Boquete, above.

EXPLORING

Parque Nacional Volcán Barú. The vast expanse of Volcán Barú's protected wilderness is home to everything from cougars to howler monkeys and more than 250 bird species. You might see white hawks, black guans, violet sabrewings, sulphur-winged parakeets, resplendent quetzals, and rare three-wattled bellbirds in the park's cloud forests. The craggy summit is topped by radio towers and a cement bunker, and unfortunately many of its boulders are covered with graffiti.

The most popular way to take in the park is the **Sendero Los Quetzales**, which has excellent bird-watching and is most easily done starting out in Cerro Punta. Several other trails penetrate the park's wilderness, including two trails to the summit. The main road to the summit begins in Boquete, across from the church, and is paved for the first 7 km (4 miles), where it passes a series of homes and farms and then becomes increasingly rough and rocky. You pay the park fee at the ANAM ranger station 15 km (9 miles) from town, which takes about 90 minutes to reach in a 4WD vehicle. Park your vehicle at the station, because the road above it can only be ascended in trucks with super-high suspension. From here it's a steep 14-km (8½-mile) hike to the summit. The other trail to the summit begins 7 km (4 miles) north of Volcán and ascends the volcano's more deforested western slope, a grueling trek only recommended for serious athletes. ☎ *507/775–3164, 507/720–3057* ⌦ *$5* ⊙ *Daily 8–3.*

VOLCÁN

60 km (36 miles) northwest of David, 16 km (10 miles) south of Cerro Punta.

A breezy little town, Volcán has the best view of Volcán Barú, several miles northeast. The town is a dreary succession of restaurants, banks, and other businesses spread along a north–south route.

Bambito and Cerro Punta are more attractive and have the area's best hotels, so there is little reason to stay in Volcán except that it's much warmer than Cerro Punta, which can get cool at night between December and March. It is also a convenient jumping-off point for summiting Barú Volcano via the southern route or bird-watching at Finca Hartmann.

GETTING HERE AND AROUND
Because Volcán's attractions are so spread out, it's best to drive there. From David, head west 22 km (14 miles) on the CA1 to Concepción, where you turn right and drive north 33 km (21 miles) through the mountains to Volcán. Buses depart from David's terminal for Volcán ($3) every 30 minutes during the day.

EXPLORING
Janson Coffee Farm. This large coffee farm near the Lagunas de Volcán gives a tour of the farming and processing of their high-quality beans that ends with a tasting. Do the tour during the December to March harvest. They also offer bird-watching and horseback-riding tours of the farm and nearby

lakes. The coffee shop serving homemade brownies and warm drinks is a great place to relax and soak in the view. *⊕pass turnoff for Cerra Punta, straight at police station, 1 km (½ mile) on left, follow signs 3 km (2 miles) down dirt road to farm ☎507/6867–3884 🌐www.lagunasadventures.com 🎫Coffee tour $25 ⏲Mon.–Sat. 8–5.*

WHERE TO EAT

$ 🍴**Burricos.** *Mexican.* This Mexican grill might seem out of place in Volcán, but it's a favorite among locals with its authentic street tacos piled high with battered fish, chorizo, and chicken. Rice, beans, slaw, and salsas come with main entrées, or you can opt for lunch classics like hamburgers or panini. The Michoacán-born Chef Jamie Ortega delivers traditional Mexican dishes of sopa de tortilla, enchiladas, mole, and chiles rellenos. Start with a sweet mango margarita and end with tasty tres leches. The colorful wooden tables and walls displaying ponchos and sombreros might make you forget where you're traveling. *[$] Average main: $5 ✉Via Volcán, next to Hotel Don Tavo ☎507/771–4325 ⏲Closed Mon. No dinner Sun. 💳No credit cards.*

4

WHERE TO STAY

$ 🏨**Hotel Dos Ríos.** *Hotel.* Build in 1975, the Dos Ríos is an original two-story wooden building fronted by a newer cabin-like lobby. **Pros:** best in central town; good views; beautiful garden pathways. **Cons:** patchy Wi-Fi; bottom-level rooms dark and basic. *[$] Rooms from: $80 ✉Road to Río Sereno ⊕2½ km (1½ miles) north of turnoff for Bambito ☎507/771–5555 🌐www.dosrios.com.pa 🛏17 rooms, 3 bungalows 🍴Breakfast.*

★ FodorsChoice 🏨**Mount Totumas Cloud Forest.** *Hotel.* Roughly
$$ 20 km (12 miles) outside of Volcán on a bumpy road, this majestic preserve at the foot of Mount Totumas is well worth the trek. **Pros:** self-sustaining property; bird-watcher's paradise; nearby hot springs; cabin discounted for couples. **Cons:** only accessible by four wheel drive vehicle; can get very windy, breakfast only included in lodge rate. *[$] Rooms from: $115 ✉Los Pozos, Volcán ⊕From Banco Nacional in Volcan, take paved road to Río Sereno for 9.8 km (6 miles). Turn right at dirt road to Los Pozos Termales. Continue 9½ km (6 miles) to Mount Totumas ☎507/ 6963–5069 🌐www.mounttotumas.com ⏲Usually closed in Oct. or Nov. 🛏8 rooms, 1 cabin 🍴Breakfast.*

BAMBITO

7 km (4 miles) north of Volcán, 8 km (4½ miles) south of Cerro Punta.

Rather than a town, Bambito is a series of farms and houses scattered along the serpentine Río Chiriquí Viejo valley on the western slope of Volcán Barú, between Volcán and Cerro Punta. Because the people who live in the valley do their shopping in nearby Volcán, it has almost no stores or other businesses—just a few hotels—so it lacks the kinds of architectural eyesores that dominate most Panamanian towns.

The valley's scenery grows more impressive with each hairpin turn. Even if your destination is Cerro Punta, make a few stops to admire the suspension bridges spanning the boulder-strewn river, lush forest clinging to hillsides, wildflowers, and neat wooden farmhouses. Small farms line the road, and several roadside stands sell vegetables, fruit, and preserves—strawberries *(fresas)* are everybody's favorite here—and fresh fruit *batidos* (smoothies).

GETTING HERE AND AROUND

Turn right at the main intersection in Volcán to reach Bambito. Hotels and restaurants are scattered along the road once it enters the valley. Buses head up and down the valley every 30 minutes and will pick you up and drop you off anywhere.

WHERE TO STAY

★ **Fodor's Choice** 🏨 **Casa Grande Bambito.** *Hotel.* The setting here is
$$$ idyllic: massive trees shade the wooden buildings and lawns,
FAMILY the Río Chiriquí Viejo is a stone's toss away, and everything is surrounded by dense forest. **Pros:** surrounded by nature; plenty of activities; children's play area. **Cons:** poor in-room lighting; weak Wi-Fi signal; often full on weekends. [$] *Rooms from: $215* ✉ *Road to Cerro Punta* ✥ *on left after Hotel Bambito* ☎ *507/771–5126, 786/228–8428 in U.S.* 🌐 *www.casagrandebambito.com* 🛏 *10 rooms, 10 suites.*

$$ 🏨 **Hotel Bambito.** *Hotel.* This alpine-style resort overlooks
FAMILY sheer rock faces and lush slopes across a wide lawn with fountains. **Pros:** lovely setting; big rooms; covered pool; good restaurant. **Cons:** dated decor; some rooms face the busy road. [$] *Rooms from: $149* ✉ *Rte. 418* ✥ *Road to Cerro Punta on right, beginning of valley* ☎ *507/771–4265* 🌐 *www.hotelbambito.com* 🛏 *39 rooms, 6 suites* 🍴 *Breakfast.*

CERRO PUNTA

75 km (45 miles) northwest of David, 15 km (9 miles) north of Volcán.

This bowl-shaped highland valley northwest of Volcán Barú offers some splendid bucolic scenery and is bordered by vast expanses of wilderness that invite bird-watchers, hikers, and nature lovers. A patchwork of vegetable farms covers the valley floor and clings to the steep slopes that surround it, and ridges are topped with dark cloud forest and rocky crags. On the eastern side of the valley, a steep slope rises up into a wedge of granite for which the area was named—*cerro punta* means "pointed hill." That eastern ridge, part of the country's Continental Divide, is often enveloped in clouds pushed there by the trade winds.

The results are frequent, fleeting rain showers that keep the valley green year-round and produce an inordinate number of rainbows.

Cerro Punta is the highest inhabited area in Panama, nearly 6,000 feet above sea level. It can get chilly when the sun goes down or behind the clouds, though it is usually warm enough for shorts and T-shirts by day. From December to March the temperature sometimes drops down to almost 4°C (40°F) at night, so bring warm clothes and a waterproof jacket, as well as sturdy boots for the slippery mountain trails. The sun is intense, so use sunblock or wear a hat when you aren't in the woods.

GETTING HERE AND AROUND

Reach Cerro Punta by turning right at Volcán's main intersection. Buses come and go every 30 minutes and will let you on and off anywhere.

EXPLORING

Finca Drácula. Interested in orchids? Finca Drácula holds one of Latin America's largest collections. The farm's name is taken from a local orchid, which has a dark red flower. The main focus here is reproducing orchids for export, but workers also give 45-minute tours, though in limited English and by prior appointment only. The farm has 2,200 orchid species from Panama and around the world, as well as a laboratory where plants are reproduced using micropropagation methods. The best time to visit is between March and May, when flowers are in bloom. If you don't have a 4WD vehicle, walk 20 minutes from Guadalupe to get here. ⊠ *Road to Los Quetzales reserve ✦ 1 km (½ mile)* *east of Guadalupe ☎ 507/771–2070 🌐 www.fincadracula.com 🎟 $10 ⏲ Daily 8–11:30 and 1–4; tours by reservation only.*

Sendero Los Quetzales. The most popular hike in Cerro Punta is the Sendero Los Quetzales, a footpath through Parque Nacional Volcán Barú that ends in the mountains above Boquete (you can hike it in reverse, but it's entirely uphill). The trail begins at the ANAM station in El Respingo, east of town, where you pay the $5 park admission fee. From there it's a 9-km (5-mile) downhill hike to Alto Chiquero, a short drive from Boquete. The trail winds through the cloud forest and follows the Río Caldera, crossing it several times en route. You might see quetzals, emerald toucanets, collared redstarts, coatis, and other wildlife on the hike, which takes most people three to four hours. Because the trail is not well marked, hire a guide or join an organized tour; the area's bird-watching guides regularly use the trail. Pack a lunch, lots of water, and rain gear, and wear sturdy waterproof boots. The best option is to have your bags transferred to a Boquete hotel and end there for the night. Hire a taxi in Cerro Punta to drop you off at El Respingo, which should cost $35, and arrange for a Boquete taxi to pick you up in Alto Chiquero. Otherwise, walk 90 minutes from the end of the trail through farmland to Bajo Mono, where you can catch public transportation to Boquete.

WHERE TO STAY

$$ 🏨 **Cielito Sur.** *B&B/Inn.* The best thing about this B&B is the service provided by its owner. **Pros:** great breakfasts; helpful owners; nice rooms. **Cons:** no restaurant; no children under 14; two-night minimum stay Nov.–May. [$] *Rooms from: $115* ✉ *Nueva Suiza, between Cerro Punta and Volcán* ⊕ *4 km (2½ miles) south of Cerro Punta center* ☎ *507/771–2038* 🌐 *www.cielitosur.com* ⏲ *Closed Oct.* 🛏 *5 rooms* 🍴 *Breakfast.*

$ 🏨 **Los Quetzales Lodge & Spa.** *Hotel.* You'll find accommoda-
FAMILY tions at this eco-lodge ranging from backpacker dorms and tents to two-bedroom suites and private cabins in the cloud forest. **Pros:** private forest reserve; good restaurant and lounge; lots of activities; green practices. **Cons:** need car to stay here; dorms and standard rooms are dark and cramped. [$] *Rooms from: $85* ✉ *Guadalupe* ☎ *507/771–2291* 🌐 *www.losquetzales.com* 🛏 *20 rooms, 9 cabins* 🍴 *Breakfast.*

SPORTS AND THE OUTDOORS

BIRD-WATCHING

The valley's feathered creatures are most easily spotted around its edges, especially near streams and along the trails that head into the nearby national parks. A good guide can significantly increase the number of species you see.

Ito Santamaría. Guadalupe resident Ito Santamaría is the area's top bird-watching guide and one of the few who speaks English. ⊠ *Cafe Ito ⊹ across from Los Quetzales Lodge* ☎ *507/6591–1621* ⊠ *From $90.*

HIKING

Between La Amistad and Volcán Barú national parks, there are enough trails around Cerro Punta to keep you hiking for several days. The area's bird-watching guides are familiar with all the local trails and are happy to guide hikers. Wherever you hike, be sure to pack plenty of water, sunscreen, a hat, and warm, waterproof clothing, even if it's sunny, since the temperature can plummet when a storm rolls in.

LAGO FORTUNA AND RESERVA FORESTAL FORTUNA

The road that connects the provinces of Chiriquí and Boas del Toro passes breathtaking views and a large hydroelectric reservoir called Lago Fortuna. The dense forests around Lago Fortuna hold a wealth of birdlife. Most people simply drive through this area or bypass it with a quick flight between Chiriquí and Boas del Toro, but if you take the time to explore its often misty landscapes, you'll be happy you strayed from the beaten path.

GETTING HERE AND AROUND

To drive from David, head east on the Interamericana 12 km (7½ miles) to Chiriquí, where you turn left and drive through Gualaca, then up the slopes toward Chiriquí Grande and Changuinola.

After Lago Fortuna, the road begins its descent to the Caribbean lowlands. Even if you visit the area as a day trip, it is worth beginning the descent toward the Caribbean for its exuberant scenery. Keep your eye out for a dirt road on the left marked by a sign that says "subestación"—it leads to an electrical tower with a great view of the Bocas del Toro Archipelago on a clear day.

If coming from Boquete, take the main road toward David and turn left before the sixth overpass. Follow the signs to

Boquete Canyon Village and head toward Caldera, staying left at the fork in the road. This scenic route is about 15 minutes longer than the right fork, but is worth the extra distance. There are several good stopping points including swimming holes at Rio Encantado and hot thermal baths beyond Caldera. Continue through the small village of Chiriquicito, and turn left at the David–Bocas highway. If turning right at the fork, head on the newly paved road toward Gualaca over a small dam and past Los Canguillones, a canyon river perfect for swimming. Continue past a baseball stadium and follow the signs to Reserva Forestal Fortuna.

WHERE TO STAY

$$ **El Refugio La Brisa Del Diablo.** *B&B/Inn.* This little stone B&B on the main road between Bocas and David looks like something out of a fairytale, with views stretching from the Pacific coast to Volcán Barú, often framed by cotton clouds and double rainbows. **Pros:** outstanding food; spectacular views; near natural attractions. **Cons:** usually closed part of low season; close to busy road; windy location. $ *Rooms from: $100* ✉ *Hornito, midway between David and Bocas, at edge of Reserva Forestal De Fortuna* ☎ *507/6852–3600, 507/6597–0296* ⏲ *Closed one month in low season, usually between June and July or Sept. and Oct.* 🛏 *2 bedrooms, 1 house* 🍴 *Breakfast* 💳 *No credit cards.*

$ **Finca La Suiza.** *B&B/Inn.* This simple, remote lodge is in a private reserve atop the Cordillera de Talamanca. **Pros:** quiet; close to nature; good hiking; great views. **Cons:** remote; few amenities; two-night minimum stay; can be cold and windy. $ *Rooms from: $58* ✥ *From Pan-American Highway intersection, take road to Chiriqui Grande/Bocas del Toro for 40.6 km (25 miles). Entrance is on right* ☎ *507/6736–4377, 507/6794–4462* 🌐 *www.fincalasuizapanama.com* 💳 *No credit cards* ⏲ *Closed Sept. and Oct.* 🛏 *3 rooms* 🍴 *No meals.*

BOCAS DEL TORO ARCHIPELAGO

Updated
by Marlise
Kast-Myers

WITH ITS TURQUOISE WATERS, SUGAR-SAND beaches, and funky island towns, the relatively isolated archipelago of Bocas del Toro has the same attractions as major Caribbean destinations with a fraction of the crowds, development, and price. An astounding variety of flora and fauna cover its six major islands, 52 cays, and 200 islets, with an overlay of a fascinating Afro-Caribbean and indigenous culture.

Bocas del Toro—the term means "mouths of the bull" and no one agrees on the origin of the name—refers to the archipelago itself, its entire province that encompasses northwest Panama, and its provincial capital. (Most visitors use the term in the last sense, but five minutes here, and you'll shorten it to "Bocas" as everyone else does.) The main center, commonly called "Bocas Town," offers an ample selection of affordable hotels and good restaurants. On any given morning dozens of boats depart from the port, carrying locals and visitors to nearby islands, beaches, reefs, and rain forests, making the town a good base from which to explore.

Whether you prefer diving, kayaking, surfing, hiking, bird-watching, partying, or swaying in a hammock cooled by an ocean breeze, the Bocas del Toro archipelago can keep you busy—or lazy—for days on end. The province incorporates a large piece of the Panamanian mainland, which is mostly covered with banana farms and a few farmworker towns. The Cordillera de Talamanca towers to the south of the archipelago and is covered with largely inaccessible wilderness, but if you travel by land between Bocas del Toro and Chiriquí, you can get a good look at its vast, unexplored jungle. Otherwise, you'll want to stick with the islands, which have plenty of sultry rain forest to complement their sand, sea, and sun.

The only caveat is that the archipelago's rain forests result from copious and frequent downpours, which have dampened more than a few vacations. Heavy showers are often over in a matter of hours, but an entire week of rain isn't out of the question some months of the year. Apart from March, September, and October, avoid booking your entire vacation here, since the likelihood of getting sunny days elsewhere in Panama is greater. But don't let the rain scare you away, because when it's sunny, Bocas del Toro is simply amazing.

TOP REASONS TO GO

Idyllic Islands. Jungle-hemmed beaches, peeling waves, secret surf spots, coconut palms growing in pale sand, emerald waters . . . the archipelago has the makings of tropical fantasies.

Funky Bocas Town. The offbeat, colorful town of Bocas offers a mix of historic architecture, mellow locals, good food, nightlife, and abundant views of the surrounding sea and islands.

Neptune's Gardens. The submarine wonders—from the sponge-studded reef beneath Hospital Point to the seemingly endless coral gardens of the Cayos Zapatillas—can keep you diving for days.

The Jungle. Though the sea and sand are the big attractions, the rain forests that cover much of the archipelago are home to hundreds of bird species as well as everything from howler monkeys to tiny poison dart frogs.

Caribbean Cultures. Bocas del Toro's cultural mix of Afro-Caribbean, Panamanian, and indigenous Ngöbe tradition adds layers to the islands' personality.

ORIENTATION AND PLANNING

GETTING ORIENTED

The Bocas del Toro Archipelago scatters across a shallow lowland gulf. Tourism centers on Bocas del Toro town, which occupies a spit of land on the southern tip of Isla Colón, the westernmost island. Many visitors arrive and depart from the tiny airport here. Water taxis and a ferry ply the waters between the town and the mainland port of Almirante, from which roads lead southeast to Chiriquí and the rest of Panama and west to banana farms and the Costa Rican border. East of Isla Colón lie several other islands with communities and isolated hotels—Islas Carenero and Bastimentos are the most popular and by day, private boats and water taxis travel regularly between the islands.

The Western Archipelago. The Western Archipelago is all about lazy days on the beach, cruising the coastline, wandering the streets, and coffees or cocktails at roadside bakeries or tin-roof shacks.

Isla Bastimentos. Cutting through the glassy waters, with Bocas Town in your wake, the "road" to Isla Bastimentos leads to picture-perfect beaches and mangrove tunnels where howler monkeys, exotic birds, and sea crabs clamber through the thick brush. Over-the-water bungalows and hillside cabanas are the perfect place to unplug, while shallow reefs beckon to an afternoon of snorkeling, surfing, or kayaking just offshore.

PLANNING

WHEN TO GO

The big drawback of Bocas del Toro is the rain. Rain sometimes falls for days on end any time of year. Statistically, March is the sunniest month. September and October are the next-driest months, and May and June tend to be nice as well. Waters are calm and ideal for snorkeling and diving from mid-August to October. Since May, June, and (especially) September and October are the rainiest months in the rest of Panama, Bocas del Toro is the place to be at those times. December is the wettest month, and July and August are right behind it, though it tends to be sunny about a third of the time. Despite this, December, July, and August are good months for surfing in the archipelago but the worst months for diving. In January and February the odds of enjoying sunny days are about fifty-fifty. Many of the outlying lodges and some restaurants close during May and June, the lowest of the low season.

PLANNING YOUR TIME

You're likely to discover that there isn't much to really "do" in Bocas del Toro since the majority of time is spent just "being." It might take a day or two to meld into the Caribbean pace, with your vacation checklist ranging from lounging on the beach to napping in a hammock. Reserve at least two days for Bocas Town on Isla Colón, overnighting at one of the colorful, laid-back hotels that line Calle 3. Get a sense of the island life (and layout) by biking north of the town center to one of the more appealing beaches like Boca del Drago, Swan's Cay, or Playa Bluff. It's worth heading across the channel to Isla Carenero for the daily catch with a side of fried plantains, before spending one night in an over-the-water bungalow for a bit of forced relaxation. For natural beauty and barefoot luxury, catch a water taxi to Isla Bastimentos and stay at least two nights at an isolated eco-lodge tucked in the jungle. Be sure to visit nearby Red Frog Beach and set aside time for an island adventure like snorkeling, kayaking, surfing, or diving.

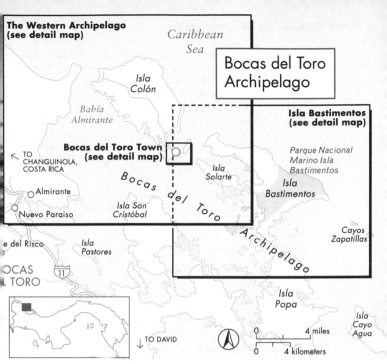

GETTING HERE AND AROUND

AIR TRAVEL

The Aeropuerto Internacional Bocas del Toro (BOC), the archipelago's tiny airport, is five blocks from the center of Bocas Town, at the west end of Avenida E. Domestic carrier Air Panama flies twice daily to and from Panama City. The flight takes 45 minutes and costs around $150. Costa Rican airline Nature Air flies four mornings weekly between Bocas and San José. You'll pay an international departure tax of $15, and an international arrival fee of $3. Note that flights from Panama City to Bocas depart from Marcus A. Gelabert Airport rather than Tocumen International Airport. A taxi ride between the two airports costs $30.

Carriers Air Panama. ☎ 507/316-9000 ⊕ www.airpanama.com.
Nature Air. ☎ 507/757-9391 in Panama, 800/235-9272 in U.S.
⊕ www.natureair.com.

BOAT AND FERRY TRAVEL

Boats are the most common means of transportation in Bocas del Toro, and the town of Bocas has several water-taxi companies and dozens of boatmen who provide transportation between Islas Colón, Carenero, and Bastimentos, as well as day tours. The water-taxi companies Bocas Marine Tours and Taxi 25 have trips every 30 minutes between Bocas and Almirante ($6), where you can catch a bus to David. It takes 25 minutes to reach Almirante, with departures every half-hour from 6 am to 6 pm. Most boat companies provide transport to Red Frog Beach and nearby islands, as do independent boatmen who depart from the dock next to the Farmacia Rosa Blanca, on Calle 3 in Bocas. The fare to Carenero is $1.50; to Old Bank, $2.

If you are heading to Isla Carenero or Bastimentos, it can be less expensive to do as the locals do and travel with boatmen who wait at the dock next to Farmacia Rosa Blanca. Most boat trips cost between $2 and $25, though the farthest lodges can be much more expensive to reach.

■TIP→ **A car is of little use here.** No in-town hotel has parking and although roads were paved in 2010, they are mostly used by taxis and a few locals with transportation. Bocas Town can easily be explored by foot or bike. A car ferry, run by Transbordadores Marinos, travels between Almirante and Bocas daily except Monday, departing from Almirante at 7 am and Bocas at 3 pm. The trip takes an hour and costs $25–$55, depending on the size of the vehicle.

Contacts Bocas Marine Tours. ⊠ *Calle 3, at Av. C, Bocas del Toro* ☎ *507/757–9033.* **Taxi 25.** ⊠ *Calle 1, at Av. Central, Bocas del Toro* ☎ *507/757–9028.* **Transbordadores Marinos** *(Ferry Baltija and Ferry Palanga).* ⊠ *Town port, Almirante* ☎ *507/391–1754, 507/391–0350* ⊕ *www.ferrybocas.com.*

BUS AND SHUTTLE TRAVEL

Transporte Boca del Drago has a shuttle van that travels the length of Isla Colón, from Bocas del Toro to Boca del Drago. It leaves from Parque Simón Bolívar every hour and will pick up passengers from hotels in Bocas Town upon request. The cost is $5 per person.

Bocas del Toro can be reached from Panama City by land and water. The direct bus from Panama City to Almirante (and vice versa) takes nine hours but is comfortable and costs $30. If you're in Chiriquí you can take a bus or taxi from David or Boquete to Almirante (3½ hours), where water taxis depart for Bocas every half-hour.

Contacts Almirante Bus. ☎ *507/774–0585.* **Transporte Boca del Drago.** ⊠ *Bocas del Toro* ☎ *507/6388–5455.*

TAXI TRAVEL

A private taxi from Bocas del Toro to Boca del Drago costs $38 round trip. Shared taxis run up and down Bocas's main streets, charging $2 for most short trips in town. Boquete-based taxi driver Daniel Higgins provides transportation between Boquete and Almirante for $150. Caribe Shuttle offers daily transportation between the Southern Caribbean coast of Costa Rica (Puerto Viejo/Manzanillo/Cahuita) and Bocas del Toro. The $36 rate includes hotel pickup and the 30-minute boat trip to Isla Colón.

Contacts Caribe Shuttle. ☏ 507/757–7048 ⊕ www.caribeshuttle. com. **Daniel Higgins.** ☏ 507/6617–0570.

HOTELS

Accommodations here range from traditional wooden buildings in town to rustic but enchanting bungalows nestled in the wilderness of Isla Bastimentos. All of them have private baths, and all but the eco-lodges have air-conditioning and Internet. Although Bocas del Toro town has an array of budget and moderately priced hotels, the out-of-town lodges tend toward the expensive, though hardly luxurious. Other advantages of staying in town are the local color and the selection of restaurants, shops, and nightlife. The downside is noise from neighbors and revelers, which is a problem at some in-town hotels. Lodges outside town provide more natural, tranquil settings. In Bocas, tap water is not potable and toilet paper must be disposed of in wastebaskets rather than flushed. Expect the occasional power outage, weak Wi-Fi signal, and water shortage certain times of the year. Despite ongoing efforts by hotel owners, a proper recycling system is not fully in place, meaning mixed garbage is taken to a nearby landfill. Sadly, litter is a problem, especially on the outskirts of town.

Hotel reviews have been shortened, for full information visit Fodors.com.

RESTAURANTS

The town of Bocas has an ample restaurant selection, with such surprising options as Thai and Indian cuisine to complement the traditional seafood. Dining is casual and the pace is slow, so be patient for your meal. Local specialties include lobster, whole-fried snapper, octopus, and shrimp served with *patacones* (fried plantain slices) or *yuca frita* (fried cassava strips). At restaurants, opt for bottled water over a glass with ice because tap water is usually unsafe to drink. Almost no restaurant here accepts credit cards.

Although tipping is not obligatory in Bocas, it is greatly appreciated by the locals.

	WHAT IT COSTS IN U.S. DOLLARS			
	$	$$	$$$	$$$$
Restaurants	under $10	$10–$15	$16–$20	over $20
Hotels	under $100	$100–$160	$161–$220	over $220

Restaurant prices are per person for a main course at dinner. Hotel prices are for two people in a standard double room, excluding service and 10% tax.

ESSENTIALS

EMERGENCIES

Although slated for major improvements in coming years, for now the hospital in Bocas is good only for minor matters. Serious medical problems should be treated in Panama City or David.

Emergency Services Fire. ⊠ *Bocas del Toro* ☎ *911 in Bocas del Toro.* **Police.** ⊠ *Bocas del Toro* ☎ *911 in Bocas del Toro.*

MONEY MATTERS

There are two ATMs at the Banco Nacional de Panama. They give cash withdrawals from Visa and MasterCard and from Cirrus- and Plus-affiliated debit and credit cards.

SAFETY

Bocas is a safe town, but it has acquired a few sidewalk hustlers and drug dealers in recent years, so don't wander its side streets late at night. It's very common to hear a local mumble "weed weed" under their breath as they pass you on the street, a discreet attempt to sell marijuana. The main dangers in the archipelago, however, are sunburn and bug bites. Take a hat, sunscreen, and insect repellent. Drowning is also a real danger, and there are no lifeguards. Don't swim at the beaches if the waves are big, unless you are an experienced surfer, and don't let a boatman take you into rough water in a dugout canoe. No matter where you're staying, don't drink the tap water.

THE WESTERN ARCHIPELAGO

The westernmost island in the archipelago, Isla Colón, is also the most developed, with a road running across it and the provincial capital occupying a peninsula on its southern tip. Across a channel from that urbanized headland is the

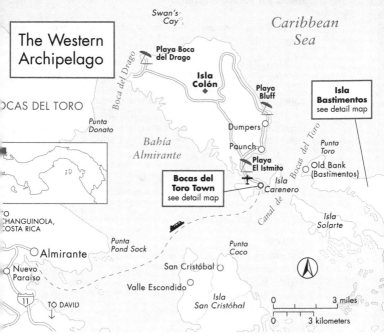

Isla Bastimentos
see detail map

Bocas del Toro Town
see detail map

smaller Isla Carenero. Boats regularly travel between the two communities that are home to the bulk of the archipelago's residents and most of its hotels and restaurants. Most travelers stay in Bocas del Toro town and make day trips to the other islands, beaches, and dive spots.

BOCAS DEL TORO

550 km (341 miles) and one hour by air northwest of Panama City, 170 km (105 miles) north of David.

The town of Bocas del Toro, which the locals simply call Bocas, sits on a little headland connected to the island's primary landmass by a narrow isthmus and is a neat grid packed with homes, businesses, and government offices. The town is surrounded by water on three sides, which gives it plenty of ocean views. The nearest beach, on the isthmus that connects it to Isla Colón, is not the island's best. The town itself holds few sights, but is a laid-back town with wide streets, weathered Caribbean architecture, and plentiful greenery. To play in the surf and sand, you either have to boat to Isla Bastimentos or take a bike, taxi, bus, or boat to one of the beaches on Isla Colón. An abundance of boatmen, dive shops, and tour operators are eager to show you paradise.

Most of Bocas's restaurants and other businesses are on or near Calle 3, its main drag sometimes called Calle Principal. This wide, north–south track stretches from one end of town to the other (seven blocks) and runs along the sea for its southern half. Boats to the mainland and other islands depart from docks along that stretch, as do tours bound for fun in the sun, while people from the other islands arrive here to shop and run errands.

GETTING HERE AND AROUND

All arrivals from elsewhere in Panama and internationally from Costa Rica put you here in Bocas Town. *(See Getting Here and Around above.)*

TOURS

Panama Excursions. Catering predominately to cruise ship passengers, Panama Excursions offers custom tours and eight-day trips highlighting the best of Panama City and Bocas del Toro. ⊠ *Bocas del Toro* ☎ *507/6265–2603* ⊕ *www. rainforestadventure.com* 🖾 *From $984.*

Panama Trails. Panama Trails organizes local flights, tailor-made itineraries, car rentals, and tours to Bocas del Toro from Panama City. ⊠ *Panama City* ☎ *507/393–8334 in Panama City, 877/290–2454 in U.S. and Canada* ⊕ *www. panamatrails.com.*

Total Adventure Inc. Bocas del Toro is a perfect town for biking, which is a good way to get to Bluff Beach. In the center of Bocas Town, Total Adventure has the best beach cruisers and mountain bikes on the island, with hourly rates ranging from $2 to $5 or $10 to $20 per day. ⊠ *Calle 3A* ✛ *Near corner of Calle 1* ☎ *507/6585–1306.*

VISITOR INFORMATION

Autoridad de Tourismo Panama (*ATP*). The local office of the Panamanian Tourism Authority, housed in a large Caribbean-style building on the water, can supply you with all the standard info about Bocas and Panama. ⊠ *Calle 1* ✛ *next to Policía Nacional* ☎ *507/757–9642* ⊕ *www.visitpanama. com* ☉ *Daily 9:30–3:30.*

Bocas del Toro Town

Avenida Norte (Avenida I) ③

Avenida H ④ ⑤

Caribbean Sea

Avenida G

Avenida F ⑥

Calle 6　Calle 5　Calle 4　Calle 3　Calle 2　Calle 1

Avenida E ⑦　❶ **Palacio Municipal** ⑧

Boat Taxi

Autoridad de Tourismo Panama (ATP) ⑨

KEY
- ❶ *Exploring Sights*
- ① *Hotels & Restaurants*

Avenida D

Avenida C ⑩ ⑪

Avenida B

⑫ **Avenida A** ⑮ ⑯ ⑭

0 — 100 yards
0 — 100 meters

⑬ **Avenida Sur**

Ferry Terminal
→ TO ALMIRANTE

① ② ❷ ③

EXPLORING

TOP ATTRACTIONS

Finca Los Monos Botanical Garden. Finca Los Monos Botanical Garden has a large collection of heliconia, ginger, palm, and fruit trees in a rain forest setting with plenty of wildlife. In addition to the standard tours offered twice a week, bird-watching tours at 6:30 am and 4:30 pm can be arranged with prior reservation. ⊠ *Idaan Hill ✧ just past the Smithsonian Institute* ☎ *507/757–9461, 507/6729–9943* ⊕ *www.bocasdeltorobotanicalgarden.com* 🖃 *$10* ☉ *Tours Mon. at 1 and Fri. at 8:30 or by appointment.*

WORTH NOTING

Parque Simón Bolívar. The town's central park site near the north end of Calle 3 is shaded by mango trees and royal palms. Children play here, and locals chat on its cement benches in the evening. North of the park stands the **Palacio Municipal,** a large cement building that houses various government offices. ⊠ *Calle 3, at Av. Central.*

BEACHES

Playa Istmito. Referred to by several names including Playa Bocas, Playa La Cabaña, and Bahia Sand Fly, this beach is the closest one to Bocas Town. It stretches along the narrow isthmus that connects the town to Isla Colón, overlooking tranquil Bahia Chitre (Sand Flea Bay). Just north of the beach is Playa Tortuga Hotel. Due to the proximity to town, this stretch of sand is popular with locals that come for an afternoon swim or cheap beers at nearby food shacks. Biting sand fleas, the sound of passing cars, occasional litter, and dark sand make this a mediocre beach, but it will do in a pinch. If you have the time and energy, rent a bike and make the *rough* 40-minute ride out to Bluff Beach (4 km [2½ miles] north of Bocas Town, on Isla Colón), which is gorgeous. **Amenities:** food and drink. **Best for:** walking; swimming. ⊠ *Av. Norte ✧ 1 km (½ mile) northwest of Calle 3.*

WHERE TO EAT

★ Fodor's Choice × **El Ultimo Refugio.** *Eclectic.* For a break from
$$$ plantains and battered fish, this darling tin-roof restaurant with live music and a menu based on the freshest-of-the-fresh, is truly the "ultimate refuge" from the typical Bocas culinary scene. Strings of bulbs dangle above wooden tables on wide-plank floors perched over the water. Vegetables are refreshing and vibrant, and salsas are sweet and tangy atop mahimahi and tuna tartare served with homemade chips. The beetroot salad with blue cheese is excellent, as are

mains like octopus on white bean puree or creamy shrimp risotto with sun-dried tomatoes and fried pumpkin seeds. The chef caters to vegans with flavorful yellow curry on coconut jasmine rice. The peanut butter Snickers pie has been known to make repeat customers out of those only in town for a week. [$] *Average main: 16* ✉ *Calle 6a* ⊕ *100 meters after ferry dock, near Casa Verde* ☎ *507/6726–9851* 🌐 *www.ultimorefugio.com* ⏲ *Closed weekends. No lunch. Usually closed Sept. or Oct.* 💳 *No credit cards.*

$$ ✕ **Gringo's.** *Mexican.* "Dive," "hole in the wall," "joint," . . . Bocas's expat community has various terms of endearment for this Mexican restaurant a block west of the central park. All agree that the fresh margaritas and Mexican food here are top-notch. The homemade salsas crafted with roasted onion, tomato, and pepper dress up the enchiladas, burritos, and taco salads. Dine inside the small restaurant itself—Mexican music videos are usually playing—or outdoors on the more spacious covered patio. [$] *Average main: $10* ✉ *Av. E at Calle 4* ☎ *507/6902–4759* 💳 *No credit cards* ⏲ *Closed Sun.*

5

★ $$$$ **Fodor's Choice** ✕ **Guari-Guari.** *Mediterranean.* Wooden tables, plastic chairs, and a tin roof hardly do justice to the spectacular six-course, prix-fixe dinner served here. A great deal of effort (and love) goes into each dish, prepared by Spanish chef Monica, who abandoned her law profession to be with German engineer "Ossi" (who serves as the restaurant's charming waiter). Together they have managed to break the barriers of Bocas's typical fare with a tasting menu that includes tuna carpaccio, spinach salad, and pork tenderloin with roasted potatoes and blue cheese sauce. Adding to the experience is the sound of crashing waves near the open-air restaurant. The menu changes daily, and special vegetarian courses can be provided upon request. Since the restaurant is surrounded by lush vegetation, mosquito coils are lit beside each table to keep the bugs away. [$] *Average main: $23* ✉ *Bocas del Toro* ⊕ *2 km (1 mile) outside Bocas Town, between La Bomba gas station and the Smithsonian* ☎ *507/6627–1825* 💳 *No credit cards* ⏲ *Closed Tues. and Wed.* ✍ *Reservations essential.*

$$ ✕ **La Casbah.** *Eclectic.* It would be an understatement to say that this tiny roadside eatery doesn't look like much. With digs like these, you have to stay on top of your kitchen to compete with restaurants on the water, and the Belgian chef does just that. His global menu hops from trout with slivered almonds to shrimp in a Sambuca cream sauce. Daily specials are a good bet, or you can stick with such local

favorites as pork loin in a Marsala wine sauce or fish of the day in a coconut sauce. The tapas and gazpacho are perfect for a lighter meal. From 8 am to 2 pm, this restaurant operates as Funfetti Bakery selling smoothies, pancakes, brownies, and other sweet treats. $ *Average main: $12* ✉ *Av. Norte, between Calles 3 and 4* ☎ *507/6477–4727* 💳 *No credit cards* ⏲ *Closed Sun. and Mon. No lunch.*

$$ 🍴 **Om Café.** *Indian.* You can get authentic Indian cuisine in Bocas del Toro at this cozy café atop a gift shop. Owner Sunanda Mehra is a Canadian of Punjabi descent who raided her aunt's cookbook before running off to Panama. You can savor such improbable delicacies as her butter chicken, shrimp masala, mattar paneer, or any of a half-dozen vegetable dishes. Choose your level of heat on the curry dishes, slowly cooked with a blend of colorful spices. You can also request to have any dish wrapped in a flour tortilla. Be sure to try a refreshing fruit *lassi,* prepared the traditional way with homemade yogurt, rosewater, sugar, and cardamom. $ *Average main: $10* ✉ *Calle 3, near Av. A* ✥ *across from La Iguana Bar* ☎ *507/6127–0671* 🌐 *www.omcafebocas.com* 💳 *No credit cards* ⏲ *Closed weekends and May–June 15. No lunch.*

$$ 🍴 **Raw Fusion.** *Sushi.* Is there any better name than "Raw" for a sushi restaurant? The Canadian owner prefers to refer to her restaurant's cuisine as Japanese fusion, and the menu here expands beyond classic sushi to include shrimp tempura and salad rolls. This lively place has become a favorite among Bocas's large expat community, but all are welcome, resident and visitor alike. Dine inside if your group counts more than two. The tables overlook the water. Smaller tables line a long pier jutting out into the bay. Raw does a brisk business each evening during its 4–6 pm happy hour. $ *Average main: $10* ✉ *Calle 3 at Av. C* ☎ *507/6938–8473* 🌐 *www.rawbocas.com* 💳 *No credit cards* ⏲ *Closed Mon. No lunch.*

$ 🍴 **Taco Surf Bocas.** *Mexican.* On the edge of Parque Central, this exalted taco stand is the go-to spot for surfers and travelers addicted to the Baja California cuisine prepared by San Diego natives Jeff and Justine Catalano. Fish burritos, carne asado nachos, and chicken tacos are piled high with organic goodness like guacamole, cilantro, cabbage, and salsas with a kick. Mains come with yummy sides of rice, beans, and chips, perfect to wash down with a ginger mint margarita or fruit smoothie mixed with green apple, banana, and spinach. Late risers can order breakfast burritos all day long, or cure hangovers with acai bowls made with maca powder, cacao nibs, and homemade granola. Broken short-boards line the walls of this cool garden setting, proving that even surfers have bad days. [$] *Average main: $7* ✉ *Mono Loco Surf School, 2nd St.* ✣ *behind the main park* ☎ *507/6951–5739* 🌐 *www.tacosurfbocas.com* ⏲ *Closed Wed., Thurs., and Sept.* 💳 *No credit cards.*

WHERE TO STAY

$ 🏨 **Bocas Inn.** *B&B/Inn.* This small lodge in an older wooden building over the water has a great location at the end of Calle 3 and is buffered from the street by a large garden, so it's relatively quiet. **Pros:** great views; organized tours; good breakfast. **Cons:** no TV; no Internet. [$] *Rooms from: $99* ✉ *Av. Norte at Calle 3* ☎ *507/757–9600, 507/269–9415 in Panama City* 🌐 *www.anconexpeditions.com* 🛏 *7 rooms* 🍴 *Breakfast.*

$ 🏨 **Gran Hotel Bahia.** *Hotel.* History abounds at the town's quaintest hotel, a two-story wooden building that was the headquarters of the United Fruit Company in the 1930s. **Pros:** good value; comfortable; historic building. **Cons:** off water; small windows; noise from neighboring disco. [$] *Rooms from: $80* ✉ *Calle 3 and Av. A* ☎ *507/757–9626* 🌐 *www.ghbahia.com* ⏲ *Closed June* 🛏 *18 rooms* 🍴 *Breakfast.*

★ $$ **Fodor's Choice** 🏨 **Hotel Bocas del Toro.** *Hotel.* This attractive waterfront hotel was designed by a boat builder, so it's no coincidence that guest rooms, with their polished hardwoods and nautical decor, look as if they could be on a yacht. **Pros:** on the water; superb staff; very clean rooms. **Cons:** ocean-view rooms are somewhat pricey for Bocas; occasional low water pressure. [$] *Rooms from: $129* ✉ *Calle 2, next to Hotel Limbo* ☎ *507/757–9771, 507/757–9018* 🌐 *www.hotelbocasdeltoro.com* 🛏 *10 rooms, 1 suite* 🍴 *Breakfast.*

$ 🏨 **Hotel Olas.** *Hotel.* Hidden at the south end of town, this large wooden hotel is one of the best deals in Bocas, comparable to more centrally located inns that charge twice as much. **Pros:** inexpensive; on the water; communal computer; quiet. **Cons:** rooms smallish; rooms pale in comparison to charming common areas. [$] *Rooms from: $50* ✉ *Av. Sur at Calle 6* ☎ *507/757–9930* 🌐 *www.hotelolas.com* 💳 *No credit cards* 🛏 *24 rooms* 🍴 *Breakfast.*

$ 🏨 **Hotel Palma Royale.** *Hotel.* At four stories, a veritable skyscraper for Bocas, this ocher hotel at the south end of town climbs in number of amenities as you climb the floors, and is the only hotel in town with an elevator. **Pros:** quiet; save money by cooking for yourself; only hotel in town with an elevator; attentive service. **Cons:** a few blocks removed from the center of action. [$] *Rooms from: $95* ✉ *Southern end of Calle 3* ☎ *507/757–9979* 🌐 *www.palmaroyale.com* 💳 *No credit cards* 🛏 *4 studios, 11 suites* 🍴 *Breakfast.*

$ 🏨 **Hotel Swan's Cay.** *Hotel.* This two-story wooden complex behind the Palacio Municipal fits into Bocas well enough, but inside the lobby feels like Old Europe with dark woods and a long staircase leading to second-story rooms. **Pros:** reasonable rates; pool by the sea. **Cons:** awkward step from bedroom to bathroom; some street noise; mediocre breakfast. [$] *Rooms from: $85* ✉ *Calle 3, between Avs. F and G* ☎ *507/757–9090, 507/757–9316* 🌐 *www.swanscayhotel.com* 🛏 *47 rooms, 2 suites* 🍴 *Breakfast.*
FAMILY

$ 🏨 **Lula's B&B.** *B&B/Inn.* Across the street from the water and a short walk from the center of town, this small B&B offers simple accommodations and a hearty breakfast. **Pros:** inexpensive; nice veranda; great breakfast. **Cons:** rooms pretty basic and small; not on water. [$] *Rooms from: $77* ✉ *Av. Norte, at Calle 6* ✣ *across from Bocas Surf School* ☎ *757–9057* 🌐 *www.lulabb.com* 🛏 *8 rooms* 🍴 *Breakfast.*

$$ 🏨 **Playa Tortuga Hotel & Beach Resort.** *Resort.* Everything, but everything is here at Bocas's largest, flashiest, resort-iest hotel. **Pros:** myriad activities; ocean views; good value for what is offered. **Cons:** not a good option if you crave solitude; outside of Bocas town. [$] *Rooms from: $125* ✉ *Bocas del Toro* ✣ *2 km (1 mile) north of town on road to Playa Bluff* ☎ *507/757–9050, 507/757–9044, 507/300–1893 in Panama City* 🌐 *www.hotelplayatortuga.com* 🛏 *74 rooms, 43 suites* 🍴 *Breakfast; Some meals.*
FAMILY

★ **Fodor's Choice** 🏨 **Tropical Suites.** *Hotel.* Completely remodeled in 2012, the spacious rooms here evoke fully furnished Florida condos, with their tropical colors, tile floors, ceiling fans, and sliding glass doors that open onto balconies (half have ocean views). **Pros:** decent value for offering; spacious rooms; great ocean views. **Cons:** questionably clean swimming area. [$] *Rooms from: $159* ✉ *South end of Calle 1* ☎ *507/757–9081, 507/757–9880* 🌐 *www.bocastropical.com* 🛏 *16 rooms, 3 suites* 🍴 *Breakfast.*
$$ FAMILY

NIGHTLIFE AND PERFORMING ARTS

Bocas livens up when the sun goes down, because the temperature becomes more conducive to movement. The decks of the town's various waterfront restaurants are pleasant spots to enjoy a quiet drink and conversation.

Barco Hundido. Barco Hundido is a funky, open-air affair with tropical gardens. Wooden platforms stretch over the water, surrounding a small shipwreck that's lit at night so you can watch the fish. It's an obligatory stop if you wish to partake of the rowdier side of Bocas. ⊠ *Calle 1, at Av. E* ☎ *507/6512–9032* ⊙ *Closed Tues.*

Bocas Bambu Beach. A large, semi-open-air bar and restaurant in the center of town projects surf videos on a big screen. You're sure to hear "No Woman, No Cry" and all the standards here. ⊠ *Calle 3, at Av. C* ☎ *507/757–9227* ⊙ *Daily 5:30–11 pm.*

★ **Fodor'sChoice Bocas Brewery.** As the only microbrewery in the province, this waterfront pub has exceptionally good beers on tap, ranging from mango-lime ale to a coconut porter. There's also greasy grub like pulled pork sandwiches, fish-and-chips, onion rings, and jalapeño cheeseburgers. Check their website for live music events. ⊠ *Las Cabanas Calle Carretera* ☎ *507/625–09037, 507/6347–5278* ⊕ *www.bocasbrewery.com* ⊙ *July–Apr., Mon.–Sat. noon–9.*

The Bookstore Bar (*Loco Dave's Bar*). Hear live music on a small stage, backed by a wall of books at this bookstore by day and bar by night. Beers run $2, cocktails $4. This local hotspot is marked by a sign reading, "Booze, Books, and Beyond." ⊠ *Av. E, at Calle 2* ☎ *507/6452–5905.*

La Iguana. In a wooden building over the water, this club gets packed with locals on Thursday nights when ladies drink free. Paper currency from around the world lines the walls of this lively spot, and there's a pizza bar for those wanting dinner between drinks. ⊠ *Calle 3, at Av. B* ☎ *507/757–9812* ⊙ *Closed Sat.*

SHOPPING

Although souvenir shops are limited in town, several Panamanian vendors sell arts and crafts at the north and south ends of Calle 3

Artisans Bri Bri. Artisans Bri Bri sells hammocks, clothing, and local handicrafts, such as the jute bags made by indigenous Ngöbe people. ⊠ *Calle 3, at Av. B* ☎ *507/757–9020* ⊙ *Daily 8–7.*

Island Traders. From handmade soaps and coconut oils to woven bags and jewelry, this small shop has locally made products created by Bocas artisans. ⊠ *Calle 1* ✛ *next to Taxi 25* ☎ *507/757–9543* ⊙ *Closed Sun.*

Mr. Mentawai. This upscale surf shop sells international brands including Volcom, Hurley, and Quicksilver. You'll find everything from sundresses and bikinis to bags and hats. They also have scooters for rent. ⊠ *Calle 3* ☎ *507/760–8102.*

Super Gourmet. Stop in at this boutique food market for a yummy selection of organic chocolate made on-site. A huge collection of kosher food items is also available. ⊠ *Calle 3 at Av. A* ☎ *507/757–9357* ⊕ *www.supergourmetbocas. com* ⊗ *Mon.–Sat. 9–7.*

SPORTS AND THE OUTDOORS

SCUBA DIVING AND SNORKELING

Bocas is primarily a base for exploring the wonders of the surrounding archipelago, the most impressive of which are the acres of colorful coral reefs. More than a dozen dive spots are within five minutes to one hour by boat from the town's several good dive centers. When booking day tours and charters, ask about the maximum passenger capacity to avoid overcrowding and accidents. Make sure the boat has a ladder, life jackets, and an English-speaking guide. Snorkeling excursions usually cost $30, depending on the destination and number of passengers, and depart at 8 or 9 am. You can guarantee a lower rate for everyone if you organize a small group. Two-tank boat dives cost $70–$150, depending on distance.

The Dutch Pirate Dive Center. This multilingual Dutch-owned outfitter offers inexpensive boat dives, snorkeling excursions, and PADI certification courses. ⊠ *Av. H, between Calles 3 and 4* ☎ *507/6567–1812* ⊠ *From $60.*

La Buga Dive & Surf. La Buga offers diving and snorkeling trips to outer reefs, ship wrecks, and Tiger Rock, as well as the complete slate of PADI courses. They also have surfboards for rent as well as lessons at nearby breaks. ⊠ *Calle 3* ⊹ *next to Farmacia Rosa Blanca* ☎ *507/757–9534, 507/678–10755* ⊕ *www.labugapanama.com* ⊠ *From $20.*

Starfleet Scuba. Starfleet Scuba offers various two-tank boat dives and snorkeling excursions, and has open-water certification courses for $250. ⊠ *Calle 1* ☎ *507/757–9630* ⊕ *www.starfleetscuba.com* ⊠ *From $225.*

SURFING

Bocas is a short boat ride from the breaks on Islas Colón, Carenero, and Bastimentos, which makes it a great base for surfers.

Mono Loco Surf. As Bocas's only surf school with certified lifeguards and instructors, Mono Loco Surf has surf lessons, board rental, and shuttle service to the best breaks. Classes are available in Spanish, English, French, Dutch, or German. ⊠ *Taco Surf Bocas, Calle 2* ✛ *next to Parque Simón Bolívar* ☎ *507/760–9877* ⊕ *www.monolocosurfschool.com* 🗐 *From $45.*

Tajada de Sandia. This surf shop is a good place to get advice, wax, or a handmade Tropix board. They also offer ding repair and have the best ATVs in Bocas. ⊠ *Calle 3* ✛ *across from Parque Simón Bolívar* ☎ *507/757–9415* ⊕ *www.tajadadesandia.com.*

ISLA COLÓN

2 km (1 mile) north of Bocas Town.

Once you're outside of Bocas Town, Isla Colón is a wild and beautiful place, with just two dirt roads, two lovely beaches, and significant swaths of tropical forest.

GETTING HERE AND AROUND

Avenida G leads north from Bocas Town over an isthmus to the rest of Isla Colón, where the road soon forks. Veer right for Playa Bluff and the surf breaks of Paunch and Dumpers, which can be reached in about 30 minutes on a very rough road by bicycle, or in an hour on foot. A taxi takes about 40 minutes, and costs $20. A boat to Paunch or Dumpers from Bocas Town should cost $10. Boca del Drago is accessible by boat, taxi, or minibus. On weekdays minibuses depart from Parque Bolívar for Boca del Drago at 6:45, 10, noon, 3, and 6, returning 40 minutes later. The trip costs $5. Taxis charge $38, but the boat trip is the same price, and includes Swan's Cay.

EXPLORING

WORTH NOTING

Swan's Cay (*Isla de los Pájaros*). Swan's Cay is a rocky islet off the north coast of Isla Colón that is commonly visited on boat tours to Boca del Drago. The swan it was named for is actually the red-billed tropicbird, an elegant white seabird with a long tail and bright-red bill that nests on the island in significant numbers. The rugged island has a narrow, natural arch in the middle of it that boatmen can slip through when the seas are calm, usually September and October. The surrounding ocean is a good scuba-diving area. ⊠ *5 km (3 miles) northeast of Boca del Drago.*

BEACHES

Boca del Drago (*Starfish Beach*). As the best beach on the island, Boca del Drago is part of a tiny fishing community in the northwest corner that overlooks the mainland. The water at the coconut palm–lined beach is *usually* calm, which makes for good swimming and snorkeling. It's a popular destination for boat tours and makes for the quintessential photo of orange starfish beaming beneath clear, shallow waters. There are several food vendors and the small Yarisnori restaurant on the beach serves decent seafood with plenty of cold beer. **Amenities:** food and drink. **Best for:** snorkeling; swimming; walking. ✉ *14 km (9 miles) northwest of Bocas Town.*

Playa Bluff. The nicest and biggest beach on Isla Colón is Bluff Beach, a 7-km (4½-mile) stretch of soft golden sand backed by tropical vegetation and washed by aquamarine waters. It's a great place to spend a day, or even an hour, but it has virtually no facilities, so pack water and snacks. When the waves are big, Playa Bluff has a beach break right on shore, but it can also develop rip currents, so swimmers beware. When the sea is calm it's a decent swimming beach—always exercise caution—and the rocky points at either end have decent snorkeling. Leatherback turtles nest here from April to September, when night tours are led by members of the Grupo Ecológico Bluff, a local Ngöbe group. If you're lucky, you may find baby turtles on the beach between June and December. A taxi will charge about $20 for the trip from Bocas to Playa Bluff, but be sure to arrange return transportation since this area is rather isolated. **Amenities:** none. **Best for:** surfing; walking. ✉ *4 km (2½ miles) north of Bocas Town* ✣ *Veer right at the "Y" heading out of Bocas Town, continue 4 km (2½ miles) north on the coastal road.*

WHERE TO STAY

$$ 🏨 **Playa Bluff Lodge.** *Hotel.* It's still pretty remote out here in Playa Bluff, but this comfy place is an oasis at the end of a rugged road. **Pros:** wonderfully secluded; eco-friendly; good restaurant. **Cons:** rough road to get here; poor lighting; no AC or Wi-Fi in room. [$] *Rooms from: $110* ✉ *Playa Bluff* ☎ *507/6798–8507* 🌐 *www.playablufflodge.com* 💳 *No credit cards* 🛏 *8 rooms* 🍴 *Breakfast.*

★ $$$$ **Fodor's Choice** 🏨 **Punta Caracol Acqua-Lodge.** *Resort.* This collection of spacious bungalows above the turquoise shallows off Isla Colón's western coast is both gorgeous and innovative, acting as a self-sustaining island within an island. **Pros:** gorgeous setting; charming rooms; eco-friendly. **Cons:** expensive for Bocas; sometimes buggy; might be too isolated for some. [$] *Rooms from: $450* ✉ *10 km (6 miles) northwest of Bocas Town* ☎ *507/757–9718* 🌐 *www.puntacaracol.com.pa* 🛏 *9 cabañas* 🍴 *Some meals.*

SPORTS AND THE OUTDOORS

SCUBA DIVING AND SNORKELING

Isla Colón doesn't have great diving, but it does have good snorkeling, mostly along the west side of the island, which has scattered reefs along the mangrove islets, one of the best of which is in front of the Punta Caracol Acqua Lodge. Excursions to Boca del Drago and Swan's Cay also include snorkeling.

SURFING

There are three good surf breaks on Isla Colón, all of them 5 to 7 km (3 to 4 miles) from Bocas. The best months for surfing are November to March, though there are often good swells in July and August. They all require intermediate or expert skills. September and October tend to be the flattest months. There are waves about half the time the rest of the year.

5

Paunch is a reef break 5 km (3 miles) north of town, around the bend from the Playa Mango Resort, that you have to walk over a coral platform to reach. The best way to get there from town is by boat. It breaks mostly left, and is for intermediate to expert surfers. **Dumpers** is an excellent left reef break on the point north of Paunch, 7 km (4½ miles) north of town. It is a quick, hollow wave that gets dangerous when big. **Playa Bluff** has a powerful beach break close to shore when there's a good swell.

ISLA BASTIMENTOS

Isla Bastimentos covers 32 square km (20 square miles) of varied landscapes, including lush tropical forest, mangrove estuaries, a lake, and several of the archipelago's nicest beaches. It also has several Afro-Caribbean and Ngöbe indigenous communities, and some excellent snorkeling and surfing spots. Old Bank, the archipelago's second-largest town, overlooks a cove on the island's western tip. The northern coast holds four beaches separated by rocky points, the longest of which, Playa Larga, lies within Parque Nacional Marino Isla Bastimentos. This park also protects a swath of rain forest and the nearby islands of

Cayos Zapatillas. Mangrove forests and islets line Bastimentos's southern side. There you can find the indigenous
community of Bahia Honda.

The island's long southeast coast is more distant and
remote, taking 40 minutes to reach from Bocas by boat.

The coast's southern point, Macca Bite, is hemmed by
mangroves, perfect for kayak exploration, and is next to
the archipelago's most popular snorkeling spot, Crawl Cay.
A short boat ride to the east of either point takes you to
the bleached sand and vast coral gardens of the paradisical
Cayos Zapatillas.

OLD BANK (BASTIMENTOS)

*4 km (2½ miles) and 10 minutes by boat east of Bocas
Town.*

Spread along a bay on the island's western tip, between
the ocean and forested hills, is a colorful, crowded, poor
collection of simple wooden buildings known as Old Bank.
It is a predominantly Afro-Caribbean community where
Guari-Guari—a mix of patois English and traces of Span-

ish—is the lingua franca. Most people live in elevated wooden houses, some awfully rudimentary, that line sidewalks and dirt paths instead of streets. Old Bank doesn't have a proper sewage system, so avoid swimming in the bay, even though the local kids do. Head to one of the nearby beaches instead.

GETTING HERE AND AROUND

Small boats regularly carry people between Bocas and Old Bank during the day. They depart Bocas from the dock next to the Farmacia Rosa Blanca and Bastimentos from the Muelle Municipal (the long dock in the middle of town). The trip takes 10 minutes and costs $2 each way.

WHERE TO EAT

$$ 🍴 **Blue Coconut.** *Caribbean.* Only in Bocas del Toro would you find the area's best bar built on stilts over the water in the middle of nowhere. Ten minutes outside of Bocas Town on Isla Solarte, this palapa bar-restaurant lures travelers who show up even before it opens at noon. Blue Coconut is known for its cold beers, fruity cocktails, reggae music, and crystal waters so clear you can see the bottom. Soak up the powerful drinks with a plate of yucca fries, fish tacos, coconut chicken, and blackened fish sandwiches. There are complimentary lounge chairs, hammocks, and snorkel gear, as well as stand-up paddleboards ($7/hour). This ultimate chill spot has excellent snorkeling, especially beneath the dock where neon fish nibble at pylons and coral. A boat taxi from Bocas runs about $10. [$] *Average main: $10* ✉ *Bocas del Toro* ✢ *west side of Isla Solarte, 10 minutes by boat from Bocas Town* ☎ *507/6762–2058* ⏲ *No dinner* 💳 *No credit cards.*

5

$$ 🍴 **Roots.** *Caribbean.* Perched over the sea near the center of Old Bank, this rustic, open-air restaurant is known for serving authentic *bocatoreña* food. House specialties include Caribbean chicken (in a mildly spicy sauce), fresh lobster, shrimp, and conch, listed as "snail" on the menu. They are served with a hearty mix of coconut rice, red beans, and a simple cabbage salad. The ambience—a thatch roof with tables and chairs made from tree trunks—is equally authentic. [$] *Average main: $12* ✉ *On the water east of police post* 💳 *No credit cards* ⏲ *Closed Tues.*

WHERE TO STAY

$$$ 🏨 **Eclypse de Mar.** *Resort.* Built over the water on stilts, this luxurious eco-lodge is the ultimate Caribbean fantasy. **Pros:** friendly staff; remote location; innovative design. **Cons:** basic breakfast; loud music can sometimes be heard from Old Bank; no AC. [$] *Rooms from: $198* ✉ *Wizard Beach* ☎ *507/6430–7576, 507/6627–3000* 🌐 *www.eclypsedemar.com* 🛏 *2 rooms, 7 bungalows* 🍴 *Breakfast.*

$$$$ 🏨 **Punta Rica Private Jungle Villa.** *Hotel.* Perched on the hillside of Isla Bastimentos, this off-grid luxury villa is constructed entirely of rich woods and is void of closed doors and glass windows, exuding a feeling of openness and connection with nature. **Pros:** gorgeous breakfasts; surrounded by wildlife; self-sustaining property. **Cons:** no children under age 6; minimum three-night stay; occasional bugs. [$] *Rooms from: $275* ✉ *South end of Old Bank, Bocas del Toro* ☎ *507/6505–6802* 🌐 *www.puntaricabocas.com* 🛏 *4 rooms* 🍴 *Some meals.*

RED FROG BEACH AND BAHIA HONDA

8 km (5 miles) east of Bocas, 4 km (2½ miles) east of Old Bank.

A couple of miles east of Old Bank, Isla Bastimentos gets narrow—a mere ½ km (¼ mile) wide—and the sea to the south is dotted with mangrove islets. Here you can find a small dock that marks the entrance to a footpath across the island to Red Frog Beach, one of the loveliest spots in the archipelago, with its golden sand shaded by tropical trees, but undergoing major real estate development since 2012. East of the beach, the island becomes wide again, and is largely covered with lush rain forest that is home to everything from mealy parrots to white-faced capuchin monkeys and countless tiny, bright-red poison dart frogs. The scattered homes of local Ngöbe line the bay to the south, known as Bahia Honda, where an indigenous organization has cut a trail through the forest and built a rustic restaurant for tourists. To the east is Parque Nacional Marino Isla Bastimentos and to the south a narrow channel through the mangroves that is the main route to the island's eastern coast and the Cayos Zapatillas.

GETTING HERE AND AROUND

Most day tours to Crawl Cay cost around $25 and include a stop at Dolphin Bay, Hospital Point, and Red Frog Beach before heading back to Bocas. Boat operators will drop you off at Red Frog Beach for $5–$8 from Old Bank and $6–$10 from Bocas, and will pick you up at a specified time.

BEACHES

Bahia Honda. About 20 Ngöbe homes are scattered around Bahia Honda, and a group of indigenous families runs a rustic restaurant about five to 10 minutes by boat from the Red Frog dock. The restaurant is administered mostly by the women of Bahia Honda. Hiking and boating tours, organized through La Loma Jungle Lodge or directly with local guide Rutilio Milton (call one day in advance to arrange the tour), include exploration of a cave with bats clinging to the stalactite-laden ceiling. The trip up the creek to get there is as spectacular as the cave itself, with plenty of opportunities to see sloths, monkeys, cayman, birds, and the occasional snake. The adventure also includes a simple lunch, a weaving demonstration, and a chance to purchase handicrafts such as *chácaras* (colorful woven jute bags). ☎*507/6592–5162 restaurant, 507/6619–5364 La Loma Jungle Lodge, 507/6726–0968 guide Rutilio Milton* ☒*Tour including transport from Bocas $25; with lunch $30.*

Red Frog Beach. Remarkable natural beauty and relative accessibility (a five-minute walk from a dock) combine to make Red Frog Beach one of the most popular spots in Bocas del Toro. The beach is almost a mile long, with golden sand backed by coconut palms, Indian almond trees, and other tropical greenery. It's the perfect spot for lounging on the sand, playing in the sea, and admiring the amazing scenery. Red Frog has unfortunately become a victim of its own popularity with a 170-acre condo development, a 150-boat marina, a jungle zip line, and an all-villas resort and spa. Although development dominates the eastern corner of Red Frog Beach, there are still plenty of unspoiled areas where expat-owned businesses provide small-scale tourism and a pleasant alternative to mass expansion. At the end of the public trail near Palmar Tent Lodge are a few relaxing spots to grab lunch and nap in the sun. Red Frog is usually a good swimming beach, but when the surf's up, rip currents can make it dangerous, so don't go beyond waist-deep if the waves are big. **Amenities:** food and drink. **Best for:** swimming; surfing; walking. ☒*4 km (2½ miles) east of Old Bank.*

WHERE TO STAY

★ $$$ **Fodor'sChoice** 🏨 **La Loma Jungle Lodge.** *Resort.* A boat ride through mangroves and a walk across wooden planks will lead you to the tastefully rustic bungalows at this eco-lodge, part of a 60-acre working cacao farm. **Pros:** in the jungle; restaurant and farm tours open to nonguests; environmentally conscientious; good tours of Bastimentos bat caves. **Cons:** very rustic; steep climb to rooms; paths are extremely dark at night. [$] *Rooms from: $200* ✉ *Bahía Honda* ☎ *507/6619–5364* 🌐 *www.thejunglelodge.com* 🛏 *3 bungalows* 🍴 *All meals.*

SPORTS AND THE OUTDOORS

Bastimentos Sky Canopy Tour (*Zip Line Red Frog Beach*). Neighboring Costa Rica gave the world the so-called zip-line canopy tour, and they have sprung up everywhere, including here in the Red Frog complex on Isla Bastimentos. The concept: A series of cables, seven in this case with one up to 1,000 feet long and 150 feet above the ground, zip you from tree to tree, courtesy of helmet and very secure harness. This facility also includes a rappel line and a Tarzan swing. Though billed as a way to get close to nature and observe life in the rain-forest canopy—hence the name "canopy tour"—your screams of delight will probably scare away any animal life within a mile. Think of it more like a two-hour amusement-park ride. Reservations are required. ☎ *507/834–7200* 🌐 *www.redfrogbeach.com* 🎟 *$55 zip line and one-way boat transport from Bocas; $5 return trip* 🕒 *Daily at 10 am, 1, and 3:30 pm.*

MACCA BITE

20 km (12 miles) southeast of Bocas.

Bastimentos's southernmost point has an odd name, and its origin is as mysterious as Bocas del Toro's, though the theory is that wild macaws once lived here. That hilly headland hemmed by mangroves and draped with lush rain forest is a mere 30 minutes from Bocas by boat, yet it feels like the end of the world.

GETTING HERE AND AROUND

Tranquilo Bay lodge provides free transportation to and from Bocas on Wednesday and Saturday but charges $100 for the trip on other days. Rates are per trip, not per passenger.

WHERE TO STAY

★ **Fodor'sChoice** ⊞ **Popa Paradise Beach Resort.** *Resort.* On the
$$$$ northeastern tip of Isla Popa, this adults-only, all-inclusive
resort sits on a white-sand beach backed by 25 acres of
tropical rain forest. **Pros:** family-friendly; excellent food;
courteous staff. **Cons:** remote; paths are dark at night; no
children under 18 allowed. ⓢ *Rooms from: $384* ⊠ *Isla
Popa* ☎ *507/6550–2505* ⊕ *www.popaparadisebeachresort.
com* ⇄ *9 cottages, 5 lodge rooms, 2 suites, 1 penthouse*
⑩ *All-inclusive.*

$$$$ ⊞ **Tranquilo Bay.** *Resort.* This all-inclusive jungle lodge is
geared toward active travelers—you can bird-watch, kayak,
snorkel, hike, surf, fish, or just stroll the beach and lounge
in a hammock, all amid amazing scenery. **Pros:** varied
activities; wild surroundings; nice rooms; good food. **Cons:**
expensive; remote; three-night minimum stay; fixed arrival
and departure days. ⓢ *Rooms from: $600* ⊠ *Macca Bite*
☎ *713/589–6952 in U.S., 507/838–0021 in Panama* ⊕ *www.
tranquilobay.com* ☉ *Usually closed June* ⇄ *6 bungalows*
⑩ *All-inclusive.*

SPORTS AND THE OUTDOORS

Macca Bite's lodges lie near some of the archipelago's best
dive sites and offer daily snorkeling excursions and kayaking. Tranquilo Bay also offers jungle hiking, sportfishing,
and surfing.

DIVING AND SNORKELING

Crawl Cay (*Coral Cay*). Just east of Macca Bite is Crawl Cay,
a large reef that holds an impressive array of coral heads,
colorful sponges, large sea fans, and hundreds of small reef
fish. It is an excellent spot for snorkelers, who can simply
float over the reef and watch the show. The reef also has
enough marine life in and around its innumerable crannies
to entertain experienced divers. It is sufficiently sheltered
that the water there is usually calm and clear, even when
the sea is too rough for diving at Cayos Zapatillas. Bring
drinking water, reef-safe sunscreen, and cash if you plan
to dine at one of the over-the-water restaurants.

PARQUE NACIONAL MARINO ISLA BASTIMENTOS

About one third of Isla Bastimentos and the Cayos Zapatillas, to the southeast, lie within Parque Nacional Marino Isla
Bastimentos. The park's 32,000 acres comprise an array of
ecosystems ranging from sea-grass beds to rain forest and
include some spectacular and ecologically important areas.

EXPLORING
Parque Nacional Marino Isla Bastimentos (*Bastimentos Island National Marine Park*). Much of the park is virtually inaccessible, especially the island's forested interior, but you can see most of its flora and fauna in the private reserves of adjacent jungle lodges. That wildlife includes tiny, bright-red poison dart frogs, green iguanas, two-toed sloths, ospreys, parrots, toucans, and collared manakins. The park's coral reefs protect even greater biological diversity, including spiny lobsters, sea stars, barracuda, various snapper species, and countless colorful reef fish.

Most people experience the park's reefs at the postcard-perfect, coconut-palmed Cayos Zapatillas, two cays southeast of Bastimentos that are the park's crown jewels. The Cayos' most impressive scenery is actually in the surrounding ocean, which holds 1,200 acres of protected coral reef ranging from a shallow platform around the islands to steep walls pocked with caves. Scuba divers explore the reef's outer expanses, while snorkelers enjoy views of the shallow platform adorned with some impressive coral formations. The park tends to have more fish than Crawl Cay and other unprotected dive spots, and divers can expect to see tiny angelfish, parrot fish, squirrelfish, octopuses, eels, stingrays, and countless other marine creatures. When seas are rough (as they often are between December and March), scuba diving is limited to the leeward side of the island, making Crawl Cay a more attractive dive spot at that time. The island has a ranger station and a small nature trail through the forest. Bring sunblock, insect repellent, a hat, a towel, water, and snorkeling gear. ☎ *507/758–6603* ✉ *$10* ☉ *Daily 6–6.*

GUNA YALA (SAN BLAS)

Updated
by Marlise
Kast-Myers
THE GUNA YALA ARCHIPELAGO AND surrounding sea are the main attractions in Guna Yala—an indigenous *comarca* (autonomous territory) stretching more than 200 km (120 miles) along Panama's northeast coast—but the traditional culture of the Guna is a close second. The comarca is composed of a thin strip of land dominated by a mountain range called the Serranía de San Blas and the 365 San Blas Islands that dot the coastal waters.

Although much of the world still refers to this region by its former name, San Blas, you'll endear yourself to residents by using the name they give to their home, Guna Yala. ■TIP→ Note that you may also see it spelled Kuna Yala, but Guna leaders voted to change the spelling from Kuna to Guna in 2011.

This is a lush and stunning region of forest-cloaked mountains, white-sand beaches, vibrant coral reefs, and timeless villages. Your trip here can consequently combine time on heavenly islands, jungle hiking, handicraft shopping, and exposure to a proud and beautiful indigenous people. Since coral reefs surround nearly every island, snorkeling is practically obligatory in the archipelago. Most lodges include the use of snorkeling equipment in their rates, and all of them provide daily trips to beaches with reefs nearby. You don't need to swim to appreciate the area's beauty, though, because the scenery topside is just as impressive; coconut groves shade ivory sand, dugout canoes with lateen sails ply turquoise waters, and cane huts with thatch roofs make up island villages.

Guna Yala's greatest beauty, however, may be in the traditional dress of its women, whose striking clothing includes hand-stitched *molas* (appliqué fabric pictures), colorful skirts and scarves, and intricate beadwork on their calves and forearms. ■TIP→ Note that women and children commonly expect a payment of $1 if you photograph them. Men, however, have gradually abandoned traditional clothing in favor of jeans, polo or tropical cabana shirts, and derby hats (for older men) or baseball caps (for younger men). Times are changing, even in Guna Yala.

TOP REASONS TO GO

Indigenous Cultures. Eastern Panama's indigenous Guna, Emberá, and Wounaan villages are amazingly traditional, colorful places that provide visitors with unforgettable cross-cultural experiences.

Beautiful Beaches. The islands of Guna Yala have ivory beaches shaded by coconut palms and washed by turquoise waters—scenery fit for the covers of travel magazines or the daydreams of snowbound accountants.

Ocean Treasures. Guna Yala's crystalline sea holds countless coral reefs awash with living rainbows of fish and invertebrates, whereas the white-sand shallows of its islands are idyllic spots for a tranquil swim.

ORIENTATION AND PLANNING

GETTING ORIENTED

Guna Yala (aka Kuna Yala) stretches along Panama's northeast coast from the Central Caribbean eastward to the border with Colombia, comprising forested mountains, coastal lowlands, the 365 Guna Yala (San Blas) Islands, and the surrounding sea. The entire province was once called San Blas, but it is known now by its indigenous name, Guna Yala, which translates as "Land of the Guna." Only one road penetrates the otherwise isolated province, a dirt track called Camino Llano-Cartí that traverses its western end.

PLANNING

WHEN TO GO

It rains almost every afternoon from May to December in Guna Yala, though the rain lets up a bit in July, August, and September. Most people consequently visit the region between January and May. The sea tends to be rough here from January to April. The best diving months are from June to November, when the seas tend to be calm and visibility is better.

PLANNING YOUR TIME

If you're a traveler with a "to do" list or a vacationer with an agenda, set it aside. Most of your time is going to be spent just relaxing, on an island possibly no larger than a basketball court. Gone are the smartphones, electricity, hot water, and feather pillows, and in their place are snorkel masks, candles, the ocean, and hammocks. For this reason, allow three days to acclimate and soak in true island life. This should give you enough time to explore the crystal waters of the Caribbean, cruise around the island in a dug-out canoe, visit Guna villages, and even buy yourself a *mola* at a craft market.

GETTING HERE AND AROUND

The Guna's autonomy over their territory has led to arbitrary taxes being placed on visitors, including a $3–$5 island tax, a $20 entry fee (per person) when arriving by car, and a $105 charge for boats visiting for more than 72 hours (you must provide documentation declaring your next destination). Independent of the country's laws, these taxes are part of an ongoing debate with the Panamanian government. Expect to show a valid passport several times throughout your journey, and have plenty of cash.

AIR TRAVEL

The easiest way to get to Guna Yala is to fly. The domestic airline Air Panama offers scheduled flights to several airstrips in Guna Yala (Achutupo, Mulatupo, Puerto Obaldia, and Playón Chico). There are neither airline offices nor airports in this region, only simple airstrips.

Contacts Air Panama. ☎ 507/316–9000 ⊕ www.airpanama.com.

BOAT TRAVEL

Motorized dugouts are the most common form of transportation in Guna Yala, where most people travel via jungle rivers. Some of the better lodges in Guna Yala transport guests in small fiberglass boats.

Boat transportation is included in the rates of all Guna Yala hotels. For day tours and boat excursions to neighboring islands, plan to pay $3–$5 for each island you visit. The company San Blas Sailing runs sailboat cruises to Guna Yala that combine visits to Guna villages with time on pristine outer islands, such as the Cayos Holandeses. Trips are a minimum of three days and run between El Porvenir and Corazon de Jesus.

Several cruise lines, including Holland America, Princess, Seabourn, and Windstar make port calls in the Guna Yala Islands on select Panama Canal and western Caribbean itineraries. You'll be tendered ashore. The total absence of restaurants means that cruise visits are kept short—usually just under a half-day—with time to be back on ship for the next meal.

CAR TRAVEL

Several companies provide transportation between Panama City and Cartí, in Guna Yala, in four-wheel-drive vehicles; you will be picked up at your hotel. It's possible to drive to Cartí in a four-wheel-drive vehicle and leave it there while you visit nearby islands. Ancon Expeditions transports guests to and from its lodge on Punta Patiño with a combination of driving and a boat. When arriving by car to Guna Yala, expect to pay $20 per person at the Nusagandi check point, and a $2 port tax once you are in the Guna Yala Indigenous Preserve; you will need to show a valid passport.

HOTELS

Most accommodations in this part of Panama range from comfortably rustic to downright primitive. Only Guna are allowed to own businesses in Guna Yala; a *waga* (foreigner) is prohibited from holding property here. Lodges are basic as a result—most have no hot water, no air-conditioning, no Internet, and only a few hours of electricity at night—but some of those thatched bungalows have priceless ocean views. There are a few nice Guna lodges, but the less expensive ones tend to be dirty and serve lamentable food, which is why few are listed in this book. Since most Guna lodges lack offices, only three accept credit cards. The alternative is to visit Guna Yala on a day trip and sleep at Coral Lodge, 26 km (16 miles) away, which has most of the comforts of home (⇨ *Santa Isabela in "The Canal and Central Panama"*).

Hotel reviews have been shortened, for full information visit Fodors.com.

RESTAURANTS

This isn't the part of Panama you head to for epicurean delights. You can count on fresh seafood in Guna Yala—and little else. If you don't eat seafood, you should mention it when you reserve, and again when you arrive. Establishments usually offer lobster, except March through May,

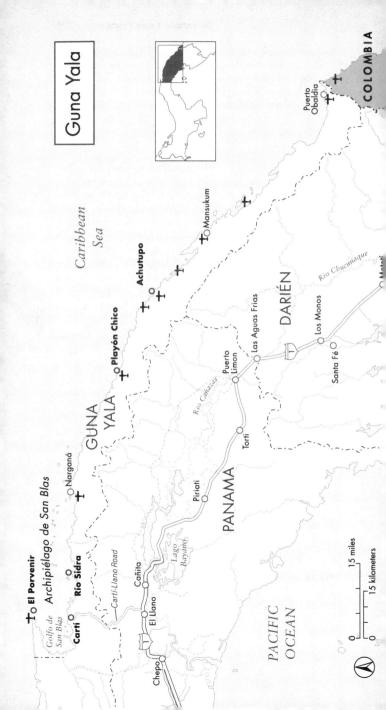

when fishing for lobster is prohibited. Nothing resembling a sit-down restaurant exists in these provinces, so hotels include three meals in their rates, usually served family-style at fixed times. Purified water, coffee, tea, and fruit juices are free; bottled soft drinks and alcoholic beverages cost extra.

WHAT IT COSTS IN U.S. DOLLARS				
	$	**$$**	**$$$**	**$$$$**
Restaurants	under $10	$11–$15	$16–$20	over $20
Hotels	under $100	$101–$160	$161–$220	over $220

Restaurant prices are per person for a main course at dinner. Hotel prices are for two people in a standard double room, excluding service and 10% tax.

ESSENTIALS

Guna Yala may have pristine nature and traditional cultures, but it lacks ATMs and pharmacies, and has only rudimentary clinics, simple stores, and few phones. Few Guna lodges have English speakers, though you can hire an English-speaking guide in Panama City to accompany you. Flights to Guna Yala depart at 6 am, and ground transportation often leaves at 5 am—at least the higher-end lodges serve you breakfast when you arrive. Bring plenty of sunblock, a hat, insect repellent, a water bottle, and cash.

■TIP→ **If you have serious health problems in Guna Yala, get on the next flight to Panama City.**

EMERGENCIES

The larger islands have police stations with radios to call Panama City for help in an emergency and tiny *centros de salud* (health centers) that can provide first aid. At the time of writing, a small hospital was being built in Cartí.

MONEY

There are no ATMs in this part of Panama, so bring all the money you'll need during your trip. Stock up on small bills in Panama City, since the indigenous vendors, and even some hotels, are usually short on change.

SAFETY

The main dangers in Guna Yala are the sun and sea creatures such as Portuguese man-of-wars, which are rare.

TELEPHONES

Telephone access is spotty in this region. Guna Yala has cell-phone reception, but connections are often weak. All island communities have pay phones provided by the government.

EL PORVENIR, CARTÍ, AND RÍO SIDRA

95 km (60 miles) northeast of Panama City.

The most accessible and popular part of Guna Yala is the cluster of islands on its western end, the most prominent of which are the provincial capital of El Porvenir, and Cartí Suitupo and Rio Sidra, which are the area's largest communities. This area holds the same kind of timeless indigenous villages and paradisiacal islands as the rest of Guna Yala. The difference is that it receives more visitors, especially during the New Year, Carnaval, and Easter holidays and its hotels are geared toward backpackers, whereas lodges to the east provide a higher level of comfort and service.

GETTING HERE AND AROUND

The easiest way to reach western Guna Yala is by flying to El Porvenir (PVE). At the time of writing, Air Panama had ceased operations to El Porvenir, but check with the airline directly to see if flights have resumed. If flights are unavailable, the main port of entry is Cartí, which has no attractions, but is where lodges pick up guests.

Cartí is the only part of Guna Yala that can be reached by land, via the Llano-Cartí road, which runs between the village of El Llano, on the Interamerican Highway, north to the rudimentary port of Cartí. Lam Tours offers daily service between Panama City and Cartí in a four-wheel-drive vehicle.

Río Sidra is accessible by land, via the Llano-Cartí road, or by air via El Porvenir when flights are available. Lam Tours offers a daily taxi service between Panama City and Cartí. Río Sidra lodges can pick you up at Cartí. Cruise ships visit Wichub Wala, Nalunega, and Carti Sugdub.

Air Panama. ☎ *507/316–9000* ⊕ *www.airpanama.com.*

TOURS

Lam Tours. The only part of Guna Yala that can be reached by road is the western El Porvenir area, via the Llano–Cartí road, which crosses the lushly forested Serranía de San Blas. Lam Tours runs a bus/taxi service from Panama City to Cartí, where boats from lodges near El Porvenir and Río Sidra pick up guests. Lam Tours will pick you up at your hotel at 5 am, reaching Cartí around 9 am, and returns to Panama City shortly thereafter. ☎ *507/395–7105, 704/469–9146 in U.S.* ⊕ *www.lamtourspanama.com* ⚓ *$35 per person.*

EXPLORING

TOP ATTRACTIONS

Río Sidra. To the east of Cartí Suitupo is the island community of Río Sidra, which is a good place to visit if you want to experience how the Guna live. Several sparsely populated islands, which are farther out, have lodges on them. To get here, lodges pick up guests in Cartí and El Porvenir.

WORTH NOTING

Cartí. This rustic port is the only part of Guna Yala accessible by land, via the Llano-Cartí road, which winds its way over the lushly forested Serranía de San Blas between the Interamerican Highway and Cartí. There is no community here, just a few buildings and docks, but it is a relatively busy place most mornings, because people and goods moving between more than a dozen Guna communities and Panama City pass through here. Lodges near El Porvenir and Río Sidra can pick up guests here.

Cartí Sugdub (*Cartí Suidup*). The closest community to the port of Cartí is the densely populated island of Cartí Sugdub (aka Cartí Suidup). Here visitors will find a collection of thatched huts, cement stores, and plenty of handicraft hawkers. Near the school is a large thatched building called the Casa de la Cultura, where *sahilas* (chiefs) from across the province gather once or twice a year. Aside from an opportunity to experience life in a Guna community, the island has a tiny museum dedicated to traditional Guna culture.

El Porvenir. Though it is technically the provincial capital, this island is practically uninhabited. It has a police station, an office of the Guna congress, a rustic hotel, and an airstrip, which makes it the arrival point for many travelers when flights are available. There are two small islands nearby that hold traditional Guna villages and rustic lodges, and are visited by cruise ships: Wichub Wala and Nalunega. These islands are fascinating to explore, but their lack of sewage systems means the sea around them is unsafe for swimming. However, there are several uninhabited, white-sand cays a short boat trip away that are idyllic swimming and snorkeling spots.

Museo de la Cultura Guna (*Guna Museum of Art and Culture*). This small, family-run museum is housed in a typical Guna home, with a thatched roof, cane walls, and sand floor. It's packed with the accoutrements of traditional Guna life, such as sleeping hammocks, woven baskets and fans, ceremonial wooden staffs and statues, and traps and gear for hunting and fishing. There is also a display of skulls of the animals they hunt for meat in the nearby rain forest. ⊠ *Cartí Sugdub* ⊠ *$5* ⊙ *Daily 8–4.*

Nalunega. The slightly larger island of Nalunega lies just to the south of Wichub Wala. Like Wichub Wala, it has a collection of huts and cement structures, including a primary school, small museum, and the archipelago's original lodge, the rundown Hotel San Blas, founded in 1972. This is a good place to see how the Guna live, and where you can purchase handicrafts. ⊠ *Nalunega.*

Río Masargandi. The Río Masargandi, a small river that flows out of the mountains near Río Sidra, provides access to the rain forest and a 30-foot waterfall. Local lodges offer half-day trips to the mainland for an additional charge. Excursions to see wildlife are best done early in the morning, but slather yourself with insect repellent. ⊠ *Waterfall entrance $10*

Wichub Wala (*Wichub Huala*). This tiny island, just south of El Porvenir, is home to a crowded Guna village with a mixture of thatch-roof huts and cement buildings that are separated by narrow sand paths. Papaya and breadfruit trees grow in back patios, dugout canoes crowd the shore, and children play in the sandy streets. Expect to encounter a number of women trying to sell you molas and other handicrafts as you explore, because this is one of the village's main sources of income. ⊠ *Wichub Wala.*

WHERE TO STAY

Accommodations in this part of Guna Yala are very rustic. Most bungalows have sand floors, cane walls, thatch roofs, and shared bathrooms. Those who can do without comforts, however, are rewarded with phenomenal island scenery and great snorkeling.

Most accommodations on or near El Porvenir are geared toward backpackers; the best option in the area is Cabañas Coco Blanco.

$$$$ 🏨 **Cabañas Coco Blanco.** *B&B/Inn.* Occupying half of the small island of Ogobsibudup, Coco Blanco has rustic bungalows with private bathrooms steps away from a white-sand beach. **Pros:** nice beach; private bathrooms; near various uninhabited islands. **Cons:** no running water at times; no English spoken; unsightly garbage on back of island. [$] *Rooms from: $340* ✉ *Ogobsibudup* ☎ *507/6738–1708 Panama Travel Unlimited, 507/6547–3651 cell* 💳 *No credit cards* 🛏 *8 bungalows* 🍴 *All meals.*

$$$ 🏨 **Cabañas Kuanidup.** *B&B/Inn.* With a small beach and hammocks strung between palm trees, this remote island is an idyllic spot. **Pros:** gorgeous island; great snorkeling. **Cons:** tiny, rustic rooms; shared bathrooms can get crowded; no English spoken. [$] *Rooms from: $180* ✉ *Kuanidup Island, near Río Sidra* ☎ *507/6635–6737, 507/6656–4673* 🌐 *kuanidup.8k.com* 💳 *No credit cards* 🛏 *12 huts* 🍴 *All meals.*

$$ 🏨 **Cabañas Narasgandup.** *B&B/Inn.* Though quite rustic, this lodge has a great setting on a sparsely inhabited island shaded by coconut palms with a lovely beach. **Pros:** great beach; friendly service; day trips. **Cons:** very rustic; no English spoken. [$] *Rooms from: $160* ✉ *Ogobsibudup, Narasgandup Bipi Island* ☎ *507/6686–7437, 507/6079–4740* 🌐 *www.sanblaskunayala.com* 💳 *No credit cards* 🛏 *6 bungalows, 2 with bath* 🍴 *All meals.*

SHOPPING

It would be a shame to visit Guna Yala and not buy a mola. Women usually set up shop outside their homes. Bring plenty of small bills, and try to buy from various vendors to benefit as many families as possible.

SPORTS AND THE OUTDOORS

The lodges in this area have good snorkeling nearby and there are several uninhabited islands that can be visited on excursions, the most popular of which is Achutupu (aka Isla Perro), which has a small shipwreck offshore. (*See Achutupu, below.*)

6

MOLAS 101

The Guna are famous for their *molas:* fabric pictures made using a reverse appliqué technique, and Panama's most famous souvenir. Guna women wear these designs on their blouses, but they are also used to decorate everything from purses to pillows to hot pads to wall hangings. The original molas echoed the geometric designs employed by the Guna as body paint—Christian missionaries' influence in the 19th century brought modest body covering to the region for the first time, and the word *mola* means "clothing" in Dulegaya, the Guna language. Over the decades, designs have taken on abstract nature scenes, and, today, even a few TV and cartoon characters show up in the artwork. Regarding the traditional geometric designs, look closely before you buy: some molas feature a reverse swastika, an ancient Guna symbol. You may not want one of those. Mola production is a major source of income in Guna Yala, and you'll often see women sewing them as they chat with neighbors. Expect to pay $20 or more for a well-made mola. Number of layers used increases the price; two is most common, but the premium works incorporate several more layers. Fineness of stitching, up to the point of being nearly invisible, also means a finer mola. Embroidery frequently enhances a mola's design, but a top-notch product creates its design strictly through reverse appliqué technique. Oddly, a bit of wear or fading is not considered to be a flaw. Perhaps a panel had a previous life as a piece of someone's blouse and is now being used in another work. Such a "blemish" adds to the mola's authenticity and means that it wasn't created strictly for tourists.

Bargaining is expected, but don't haggle too hard. Molas are usually already reasonably priced when you consider the labor that went into their production, and those few extra dollars will mean much more to the vendor than to you. If you plan on buying multiple molas, try to buy from a variety of women. You'll benefit more families that way.

PLAYÓN CHICO

150 km (93 miles) northeast of Panama City.

This community of about 3,000 people lies just offshore, with a wooden footbridge connecting it to the mainland, where the town's school and landing strip are located. Most homes in Playón Chico are traditional thatched buildings, with small gardens shaded by breadfruit, mango, or citrus trees. It was an important place in the 1925 revolution that led to Guna autonomy, because it held one of the Panama military outposts that were captured by Guna warriors.

The lowlands around the landing strip hold farms, but a nearby hill is topped with the burial ground that resembles a small village. The Guna bury family members together under thatched shelters complete with the tools and utensils that their spirits require to survive. Forested mountains stand beyond the farmland where a trail leads to a waterfall. Insect repellent is essential on the mainland due to sand fleas. There are several uninhabited islands in the area with pale beaches and coral reefs offshore that local lodges take guests to for snorkeling and beach time.

GETTING HERE AND AROUND

Air Panama flies to Playón Chico airstrip (PYC) most days, departing from Panama City's Albrook Airport at 6 am and returning at 7 am. A guide from your lodge will meet you at the airstrip.

WHERE TO STAY

$$$$ **Sapibenega** (*Sapibenega The Kuna Lodge*). *B&B/Inn.* With spacious rooms and an attractive restaurant perched over the sea, this is one of the better lodges in Guna Yala, but it is also the most expensive. **Pros:** big rooms; good food; friendly staff. **Cons:** rooms lack privacy; no beach on island; little English spoken; overpriced. [$] *Rooms from: $340* ✉ *Playón Chico* ☎ *507/215–1406* 🌐 *www.sapibenega.com* 🛏 *5 rooms* 🍴 *All meals.*

★ Fodor's Choice **Yandup Island Lodge.** *B&B/Inn.* Yandup's over-the-water bungalows are the nicest accommodations in Guna Yala, each with 360° views, wraparound balconies, hardwood floors, private baths, orthopedic mattresses, and plenty of hammocks to sway away the day. **Pros:** lovely bungalows and island; friendly staff; good food. **Cons:** sand fleas can be a problem at night; use of snorkeling gear costs extra; additional $10 per person tax. [$] *Rooms from: $384* ✉ *Yandup Island* ☎ *507/203–7762* 🌐 *www.yandupisland.com* 🛏 *10 bungalows* 🍴 *All meals.*

$$$$

ACHUTUPO

190 km (118 miles) northeast of Panama City.

Achutupo, or Isla Perro in Spanish, is a medium-size community on an island near the mainland in the eastern half of Guna Yala. Because this is the most distant area that you can visit in Guna Yala, it's a good destination if you're especially interested in Guna culture. The people on Achutupo and nearby Aligandi see few tourists, and offer handicrafts of a higher quality than you'll find on the province's western end.

GETTING HERE AND AROUND

Air Panama flies from Panama City's Albrook Airport to the airstrip at Achutupo (ACU) departing from Albrook at 6 am and returning at 7 am. A guide from your lodge will meet you at the airstrip. It is not recommended to arrive by boat because of rough seas.

EXPLORING

Aligandi. A short trip to the west of Achutupo is the island community of Aligandi, which played an important role in the Guna revolt of 1925. There is a small museum and cultural center focusing on the Guna Revolution. You'll see the Guna flag displayed here, as well as a statue of the local revolutionary Simral Colman, one of the architects of the autonomous Guna Indigenous Preserve. ✉ *Achutupo.*

WHERE TO STAY

$$$$ 🏨 **Akwadup Lodge.** *B&B/Inn.* This lodge's wooden bungalows are perched over the sea and just a short walk from a small beach. **Pros:** comfortable bungalows; relaxing property; friendly staff. **Cons:** island has trash on it; no-see-ums can be a problem; unimpressive food. [$] *Rooms from: $260* ✉ *Akwadup Island* ☎ *507/832–5144, 507/6070–0964* 🌐 *www.akwaduplodge.com* 💳 *No credit cards* 🛏 *7 bungalows* 🍴 *All meals.*

$$$$ 🏨 **Dolphin Island Lodge** (*Dolphin Lodge San Blas*). *B&B/Inn.* One of the oldest hotels in Guna Yala, this lodge occupies most of the small Uaguinega Island, which is across a channel from Achutupo. **Pros:** spacious bungalows; friendly staff; two daily tours included in rate. **Cons:** no beach on island; charge for drinking water; no hot water. [$] *Rooms from: $260* ✉ *Uaguinega Island* ☎ *866/390–3451 in U.S., 507/396–4805 in Panama* 🌐 *www.dolphinlodgesanblas.com* 🛏 *6 bungalows* 🍴 *All meals.*

TRAVEL SMART
PANAMA

GETTING HERE AND AROUND

Panama is the southernmost part of an isthmus that stretches between Colombia and Mexico. Although relatively narrow, the country still has hundreds of miles of Pacific and Caribbean coastline. It is bisected by the Panama Canal, which runs north–south across the center of the country. To the east, the Carretera Panamericana (Panamerican Highway) heads toward the Darién, home to a vast, near-impenetrable jungle, which creates the only break in the whole highway between North and South America. The road starts again on the other side of the Colombian border and continues to Patagonia. The 350 San Blas Islands, which lie off the Caribbean coast in this region, are accessible only by light airplane or boat. The Carretera Panamericana runs west from Panama City to Costa Rica, passing through David. Two provinces border Costa Rica: Chiriquí, to the south, and Bocas del Toro, to the north. You can reach Bocas by land and boat from Chiriquí.

▌ AIR TRAVEL

From New York or Chicago flying time to Panama City is 5½ hours; from Atlanta 4 hours; from Miami 3 hours; from L.A. 6½ hours; and from Houston 4¼ hours.

FLIGHTS

Copa, a United partner, is Panama's flagship carrier. It operates flights from Atlanta, Boston, Chicago, Dallas, Fort Lauderdale, Houston, Las Vegas, Los Angeles, Miami, Newark, New Orleans, New York–JFK, Orlando, Philadelphia, Toronto, San Francisco, Seatle, Tampa, and Washington Dulles. Copa also flies to many Central and South American cities. You can fly to Panama from Houston and Newark on United, from Atlanta on Delta, from Miami, Dallas, New York, and Newark on American, and from Fort Lauderdale on Spirit.

Air Panama is Panama's domestic carrier and serves destinations all over the country, including Contadora, Guna Yala, Bocas del Toro, David, and the Darién. Domestic flights usually cost $100 to $250 round-trip; you can buy tickets directly from the airline or through a travel agent. Air Panama offers charter flights as well, although these tend to be quite pricey.

Airline Contacts American Airlines. ☏ 800/433–7300 in North America, 507/269–6022 in Panama ⊕ www.aa.com. **Copa.** ☏ 800/359–2672 in North America, 507/217–2672 in Panama ⊕ www.copaair.com. **Delta Airlines.** ☏ 800/241–4141 in North America, 507/214–8118 in Panama ⊕ www.delta.com. **Spirit Airlines.** ☏ 801/401–2200 in North America, 507/836–7701 in Panama ⊕ www.spirit.com. **United Airlines.** ☏ 800/864–8331 in North America, 507/265–0040 in Panama ⊕ www.united.com.

Airline-Security Issues Transportation Security Administration. ⊕ *www.tsa.gov.*

Domestic Airlines Air Panama. ☎ *507/316–9000 in Panama* ⊕ *www. airpanama.com.*

AIRPORTS

Panama's main air hub is Aeropuerto Internacional de Tocumen (PTY), about 17 km (11 miles) northeast of Panama City. All scheduled international flights land here. The airport underwent a $600 million expansion in 2012 that included the addition of airy, glass-walled corridors; construction of a new terminal began in 2014. Tocumen has two tourist-information booths, shops, a few eating places, ATMs, 24-hour luggage storage, car-rental agencies, and a telephone and Internet center. Arrival and departure formalities are usually efficient. Minimum check-in time is two hours prior to departure; your airline may recommend longer.

Domestic flights operate out of Aeropuerto Marcos A. Gelabert (PAC), more commonly known as Albrook Airport, after the U.S. military base that once stood there. Albrook has a tourist-information stand, an ATM, a small food court, and some car-rental offices.

Airport Information Aeropuerto Internacional de Tocumen. ⊠ *Av. Domingo Díaz s/n, Achutupo* ☎ *507/238–2761* ⊕ *www. tocumenpanama.aero.* **Aeropuerto Marcos A. Gelabert (Albrook Airport).** ⊠ *Av. Diógenes de la Rosa* ☎ *501–9272.*

CUSTOMS AND DUTIES

You may import 500 cigarettes (or 500 grams of tobacco or 50 cigars) and three bottles of alcohol duty-free. You can import duty-free up to $2,000 of various goods; customs is not overly strict on applying duty to items that are obviously yours for personal use. Prescription drugs should always be accompanied by a doctor's prescription.

U.S. Information U.S. Customs and Border Protection. ☎ *877/ 227–5511* ⊕ *www.cbp.gov.*

GROUND TRANSPORTATION

Taxis are the quickest way into Panama City from Tocumen Airport. The fare is $30 to $40, depending on your hotel's location, but a few hotels offer a shuttle service. Only licensed operators are allowed to offer services as you leave the airport doors. The trip can take between 20 and 60 minutes, depending on traffic and your hotel's location.

The 15-minute taxi ride from Albrook Airport to the city center costs $4 to $6.

Public buses stop far from Tocumen's terminal and take well over an hour to get into the city, so we recommend taking a taxi or shuttle, if your hotel offers one.

TRANSFERS BETWEEN AIRPORTS

A taxi ride between Tocumen and Albrook airports can top $40, though if you're catching the cab at Albrook, you might be able to negotiate a cheaper price. The trip takes about 30 minutes. Alternatively, buses to both airports start and finish at Plaza Cinco de Mayo.

▌ BOAT AND FERRY TRAVEL

⇨ *For information about Panama Canal boat trips, see The Canal and Central Panama Essentials in Chapter 3.* Ferry Panama Cartagena operates weekly service between Colón and Cartagena, Colombia. The ship departs the Colón 2000 port each Monday, and Cartagena's Puerto de Cruceros each Tuesday from November to May. Departure time is 7 pm and the trip takes 18 hours. The ship carries up to 1,320 passengers and 300 motor vehicles. One-way tickets are $130 for seats, and $170–$280 for private cabins.

Within Panama, boats are the only way to get between points in the islands of Guna Yala and Bocas del Toro. There are regular, inexpensive water-taxi services connecting the city of Almirante with Bocas del Toro.

Ferry Panama Cartagena. ☎ *507/ 836–5351 in Panama* ⊕ *www. ferrypanamacartagena.com.*

▌ BUS TRAVEL

DOMESTIC BUS SERVICES

Getting around Panama by bus is comfortable, cheap, and straightforward. Panama City is the main transport hub. Services to towns all over the country (and to the rest of Central America) leave from a huge terminal/mall in Albrook with shops, ATMs, Internet access, and restaurants. To get to smaller cities and beaches, you need to catch

> ## THE MATTER OF METERS
>
> In directions and addresses in Panama, "100 meters" means one block, regardless of actual measurements. Likewise, 200 meters is two blocks and 50 meters is half a block.

minibuses out of regional transit hubs.

Long-distance buses are usually clean and punctual. Routes are operated by many different bus companies, and there's no centralized timetable service. Call the bus company or go to the terminal to get departure times. Rates are not set in stone, but estimate $1 to $2 per hour of travel.

For bus company and terminal information, see Getting Here and Around in each destination chapter.

INTERNATIONAL BUS SERVICES

You can reach Panama by bus only from Costa Rica. Services cross the border at Paso Canoas. The Darién jungle causes a gap in the Panamerican Highway, meaning bus travel to Colombia is impossible.

Ticabus is an international bus company connecting all of Central America. Air-conditioned coaches leave Panama City daily at 11 am and noon and take 16 hours to get to San José, Costa Rica. One-way tickets cost $55 for the more comfortable "executive service" daytime departure and $40 for the nighttime departure. Ticabus continues to Nicaragua, El Salvador, Honduras, Guatemala, and Mexico.

Panamanian company Expreso Panamá operates air-conditioned coach service from Panama City nightly at 11 pm arriving at San José, Costa Rica 16 hours later. The one-way fare is $40.

International Bus Companies
Expreso Panamá. ☎ *507/314–6837* ⊕ *www.expresopanama.com.* **Ticabus.** ☎ *507/314–6385* ⊕ *www.ticabus.com.*

▌ CAR TRAVEL

Driving is a great way to see Panama. The Panamerican Highway takes you to or near most towns in the country, and with a car you can also visit small villages and explore remote areas more easily. Most secondary roads are well signposted and in reasonable condition.

Panamanian drivers can be a little aggressive, but they're not much worse than New Yorkers or Angelenos. We recommend saving the car for outside Panama City: traffic jams, a dearth of road signs beyond major avenues, and lack of safe parking can make downtown driving stressful.

GASOLINE
Gas stations are plentiful in and near towns in Panama, and along the Panamerican Highway. Some are open 24 hours. On long trips fill your tank whenever you can, as the next station could be a long way away. An attendant always pumps the gas and doesn't expect a tip, though a small one is always appreciated. Both cash and credit cards are usually accepted.

Most rental cars run on premium unleaded gas, which is generally a bit more expensive than in the United States. Gas is sold by the liter.

PARKING
On-street parking generally isn't a good idea in Panama City. Instead, park in a guarded parking lot—most hotels have them. Many rental agencies insist you follow this rule. Restaurants often have free parking.

RENTAL CARS
Compact cars like a Kia Pinto, Ford Fiesta, VW Fox, or Toyota Yaris start at around $35 a day; for $40–$50 you can rent a Mitsubishi Lancer, a VW Golf, or a Polo. Four-wheel-drive pickups start at $70 a day. International agencies sometimes have cheaper per-day rates, but locals undercut them on longer rentals. Stick shift is the norm in Panama, so check with the rental agency if you only drive an automatic.

Rental-car companies routinely accept driver's licenses from the United States, Canada, and most European countries. Most agencies require a major credit card for a deposit, and most require that you be over 25. Panamanian rental vehicles may not leave the country.

Contacts Avis. ☎ *800/633–3469 in North America, 507/278–9444 in Panama* ⊕ *www.avis.com. pa.* **Budget.** ☎ *800/472–3325 in North America, 507/263–8777 in Panama* ⊕ *www.budgetpanama.*

com. **Dollar.** ☎ *866/700–9904 in North America, 507/270–0355 in Panama* ⊕ *www.dollarpanama.com.* **Hertz.** ☎ *800/654–3001 in North America, 507/260–2111 in Panama* ⊕ *www.hertz.com.* **National.** ☎ *800/654–3001 in North America, 507/275–7222 in Panama* ⊕ *www.nationalpanama.com.* **Thrifty.** ☎ *800/334–1705 in North America, 507/204–9500 in Panama* ⊕ *www.panamathrifty.com.*

RENTAL-CAR INSURANCE

If you own a car, your personal auto insurance may cover a rental to some degree, though not all policies protect you abroad; always read your policy's fine print. If you don't have auto insurance, then seriously consider buying the collision- or loss-damage waiver (CDW or LDW) from the car-rental company, which eliminates your liability for damage to the car. Some credit cards offer CDW coverage, but it's usually supplemental to your own insurance and rarely covers SUVs, minivans, luxury models, and the like. If your coverage is secondary, you may still be liable for loss-of-use costs from the car-rental company. But no credit-card insurance is valid unless you use that card for *all* transactions, from reserving to paying the final bill. All companies exclude car rental in some countries, so be sure to find out about the destination to which you are traveling. It's sometimes cheaper to buy insurance as part of your general travel insurance policy.

Car-rental agencies in Panama require basic third-party liability insurance, and the fee is included in their cheapest quoted rental price.

Optional insurance to cover occupants and the deductible if you are in an accident deemed your fault is about $20 extra per day for a compact car.

ROADSIDE EMERGENCIES

Panama has no private roadside assistance clubs—ask rental agencies carefully about what you should do if you break down. If you have an accident, you are legally obliged to stay by your vehicle until the police arrive, which could take awhile, depending on your location. You can also call the transport police or, if you're near Panama City, the tourist police.

Emergency Services National police. ☎ *911 for emergencies.* **Tourist police.** ☎ *507/511–9262 for information, 911 for emergencies.* **Transport police.** ☎ *911 for emergencies.*

ROAD CONDITIONS

The Panamerican Highway is paved along its entire length in Panama, and most secondary roads are paved, too. However, maintenance isn't always a regular process, so you may encounter worn, pockmarked surfaces if you stray from the main routes. Turnoffs are often sharp, and mountain roads can have hairpin bends.

In and around Panama City, traffic is heavy. An efficient toll highway ($5 one-way) connects the capital and the Caribbean port of Colón in an hour.

Turnoffs and distances are usually clearly signposted. Be especially watchful at traffic lights, as crossing on yellow (or even red) lights is common practice.

FROM PANAMA CITY	TO
Colón	89 km (55 miles)
David	486 km (302 miles)
Boquete	515 km (320 miles)
Costa Rican Border	592 km (368 miles)

TRAVEL TIMES FROM PANAMA CITY		
To	By Air	By Bus
Bocas del Toro	1 hour	12 hours (to Almirante)
Colón	N/A	1 hour
David	1 hour	6 hours
Guna Yala	½ hour	N/A

RULES OF THE ROAD

You cannot turn right on a red light. Seat belts are required. Cell phone use and texting while driving is prohibited. As you approach small towns, watch out for *topes*, the local name for speed bumps.

▋ TAXI TRAVEL

Panamanian taxis range from sleek air-conditioned sedans to stuffy, banged-up rust buckets that seem to run off the sheer will of the driver. Hailing cabs on the street is widely considered safe during the day and is your cheapest option for private transportation around the city. Short hops are as little as $1; fares within town shouldn't top $3; a trip to an outlying area should run about $5. Airport taxis and hotel taxis are nicer but considerably more expensive, so check to see if your hotel has shuttle service. Don't feel obliged to tip, but city cab drivers who strictly adhere to low city fares are genuinely appreciative (and sometimes surprised by) the extra quarter or two. You may want to ask how much the fare is before getting aboard to avoid a tourist premium.

▋ TRAIN TRAVEL

Panama's only train service is the Panama Canal Railway, which operates between Panama City and Colón on weekdays. Tracks run alongside the canal itself and over causeways in Gatún Lake. The hour-long trip costs $25 each way; trains leave Panama City at 7:15 am and Colón at 5:15 pm. You can buy tickets at the station before you leave.

Information Panama Canal Railway. ☎ *507/317–6070* ⊕ *www.panarail.com.*

ESSENTIALS

■ ACCOMMODATIONS

Panama has plenty of lodging options. "Hotel" isn't the only tag you'll find on accommodation: *hospedaje, pensión, casa de huespedes,* and *posada* also denote somewhere to stay. There are no hard-and-fast rules as to what each name means, though hotels and *posadas* tend to be higher-end places, whereas *hospedajes, pensiones,* and *casas de huespedes* are small, often family run. A *residencial* is usually a by-the-hour sort of place. Breakfast isn't always included in the room price.

The usual big international chain hotels have rooms and facilities equal to those at home, but may lack a sense of place. If five-star luxury isn't your top priority, the best deals are undoubtedly with midrange local hotels. Granted, there's no gym or conference center, but comfortable rooms with private bathrooms, hot water, and more local character often come at a fraction of the cost of a big chain.

Lodges—both eco- and not-quite-so—are the thing in Guna Yala and the mountains of Central Panama and Chiriquí. Some are way off the beaten path, so plan on staying a few nights to offset travel time.

■TIP→ Assume that hotels offer no meals unless we specify that they serve breakfast, some meals, all meals, or are all-inclusive with all meals and most activities).

FODORS.COM CONNECTION

Before your trip, be sure to check out what other travelers are saying in our Forums on www.fodors.com.

APARTMENT AND HOUSE RENTALS

Short-term furnished rentals are increasingly common in Panama. Airbnb has the widest selection of rentals, in the city and provinces. Villas International mainly offers premium villa and apartment rentals. VRBO has an ample selection of accommodations all over the country.

Contacts Airbnb. ⊕ *www.airbnb. com.* **Villas International.** ☎ *800/ 221–2260 in U.S.* ⊕ *www.villasintl. com.* **VRBO.** ⊕ *www.vrbo.com.*

BED-AND-BREAKFASTS

The Panamanian definition of B&B might not coincide with yours: the term is frequently extended to luxury hotels that happen to include breakfast in their price. Indeed, these make up most of the pickings at BnBFinder.com. BedandBreakfast.com lists a small but authentic selection of B&Bs. For cheap, family-run places, search for 'guesthouses' on Travellers' Point.

Reservation Services BedandBreakfast.com. ⊕ *www. bedandbreakfast.com.* **BnBFinder.** ⊕ *www.bnbfinder.com.* **Travellers' Point.** ⊕ *www.travellerspoint.com.*

ECO-LODGES

In addition to hotels and hostels, Panama does a brisk trade in so-called eco-lodges, most of which are in the mountains of Central Panama and Chiriquí or Guna Yala. If you are seriously interested in sustainable accommodation, it pays to do your research. The term *eco-lodge* is used freely, sometimes simply to describe a property in a rural or jungle location rather than somewhere that is truly sustainable. The International Ecotourism Society offers tips to help you organize a truly green vacation. Responsible Travel is an online travel agency for ethical holidays.

Information **The International Ecotourism Society.** ⊕ *www. ecotourism.org.* **Responsible Travel.** ⊕ *www.responsibletravel.com.*

▌COMMUNICATIONS

PHONES

The country code for Panama is 507. To call Panama from the United States, dial the international access code (011), followed by the country code (507), and the seven digit phone number, in that order. Note that cell phones have eight digits. Panama does not use area codes. To make collect or calling-card calls, dial 106 from any phone in Panama and an English-speaking operator will connect you.

CALLING WITHIN PANAMA

Panama's telephone system, operated by Cable & Wireless, is cheap and highly efficient. You can make local and long-distance calls from your hotel—usually with a surcharge—and from any public phone box.

The bright blue public phone boxes all take phone cards and some also accept coins; you insert coins or your card first, and then dial. You can also use prepaid calling cards from them free of charge. Standard local calls cost 10¢ a minute, less with a prepaid calling card *(Calling Cards, below)*. For **local directory assistance** (in Spanish), dial 102.

CALLING OUTSIDE PANAMA

To make international calls from Panama, dial 00, then the country code, area code, and number. The country code for the United States is 1.

Many cybercafés have Internet phone services with cheap rates (they're usually posted outside the shop), but communication quality can vary. You can also make international calls from pay phones using a prepaid Telechip or card, which are sold in the abundant convenience stores. Dialing the international operator lets you make collect international calls. It's also possible to use AT&T, Sprint, and MCI services from Panama, but using a prepaid card is cheaper.

CALLING CARDS

Ovinicom prepaid calling cards can be used to make local and international calls from any telephone in Panama. Calls both within Panama and to the United States cost as little as 5¢ a minute; cards come in denominations of $3, $5, $10, and $20. To use them, you dial a free local access number, then enter your PIN and the number you want to call. You can buy cards at supermarkets, convenience stores, and pharmacies. Ask for *una tarjeta telefónica de prepago.*

Calling Card Information

Cable & Wireless Panama. Cable & Wireless Panama's Telechip cards can be used in payphones for national or international calls. ☎ *507/800–2102* ⊕ *www. cwpanama.com.* **Ovnicom.** ☎ *507/ 200–5555 in Panama* ⊕ *www. ovnicom.com.*

MOBILE PHONES

Mobile phones are immensely popular in Panama. If you have an unlocked tri-band phone and intend to call local numbers, it makes sense to buy a prepaid Panamanian SIM card on arrival—rates will be much better than using your U.S. network. Alternatively, you can buy a cheap handset in Panama for $10–$20.

There are four main mobile-phone companies in Panama: +Móvil (owned by Cable & Wireless), Claro, Movistar, and Digicel. Their prices are similar, but +Móvil has better coverage in farther-flung areas of the country. You pay only for outgoing calls, which cost between 5¢ and 50¢ a minute. You can buy a SIM card (*tarjeta SIM*) from any outlet of either company; pay-as-you-go cards (*tarjeta de prepago para celular*) to charge your account are available from supermarkets, drugstores, gas stations, and kiosks.

You can also rent from companies such as cellular Abroad, Mobal, or PlanetFone. A basic phone costs $7 a day, but you have to pay for incoming and outgoing calls, and for theft insurance, so buying a phone in Panama is usually cheaper.

■**TIP→ If you travel internationally frequently, save one of your old mobile phones or buy a cheap one on the Internet; ask your cell phone company to unlock it for you, and take it with you as a travel phone, buying a new SIM card with pay-as-you-go service in each destination.**

Contacts Cellular Abroad. ☎ *800/287–5072 in North America* ⊕ *www.cellularabroad.com.* **Mobal.** ☎ *888/888–9162* ⊕ *www.mobal. com.* **PlanetFone.** ☎ *888/988–4777* ⊕ *www.planetfone.com.*

▌ EATING OUT

Panama's cosmopolitan history is reflected in its food. Panama City has a great range of restaurants serving both local and international fare. Among the latter, Greek, Chinese, Italian, and American eateries are the most common. Fast-food outlets abound—some are names you'll recognize, others are local chains.

Eateries offering traditional Panamanian fare for locals are cheap—you can get a full plate of beans or lentils and rice and fried chicken for as little as $4. Most restaurants, however, charge U.S.-level prices for meals.

MEALS AND MEALTIMES

A typical Panamanian breakfast (*desayuno*) consists of eggs or beef served with deep fried tortillas or *hojaldre* (fried bread), washed down with coffee. Most hotels catering to foreigners also offer fruit, toast, and cereal, and you can expect breakfast buffets at the four- or five-star hotels.

Lunch (*comida* or *almuerzo*) is the main meal and is generally served around midday. Many restaurants do set-price meals of two or three courses at lunch. In Panamanian homes dinner is often merely a light snack eaten around 9 pm. If you're eating out, dinner is just as big a deal as in the United States, but is usually served until 10:30 pm.

Unless otherwise noted, the restaurants listed here are open daily for lunch and dinner.

PAYING

In restaurants with waiter service you pay the check (*la cuenta*) at the end of the meal. You'll usually have to ask for the check, sometimes more than once. In fast-food restaurants and at food stands, you generally pay up front. Credit cards are accepted in most restaurants, but it's always a good idea to check before you order, especially as some establishments only accept one kind of credit card.

RESERVATIONS AND DRESS

We only mention reservations when they are essential (there's no other way you'll ever get a table) or when they are not accepted. We mention dress only when men are required to wear a jacket or a jacket and tie.

WINES, BEER, AND SPIRITS

Alcohol is available in just about every restaurant in Panama, though cheaper places have limited selections.

For meals and light drinking, beer—usually lager—is the local favorite. Good brands made in Panama include Balboa, Atlas, Panamá, and Soberana, but North American and European brands are also widely available. For more serious drinking, Panamanians reach for a bottle of *seco,* a fierce white rum that gets you under the table in no time. Seco is often mixed with cranberry juice.

Wine still isn't a big thing in Panama, but most decent restaurants have imported bottles from the United States or Chile and Argentina. Imported liquor is also easy to find in supermarkets.

▌ ELECTRICITY

Electrical current in Panama is 110 volts, the same as in the United States. Outlets take either plugs with two flat prongs or two flat prongs with a circular grounded prong. No converters or adapters are needed.

▌ EMERGENCIES

Dial 911 nationwide for police, fire, and ambulance. In a medical or dental emergency, ask your hotel staff for information on and directions to the nearest private hospital or clinic. Taxi drivers should also know how to find one, and taking a taxi may be quicker than waiting for an ambulance. Many private medical insurers provide online lists of hospitals and clinics in different towns. It's a good idea to print out a copy of these before you travel.

For theft, wallet loss, small road accidents, and minor emergencies, contact the nearest police station. Expect all dealings with the police to be a bureaucratic business—it's probably only worth bothering if you need the report for insurance claims.

Most embassies in the capital open at 8:30 and close by noon.

The private Hospital Punta Pacifica is affiliated with Johns Hopkins Medicine International and has many English-speaking doctors. The Hospital Nacional is an excellent private hospital with English-speaking doctors, a 24-hour emergency room, and specialists in many areas. The Centro Médico Paitilla is one of the country's best, and most expensive, hospitals.

■TIP→ **Medical staff at Panamanian public hospitals are well-trained and professional. However, hospitals are underfunded and often lack supplies: as a rule, you're best going to a private clinic, which means medical insurance is a must.**

Pack a basic first-aid kit, especially if you're venturing into more remote areas. If you'll be carrying any medication, bring your doctor's contact information and prescription authorizations. Getting your prescription filled in Panama might be problematic, so bring enough medication for your entire trip.

Foreign Embassies U.S. Embassy. ✉ *Av. Demetrio Basilio Lakas, Building 783* ☎ *507/317–5000* ⊕ *panama. usembassy.gov.*

■ HEALTH

It's safe to drink tap water and have ice in your drinks in urban areas, but stick to bottled water everywhere else.

Two mosquito-borne diseases are prevalent in Panama: dengue fever (especially in Bocas del Toro) and malaria (in the Guna Yala and parts of Chiriquí). Prevention is better than a cure: cover up your arms and legs and use a strong insect repellent containing a high concentration of DEET. Don't hang around outside at sunset, and sleep under a mosquito net in jungle areas.

Sunburn and sunstroke are potential health hazards when visiting Panama. Stay out of the sun at midday and use plenty of high-SPF-factor sunscreen when on the beach or hiking. You can buy well-known brands in most Panamanian pharmacies. Protect your eyes with good-quality sunglasses, and bear in mind that you'll burn more easily at higher altitudes and in the water.

OVER-THE-COUNTER REMEDIES

In Panama *farmacias* (drugstores) sell a wide range of medications over the counter, including some, but not all, drugs that would require a prescription in the United States. Familiar brands are easy to find, otherwise ask for what you want with the generic name. Note that acetaminophen—or Tylenol—is called *paracetamol* in Panama (just as in the U.K.). Farmacias Arrocha and Farmacias Rey, which are located inside Rey supermarkets, are two Panamanian drugstore chains with branches all over the country, many of which are open 24 hours.

Information Farmacias Arrocha. ☎ *507/279–9000* ⊕ *www.arrocha.com.* **Farmacias Rey.** ☎ *507/270–5535* ⊕ *www.smrey.com.*

SHOTS AND MEDICATIONS

If you're traveling anywhere east of Panama City and the former Canal Zone, a yellow fever vaccination is recommended. Remember to keep the certificate and carry it with you, as you may be asked to show it when entering another country after leaving Panama.

The CDC recommends mefloquine, proguanil, or doxycycline as preventive antimalarials for adults and infants in Panama if entering a malaria zone east of the Panama Canal. Chloroquine is sufficient for western Panama malarial regions. To be effective, the weekly doses must start a week before you travel and continue four weeks after your return. There is no preventive medication for dengue.

Health Warnings Centers for Disease Control and Prevention (*CDC*). ☎ *800/232–4636 in North America* ⊕ *wwwnc.cdc.gov/travel.* **World Health Organization** (*WHO*). ⊕ *www.who.int.*

▌ MONEY

Although Panama is Central America's most expensive destination, prices compare favorably to those back home. Midrange hotels and restaurants where locals eat are excellent value. Rooms at first-class hotels and meals at the best restaurants, however, approach those in the United States. Trips into remote parts of the country and adventure travel are also relatively inexpensive.

You can plan your trip around ATMs—cash is king for day-to-day dealings—and credit cards (for bigger spending). U.S. dollars are the local currency; changing any other currency can be problematic. Traveler's checks are useful only as a reserve.

Using large bills is often a problem in Panama, even in big shops or expensive restaurants. Have plenty of ones and fives at hand. Counterfeiting is a problem with $50 or $100 bills. Many businesses won't accept anything larger than $20.

Prices are given for adults. Substantially reduced fees are almost always available for children, students, and senior citizens.

ATMS AND BANKS

ATMs—known locally as *cajeros automáticos*—are extremely common in Panama. In big cities even supermarkets and department stores usually have their own ATMs. On-screen instructions appear in English; you are usually prompted to select your language. Make withdrawals from ATMs in daylight rather than at night.

The main ATM network accepts cards with both Cirrus and Plus symbols. ATMs are located all over the country, with the exceptions of Isla Contadora and Guna Yala. Many international banks have branches in Panama City.

CREDIT CARDS

Inform your credit-card company before you travel, especially if you're going abroad and don't travel internationally very often. Otherwise, the credit-card company might put a hold on your card owing to unusual activity—not a good thing halfway through your trip. Record all your credit-card numbers—as well as the phone numbers to call if your cards are lost or stolen—in a safe place, so you're prepared should something go wrong. Both MasterCard and Visa have general numbers you can call (collect if you're abroad) if your card is lost, but you're better off calling the number of your issuing bank, since MasterCard and Visa usually just transfer you to your bank; your bank's number is usually printed on your card.

Credit cards are widely accepted in Panama's urban areas. Visa is the most popular, followed by MasterCard and American Express. Discover is gaining ground. Diners Club is rarely accepted. If possible, bring more than one credit card, as smaller establishments sometimes accept only one type. In small towns only top-end hotels and restaurants take plastic.

Reporting Lost Cards American Express. ☎ 336/393–1111 collect from abroad, 800/528–4800 in

North America ⊕ www.americanexpress.com. **MasterCard.** ☎ 800/627–8372 in U.S., 636/722–7111 collect from abroad ⊕ www.mastercard.com. **Visa.** ☎ 800/847–2911 in U.S., 410/581–9994 collect from abroad ⊕ www.visa.com.

CURRENCY AND EXCHANGE

Panama's national currency is the U.S. dollar. Don't get confused if you see prices expressed in *balboas*: it's just the local name for the dollar. All bills come in standard U.S. denominations, although Panama also issues its own version of pennies, nickels, dimes, quarters, and 50-cent pieces. New as of 2012 are one-balboa coins, still newfangled enough that much of the population is suspicious of them, with plans for a two-balboa coin on the way. Try to avoid coming to Panama with other currencies, as the exchange rates are generally unfavorable.

▍ PACKING

Think capri pants, skirts, or khakis for urban sightseeing, with something a little dressier for eating out at night. Shorts, T-shirts, tank tops, and bikinis are all acceptable at the beach or farther afield. Leave flashy jewelry behind—it only makes you a target.

"Insect repellent, sunscreen, sunglasses" is your packing mantra; long-sleeve shirts and long pants also help protect your skin from the relentless sun and ferocious mosquitoes. Panama's rainy season lasts from mid-April to December, and rain is common at other times, too, so a foldable umbrella or waterproof jacket is a must. So are sturdy walking boots if you're planning any serious hiking, otherwise sneakers or flats are fine. A handbag-size flashlight is also very useful: blackouts are more common than at home.

Tissues and antibacterial hand wipes make trips to public toilets more pleasant. Finding your preferred brands of condoms and tampons in Panama can be hit and miss, so bring necessary supplies of both. Familiar toiletry brands are widely available.

▌ PASSPORTS AND VISAS

Most travelers from Western countries can visit Panama for up to 90 days with the purchase of a $5 tourist visa; you can buy this upon arrival or at the check-in desk of some airlines. Your passport must be valid for at least six months. The visa may actually say it is valid for only 30 days so ask the usually friendly officer to write "*90 días*" by the stamp on the visa.

Arriving tourists are technically required to show proof that their travels continue beyond Panama. A return ticket will suffice. Airlines are often more demanding than immigration officials on this particular issue: If you don't have a return ticket they might not let you board the plane.

It is nearly impossible to extend your stay in Panama unless you are a retiree investing in property or sponsored by an employer. If you need to stay longer, it's easier to simply leave the country for 72 hours by grabbing a cheap round-trip flight to Colombia or Costa Rica and then returning.

Information Consulate of Panama in Washington, D.C. ☎ 202/483–1407 ⊕ www.embassyofpanama. org. **Oficina de Migración.** ✉ Av. Cuba and Calle 28 ☎ 507/507–1800 ⊕ www.migracion.gob.pa.

▌ SAFETY

Panama is relatively safe. In most of the country crime against tourists is usually limited to pickpocketing and bag snatching. Taking a few simple precautions is usually enough to keep you from being a target.

In urban areas, strive to look aware and purposeful at all times. Look at maps before you go outside, not on a street corner, and keep a firm hold on your purse. At night exercise the same kind of caution you would in any big American city and stay in well-lit areas with plenty of people around. Ask hotel or restaurant staff to call you a taxi at night, rather than flagging one down. If you're driving, park in guarded lots, never on the street, and remove the front of the stereo if possible.

In Panama City it's best to steer clear of the neighborhoods of El Chorrillo, parts of Calidonia away from the parallel thoroughfares of Peru and Cuba avenues, and El Marañón, where muggings are commonplace. (We shade dangerous neighborhoods on our Panama City maps.) Finally, local drivers are a danger to pedestrians in all the city's neighborhoods, so look twice (or thrice) before crossing the street.

Two places in the country are blots on Panama's safety reputation. The city of Colón is a hot spot for violent crime, and locals warn against wandering its streets alone. Bordering Colombia, the Darién Province is a largely impenetrable jungle far from the reach of the law, and thus a hotspot for paramilitary activity and drug smuggling. An organized tour should be your only choice for visiting the Darién.

In the unlikely event of being mugged or robbed, do not put up a struggle. Nearly all physical attacks on tourists are the direct result of their resisting would-be pickpockets or muggers. Comply with demands, hand over your stuff, and try to get the situation over with as quickly as possible—then let your travel insurance take care of it.

Report any crimes to the nearest police station. In Panama City you can also ask English-speaking tourist police (identifiable by a white armband) for help. Panamanian police are usually helpful when dealing with foreigners. However, their resources are limited: they'll happily provide you with reports for insurance claims, but tracking down your stolen goods is pretty unlikely.

In Panama you're legally obliged to carry ID—preferably your passport—with you at all times. If you prefer to keep your passport safe, laminate a color copy of the photo page and carry that, together with your driver's license or other photo ID. You may be asked for proof of your identity when dealing with the police, and you can be fined $10 or hauled away if you don't have ID.

■ TIP→ Distribute your cash, credit cards, IDs, and other valuables between a deep front pocket, an inside jacket or vest pocket, and a hidden money pouch. Don't reach for the money pouch once you're in public.

Contact **Transportation Security Administration** (*TSA*). ☎ *866/289–9673* ⊕ *www.tsa.gov.*

GOVERNMENT ADVISORIES

U.S. State Department travel advisories are known for being very cautious. A perusal of the corresponding sites for other English-speaking countries (Australia, Canada, and the United Kingdom) gives a larger sampling. All warn against independent travel to the Darién region and recommend avoiding rougher neighborhoods of Panama City and most of Colón.

General Information and Warnings **Australian Department of Foreign Affairs and Trade.** ☎ *262/613–305 in Australia* ⊕ *www.smartraveller.gov.au.* **Foreign Affairs and International Trade Canada.** ☎ *800/387–3124 in North America* ⊕ *www.voyage.gc.ca.* **U.K. Foreign & Commonwealth Office.** ☎ *300/200–3500 in the U.K.* ⊕ *www.gov.uk.* **U.S. Department of State.** ⊕ *www.travel.state.gov.*

▌ TAXES

Panama has a value-added sales tax (IVA) of 7%, which is usually included in the displayed price. No tax-refund scheme exists for visitors. Hotels also have a 10%

tax. Visitors departing by air are charged an exit tax of $40, though this is usually included in your ticket.

TIME

Panama is five hours behind GMT, the same as U.S. Eastern Standard Time (GMT-5). Panama does not observe Daylight Saving Time.

Time Zones Timeanddate.com. ⊕ *www.timeanddate.com/worldclock.*

TIPPING

In Panama tipping is a question of rewarding good service rather than an obligation. Restaurant bills don't include gratuities; adding 10% is customary. Bellhops and maids expect tips only in more expensive hotels, and $1–$2 per bag is the norm. You should also give a tip of up to $10 per day to tour guides. Rounding up taxi fares is a way of showing your appreciation to the driver, but it's not expected.

VISITOR INFORMATION

The Autoridad de Turismo Panamá (Panamanian Tourism Authority, ATP) is Panama's official tourism organization.

ATP has 17 offices around Panama, open weekdays 8–3:30. The English-speaking staff at ATP offices are friendly and helpful. Their resources—mostly brochures—tend to plug local tour companies rather than aid independent touring.

Other resources include *The Visitor,* a small, free paper that can be found at most hotels and travel agencies, and *Panama Planner,* an excellent tourism magazine available at large hotels.

Contacts Autoridad de Turismo de Panamá (*ATP*). ☏ *507/526–7000 in Panama* ⊕ *www.atp.gob.pa.*

ONLINE TRAVEL TOOLS
All About Panama Explore Panama. ⊕ *explorepanama.com.* **Panama Guide.** ⊕ *www.panama-guide. com.* **Panama Info.** ⊕ *panamainfo. com.* **The Panama Report.** ⊕ *www. thepanamareport.com.*

INDEX

PHOTO CREDITS

Cover credit: Hemis / AWL Images [Description: San Blas, Panama]. Spine: Oliviermeerson | Dreamstime.com 1, Alex Bramwell / age fotostock. 2, Lmseco | Dreamstime.com. 3 (top), Thompson Paul / age fotostock. 3 (bottom), Piumatti Sergio / age fotostock. 4 (top), Sergio Pitamitz / age fotostock. 4 (bottom), Alfredo Maiquez / age fotostock. 5, Vilainecrevette | Dreamstime.com. 6, Philippe Michel / age fotostock. 7 (top left), Carver Mostardi / Alamy. 7 (top right), Melba / age fotostock. 7 (bottom), Scott B. Rosen / Alamy. 8 (top), Oliviermeerson | Dreamstime.com. 8 (bottom), Alvaro Leiva / age fotostock. Chapter 1: Experience Panama: 11, Picturemakersllc | Dreamstime.com. Chapter 2: Panama City: 31, Sergio Pitamitz/age fotostock. Chapter 3: The Canal and Central Panama: 95, Ken Welsh/age fotostock. Chapter 4: Chiriqui Provence: 153, David Cantrille / Alamy. Chapter 5: Bocas del Toro Archipelagio: 193, Juan Carlos Muñoz/age fotostock. Chapter 6: Guna Yala (San Blas): 221, Simon Dannhauer/iStockphoto.

About Our Writers: All photos are courtesy of the writers except for the following: Marlise Kast-Myers, courtesy of Benjamin Myers.

NOTES

NOTES

NOTES

Fodor's InFocus PANAMA 2016

Publisher: Amanda D'Acierno, *Senior Vice President*

Editorial: Arabella Bowen, *Editor in Chief*; Linda Cabasin, *Editorial Director*

Design: Tina Malaney, *Associate Art Director*; Chie Ushio, *Senior Designer;* Erica Cuoco, *Production Designer*

Photography: Jennifer Arnow, *Senior Photo Editor*; Mary Robnett, *Photo Researcher*

Production: Linda Schmidt, *Managing Editor*; Evangelos Vasilakis, *Associate Managing Editor*; Angela L. McLean, *Senior Production Manager*

Maps: Rebecca Baer, *Senior Map Editor*; Mark Stroud (Moon Street Cartography) and David Lindroth, *Cartographers*

Sales: Jacqueline Lebow, *Sales Director*

Marketing & Publicity: Heather Dalton, *Marketing Director*; Katherine Punia, *Publicity Director*

Business & Operations: Susan Livingston, *Vice President, Strategic Business Planning*; Sue Daulton, *Vice President, Operations*

Fodors.com: Megan Bell, *Executive Director, Revenue & Business Development*; Yasmin Marinaro, *Senior Director, Marketing & Partnerships*

Writers: Mark Chesnut, David Dudenhoefer, Marlise Kast-Myers
Editor: Eric Wechter
Production Editor: Evangelos Vasilakis

2nd Edition

ISBN 978-0-8041-4353-0

ISSN 2324-9609

All details in this book are based on information supplied to us at press time. Always confirm information when it matters, especially if you're making a detour to visit a specific place. Fodor's expressly disclaims any liability, loss, or risk, personal or otherwise, that is incurred as a consequence of the use of any of the contents of this book.

SPECIAL SALES

This book is available at special discounts for bulk purchases for sales promotions or premiums. For more information, e-mail specialmarkets@penguinrandomhouse.com.

PRINTED IN THE UNITED STATES OF AMERICA
10 9 8 7 6 5 4 3 2 1

ABOUT OUR WRITERS

New York City–based freelance journalist **Mark Chesnut** has been criss-crossing Latin America since 1994 for a variety of media. Panama is one of his all-time favorite places to visit, thanks to its diverse natural and cultural attributes. He updated the Panama City chapter and The Canal and Central Panama chapter.

Freelance journalist **David Dudenhoefer** began visiting Panama in the early 1990s, when he lived in neighboring Costa Rica. He has returned dozens of times since then to write about everything from the country's politicians to its indigenous peoples. David now lives in Lima, Peru, from where he covers much of South America, but he tries to get back to Panama at least once a year.

Journalist and author **Marlise Kast-Myers** has traveled to more than 80 countries and has lived in Switzerland, Dominican Republic, Spain, and Costa Rica. Before settling in Southern California, she completed a surfing and snowboarding expedition across the world. Following the release of her memoir, *Tabloid Prodigy*, Marlise appeared on CNN, FOX News, CBN, CNBC, The O'Reilly Factor, NPR, Good Morning America, and Entertainment Tonight. Marlise has co-authored over 20 Fodor's guidebooks including Mexico, San Diego, Panama, Puerto Rico, Peru, Los Cabos, Corsica, Sardinia, Vietnam, and Costa Rica. She served as a photojournalist for Surf Guide to Costa Rica and authored *Day and Overnight Hikes on the Pacific Crest Trail*. Now based in San Diego County, she lives on a small farm with her husband Benjamin.
⊕ *www.marlisekast.com*

EUGENE FODOR

Hungarian-born Eugene Fodor (1905–91) began his travel career as an interpreter on a French cruise ship. The experience inspired him to write *On the Continent* (1936), the first guidebook to receive annual updates and discuss a country's way of life as well as its sights. Fodor later joined the U.S. Army and worked for the OSS in World War II. After the war, he kept up his intelligence work while expanding his guidebook series. During the Cold War, many guides were written by fellow agents who understood the value of insider information. Today's guides continue Fodor's legacy by providing travelers with timely coverage, insider tips, and cultural context.